KANSAS CITY
BARBEQUE
SOCIETY

COOKBOOK

OTHER BOOKS FROM THE KANSAS CITY BARBEQUE SOCIETY

The Passion of Barbeque

The Kansas City Barbeque Society Cookbook

THE KANSAS CITY BARBEQUE SOCIETY COOKBOOK

KC BS

KANSAS CITY
BARBEQUE
SOCIETY

BARBEQUE . . .
IT'S NOT JUST FOR
BREAKFAST ANYMORE

Ardie A. Davis, PhB,
Chef Paul Kirk, PhB,
and Carolyn Wells, PhB

COOKBOOK

KCBS
25th
Anniversary
Edition

Andrews McMeel Publishing, LLC
an Andrews McMeel Universal company
1130 Walnut Street, Kansas City, Missouri 64106

www.andrewsmcmeel.com

11 12 13 14 WKT 10 9 8 7 6 5 4 3 2

ISBN: 978-0-7407-9010-2

Library of Congress Control Number: 2009939469

www.kcbs.us

ATTENTION: SCHOOLS AND BUSINESSES

Andrews McMeel books are available at quantity discounts with bulk
purchase for educational, business, or sales promotional use. For
information, please e-mail the Andrews McMeel Publishing Special Sales
Department: specialsales@amuniversal.com

For **GARY WELLS**, PhB, KCBS

co-founder, leader, friend, and mentor.

Gary is loved by all and we sorely miss him!

CONTENTS

ACKNOWLEDGMENTS

We gratefully acknowledge and thank the many teams and individuals who contributed to this book. All are listed in the Index of Contributors at the back of the book.

We are also grateful to the individuals and teams significant to the growth of the KCBS over the last twenty-five years. Many are acknowledged by name with recipes or anecdotes throughout the book.

This book would not have happened without the exemplary teamwork of the book division staff at Andrews McMeel. Kirsty Melville, head of the book division; Lane Butler, our editor par excellence; Diane Marsh; Tim Lynch; John Carroll; and Blake Stevens; plus Tammie Barker and the marketing team: thank you!

Finally, Dennis Hayes, our stellar agent, percolated the idea for this cookbook more than five years ago. Dennis, we thank you for your vision and persistence in seeing this project through to fruition.

PREFACE: THE HISTORY OF THE KANSAS CITY BARBEQUE SOCIETY

When Carolyn Wells set out to write this history of the Kansas City Barbeque Society (KCBS), she strove to be factual. She read twenty-three years of board minutes and highlighted something from each meeting. "Not a good move," she concluded, but "an excellent remedy for insomnia." Board meetings are important because they are where major decisions are made to advance the organization, but they are not the essence of KCBS. KCBS is a cultural phenomenon. It was at the right place at the right time. As Carolyn puts it, "The real story is the people, their camaraderie, their love of barbeque, and their competitive nature."

KCBS, along with other new barbeque associations, was born in the 1980s. The sport of barbeque was so new then that there was little organization anywhere. John Raven, the "Commissioner of Barbecue," had founded the International Barbecue Society (IBS) in Tempe, Texas. Another fledgling group, the International Barbecue Cookers Association (IBCA), formed in Dallas. Memphis hosted the Memphis in May World Championship Barbecue Cooking Contest. Kansas City had the American Royal Barbecue Contest, the Great Lenexa Barbeque Battle, and the Blue Springs Barbeque Blazeoff. Each contest was independent, setting its own rules and judging procedures.

KCBS was born one evening in 1986, when Carolyn and her husband, Gary, were enjoying drinks and conversation with their friend Rick Welch. By then Gary and Carolyn had competed in every contest in metropolitan Kansas City and beyond. They had been hooked by the passion of barbeque. The topic of discussion with Rick was, of course, barbeque.

Carolyn mentioned that cookers were constantly calling her to find out when and where the next competition was going to be held. "Why not start a club for cookers?" the three asked themselves. "Why not call it the Kansas City Barbeque Society?" After all, Kansas City had long been known as a barbeque capital, the epicenter of the barbeque universe. Plus, they liked the acronym, KCBS. It left lots of room for interpretation. They agreed that the only requirement for membership was to take nothing seriously. To do so was grounds for expulsion. Fellow cookers would be reached by a newsletter, published occasionally for anyone who cared to read it. Thirty cooks signed on and paid the $12 yearly dues.

Since there were so few contests in the KC metro area at the time, KCBS members decided to have a Spring Training practice competition every April. Dan Haake offered his farm as the venue. There was no prize money, and the cheap plastic trophies bore typed stick-on labels. The entry fee was $69, which included all contest meats and a heavy-duty Styrofoam container. The concept was well received. It was all about the competition and the camaraderie. Spring Training continued for ten years, until it was no longer needed. Competition barbeque was thriving in Kansas City and beyond.

Meanwhile, calls began pouring in to Gary and Carolyn asking for KCBS "sanctioning" of community contests. This was getting serious! Now the society needed rules, judging procedures, a method of tabulating scores, and all those other things that make an official governing organization.

More organizational formalities were established in 1987, after the first KCBS New Year's party, a potluck dinner designed to allow members to reconnect with barbeque buddies they hadn't seen much of since late fall. Gary appointed a board of directors from active charter members: Gary Wells, Carolyn Wells, Rick Welch, Alan Uhl, Paul Kirk, Guy Simpson, John Lillich, Donna McClure, and Dale Shockey. KCBS was incorporated as a 501(c)7 fraternal organization. Rules and a logo were approved. The newsletter was named the *Kansas City Bullsheet*, with the subhead "It Just Doesn't Matter." Later that year a computerized tabulation program was used successfully at Spring Training. KCBS was state of the art, and the membership roster had grown to 168!

A cookbook with KCBS member recipes, *The Passion of Barbeque*, was released in June 1988. Owned by Rick Welch and Karen Adler, the book sold 3,500 copies the first month after release. Royalties helped fund the society. Later the book was sold to Hyperion, a national publisher in New York, and sales gave the KCBS significant national exposure.

When the sun set on the 1980s, many other important organizational changes and initiatives followed in the next decade. Among them:

- The *Bullsheet* was changed to a newspaper format. Bunny Tuttle was hired as editor and the first KCBS employee.

- Gary Wells was named Chairman of the Board and permanent voting member.

- Contests where teams sold barbeque to the public and competed against each other asked that KCBS officiate at their events to validate the judging.

- A KCBS Seal of Approval program was initiated.

- The board approved contracting with Favorite Recipes Press to produce a new cookbook of member recipes, with Janeyce Michel-Cupito, Ardie A. Davis, Paul Kirk, and Carolyn Wells as co-authors. *The Kansas City Barbeque Society Cookbook*,

IT JUST DOESN'T MATTER.

subtitled, *Barbeque . . . It's Not Just for Breakfast Anymore*, was released on December 7, 1995.

- A Certified Barbeque Judge training curriculum was finalized by Ardie Davis and Ed Roith, and the first classes were taught.

- Carolyn Wells was appointed Executive Director.

The first decade of the twenty-first century has seen phenomenal growth in KCBS membership and sanctioned contests. The decade also saw the adoption of a new KCBS logo, a new marketing initiative, formalized Contest Rep training and training procedures, and the start of a very successful Great American BBQ Tour. Regrettably, it was also the decade when Gary resigned as KCBS president due to health issues, from which he later passed away.

Carolyn has enough information and experiences to write *the* definitive book of KCBS history. Thanks to Carolyn's research and recollections, we have highlighted some key people, events, and initiatives of the first 25 years. However, no one could sum up KCBS history better than Carolyn when she says, "The real history of KCBS is that of the members. It is the extended family. Like most families, there is some dysfunction from time to time. But generally these folks like each other. They compete against each other, but cheer loudly when their friends and neighbors win. They judge together, and take field trips to contests where they renew acquaintances, and sample world-class 'Que.

"They are organizers, showcasing their communities and/or fund-raising for worthy causes. They are folks who enjoy the outdoor lifestyle and the camaraderie of fellow enthusiasts in the name of barbeque. Each group is a necessary part of the whole society and interdependent. The sense of community is the heart and soul of the group."

The story we want to tell here in this book is that of the people—the lives touched, the places seen, the sense of community. You'll get many glimpses of that story throughout this book. The rest of the KCBS story will be told over the next 25 years. If you are not already involved in making KCBS history, now is the time to take the leap! We invite you to join. Please visit us at wwww.kcbs.us/join.

INTRODUCTION

25 Years and Still Smokin'!

If you like great food, welcome to the Kansas City Barbeque Society!

The Kansas City Barbeque Society (KCBS) is an international not-for-profit organization of people who love barbeque. We love to cook it, eat it, talk about it, learn better ways to cook it—and most of all we love the camaraderie that happens when smoke is in the air and the pits are full of meat. Besides sharing recipes or asking for honest opinions on a new rub or sauce, we enjoy keeping up with one another's families, careers, joys, and sorrows—and we're always ready to hear a new joke or tall tale.

In the beginning there were only three members: co-founders Gary Wells, Carolyn Wells, and Rick Welch. When our first cookbook was published in 1995, we had fifteen hundred members. Today KCBS is more than eleven thousand strong. That's a lot of growth in a mere fifteen years! That phenomenal growth is due in large part to a steadfast focus on the fulfillment of our mission: "Our mission is to celebrate, teach, preserve, and promote barbeque as a culinary technique, sport and art form. We want barbeque to be recognized as America's Cuisine."

Although KCBS is a quarter century old as we introduce this new cookbook, barbeque's roots are deep. Food historians have yet to put a date or location on the world's first meat fire, but when that momentous day arrives, we expect it will be tagged at at least ten thousand years ago. We won't even blink at a hundred thousand years. Archaeological finds in Africa, China, France, and Spain have been promising. Some even say barbeque first happened in North Carolina. The jury is still out. While the jury digs, ponders, and debates, we're grateful for the first meat fire, wherever and whenever it was, and we're proud to embrace the earliest barbequers as our own. We stand on their shoulders and the shoulders of the many legends, known and unknown, who have followed.

While barbeque as a method of cooking has been around for many years, barbeque as a sport is new. As you'll note in the KCBS history (see page ix), barbeque contests that evolved into full-fledged sanctioned contests with rules and regulations date back to the early 1980s. Granted, when backyard barbeques first emerged in 1930s America as "outdoor suppers" featuring Dad at the grill, and then became a full-fledged national pastime in the 1950s, a few contests were held, but they didn't get enough traction to last past one or two events. Kaiser Aluminum, for example, sponsored and conducted two national barbeque contests in the 1950s. Participation was limited to men. Imagine trying that exclusion today—no way! The recipes in this book reflect the KCBS gender, ethnic, and geographic diversity.

Although some of our members think, "If it isn't barbeque, it isn't food," we really do think bigger than that. The proof is in this cookbook. Along with our growth in membership has come an exciting culinary mosaic. While KCBS-sanctioned contests still feature our four basic food groups—chicken, pork shoulder, beef brisket, and pork ribs—this book goes much further. Our recipes reflect the global reach of KCBS—states from coast to coast and border to border, plus the United Kingdom, Canada, and Australia. New and seasoned cooks will get valuable tips from seven-time world champion pitmaster Paul Kirk in our chapter on the four KCBS food froups.

From Ron Buchholz's Fire in the Pasture! (page 34) stuffed smoked jalapeños—topped with Doc K's Level 1 Trauma Salsa (page 16) if you dare—to Smoked Trout–Stuffed Potatoes (page 42) à la Ruben Gomez, we give you appetizers that will jolt you or comfort you.

ANIMAL RIGHTS AND BBQ

I think every animal has a right to be barbequed!

—Al Lawson, KCBS Hall of Flame member, as quoted at the Blue Devil BBQ Cookoff, May 19, 1990

A side of beans is a hands-down favorite with KCBS members. We know because of the number of bean recipes we received for the book. We couldn't include them all, but we're sharing a hefty dozen with you. And as they say about the free pinto beans at Cooper's Old Time Pit Bar-B-Que in Llano, Texas, "Our beans speak for themselves."

OUR MISSION IS TO CELEBRATE, TEACH, PRESERVE, AND PROMOTE BARBEQUE AS A CULINARY TECHNIQUE, SPORT AND ART FORM. WE WANT BARBEQUE TO BE RECOGNIZED AS AMERICA'S CUISINE.

Beyond the beans you'll find a rich selection of sides—potatoes, onions, corn, asparagus, fruit, grits, and more—to enhance your repertoire. Several of our sides—BBQ Spaghetti Pie (page 99) or Carolina Smashed Potato Pig Butt Bake (page 70), for example—can be served in smaller quantities as a side dish or in larger quantities as a meal.

When the four basic competition categories aren't up for judgment, KCBS members are very talented at cooking outside the Styrofoam contest-entry box. The contest category "Anything Butt" refers to dishes that are anything but the four sanctioned meat categories. For "Anything Butt" we have salmon, tuna, pasties, stromboli, steaks, brats, meat loaf, spiedies, lots of chicken, eggs—from Bad's Quihi Migas (page 154) to Scotch Eggs (page 178)—pizzas, chilis, and stews. You'll never run out of ideas, even if you need or want strictly vegetarian fare.

We also have you covered when you're looking for something new to spice up your barbeque—Snail's Simple Sauce (page 228), Voodoo Glaze (page 230), Al Lawson's Dry Rib Seasoning (page 224), and Kathy's Pig Powder Sauce (page 233), to name a few. We top off our seasonings chapter with Ken Mishoe's easy and tasty 3 X BBQ Sauce (page 234).

Desserts were introduced as a nonsanctioned contest category in the late 1990s. They were an instant hit with judges. We won't promise our desserts will get you a blue ribbon in a contest, but we know you'll find some keepers in our collection. Food historians take note: Here, for the first time ever, is an original recipe for Valomilk Moon Pie (page 258), thanks to Mary Beth Lasseter.

Be an animal at

To most people, *boneyard* means a place where unwanted objects are discarded. Not so with us. Our "Boneyard" contains culinary jewels that don't fit into our other recipe categories. We just couldn't throw them out. We could have said *miscellaneous*, but *boneyard* resonates best with barbequers.

The first KCBS cookbook featured recipes donated by members. That tradition continues in this book. The emphasis here is on barbequed or grilled meats and dishes that go well with them. However, because even barbeque lovers don't eat barbeque for every meal, there are also a lot of recipes for grilling, baking, and stovetop cooking. You'll get everything from fried chicken, to burger rolls, country ham pie, and a few of the favorite breakfast dishes that have fueled more than a few barbequers as they manned the smoker through those long morning hours. Vegetarians will also find a few fabulous nonmeat dishes here to earn a place in their kitchen cookbook collection. Most of our recipes are original and previously unpublished. Some are adapted from other published recipes and are so noted. Some have appeared in other publications and appear here with permission. To top it all off, the book is sprinkled liberally with quips, quotes, anecdotes, and other "barbequephernalia," sort of like seasonings that are added here and there.

To all whose shoulders we stand on in making this book possible, we give our hearty thanks. To all who buy and use this book and love the results of the barbeque method of cooking, we thank you for your support and welcome you into our fellowship. Let's start cooking!

THE 4 KANSAS CITY BARBEQUE SOCIETY FOOD GROUPS REQUIRED AT SANCTIONED CONTESTS

When the **KCBS** was founded and contest rules were established, chicken, pork ribs, pork, and beef brisket were the four basic meats required at sanctioned contests. Specific allowable parts of the animal have changed over the years, but the categories have remained constant.

Here we offer a basic contest-quality generic recipe for each category. Please remember that KCBS rules and regulations are revisited and revised each year. Check the current rules and regulations on the Web site at www.kcbs.us for up-to-date information.

KCBS BARBEQUE CONTEST BASICS

In a Kansas City Barbeque Society—sanctioned contest, four categories count for the Grand Championship: chicken or Cornish hen, pork ribs (spareribs, St. Louis–style ribs, loin back ribs/baby back ribs), pork (shoulder, butt, or picnic), and beef brisket (whole, flat, or point). This chapter covers those four basic categories with some general cooking instructions and advice.

The procedures we give you in this section are Paul's way of doing barbeque. These procedures have helped him win more than five hundred awards, including seven World Barbeque Championships. They have been successful for Paul and his students, but keep in mind that Paul's way is *not* the only way. There are as many ways to barbeque as there are barbequers. You can marinate, brine, rub, baste, and sauce meat almost any way you want. Your choice of charcoal and wood makes a difference. Cooking times can vary according to your preference. The longer you're at this, and the more you practice, the more you'll learn, and maybe you'll have a few tips, tricks, and award-winning recipes to share with KCBS one day for a future cookbook.

Before we get into how-to, let's talk about the smoker or cooker. For competition, you can use anything from a Weber kettle grill to a tow-behind. You can buy one from a manufacturer, or you can make one yourself, though we don't see as many homemade cookers these days. In the past, teams have cooked in everything from smokers made from industrial metal drums to refrigerators, Dumpsters, and a Volkswagen Beetle, and a team called Swine Flu even used a Cessna airplane, complete with a sign that read, "Meat-Seeking Missiles." Whatever you choose, make sure you cook at a constant temperature of 230° to 250°F. Most smokers can be controlled at these temperatures.

As for fuel, no gas or electric cooking is allowed. You can use an electric source to feed pellets or power a blower, and you can use a gas or electric source to light your fire (and cook your breakfast while you man the fire), but you can't cook your competition meat with either one.

You can use either charcoal briquettes, lump charcoal, hardwood, or pellets. Since charcoal has no flavor, most people add wood chips or pellets to a charcoal fire. Most barbequers use what's indigenous to their area—alder in the Pacific Northwest, mesquite in Texas, maple in Vermont, and pecan, cherry, and oak in many parts of the United States. Hickory and mesquite can add a slightly bitter flavor. Pecan, cherry, and oak all impart a mild smoke. There's a wood chart on page 291 that lists the flavor properties and suggested uses of a variety of woods.

MARINATING: Most competition cooks marinate their meat before smoking it. Marinades are simply flavor-infused liquids. In addition to herbs, condiments, spices, and oils, marinades typically include an acid, such as lemon or lime juice, wine, vinegar, beer, or dairy. The acids work on the proteins, lightly tenderizing the meat while balancing out sweet or spicy flavors in the marinade. Adding sweet ingredients to the marinade can help form appealing caramelized, crispy coatings on grilled meats. Marinades are suitable for any type of meat, fish, poultry, or vegetables. Do your marinating under refrigeration—either in a refrigerator at home or in a cooler at competition. Meat should be kept below 40°F. There is a marinating chart on page 291 with suggested marinating times for various meats.

WHY THE GREEN LETTUCES IN KCBS CONTEST ENTRY BOXES?

Since the early days of the KCBS, contestants have been required to present their meat entries on a bed of green lettuce. Curly parsley or cilantro may also be used. This rule has stirred up some controversy over the years, but the organization has remained steadfast in upholding it. When he proposed the rule, Gary Wells said that lettuce, instead of grease and sauce on Styrofoam, would make the meat look more appealing to judges. Yet the debate goes on, and you'll still hear critics ask, "Is it meat we're judging or meat salad?"

BRINING: A lot of people brine their meat for contest cooking. The basic components of a brine are salt, water, and any seasonings you want. It used to be that brines were a supersaturated water you could float an egg in. Now brines are usually lighter, with about ½ to 1 cup of kosher salt per gallon of water. Most people prefer kosher salt to any other kind because the flavor is pure. There is a brining chart on page 291 with suggested brining times for various meats.

BASTING: Many cooks use apple juice as a baste, since it tends to add moisture without significantly altering the flavor of the meat. You could even add a little liquor to the apple juice if you do want to change or boost the flavor. About halfway through the cooking time, start basting the meat every hour or so, or when you are in the pit for a good reason. Adding something to the pit and turning the meat are good reasons. Just checking to see how the meat is doing is not a valid reason!

CHICKEN OR CORNISH HEN

KCBS contest rules allow whole chicken or Cornish hen, or any parts of chicken or Cornish hen, to be entered in this category. Both are in the same genus, scientifically speaking, and all the same rules apply to cooking them for a contest. However, chicken is much more common in contests, and chicken thighs are the most popular cut of choice, due to their tenderness and juiciness. Despite that, we're giving you a recipe for whole chicken here.

When selecting chicken, look for chicken that has been chill-packed. That means the chicken has not been pumped or tumbled in a broth or water to add weight and give it a longer shelf life. It will not be in a sealed pouch and should not be full of water. The same goes for any piece of chicken you buy.

BARBEQUED CHICKEN

Serves 2 to 4

1 (3½- to 4½-pound) whole chicken

2 cups of your favorite marinade

¼ to ½ cup of your favorite barbeque rub

To prepare the chicken, rinse it inside and out with cold water. If possible, do that at home before you go to a contest. Rinse the chicken and pat dry with paper towels. Most people marinate or brine their meat—especially chicken. To marinate the chicken, place it in a 1-gallon resealable plastic bag, pour the marinade into the cavity of the chicken, seal the bag, and roll the chicken around, making sure the marinade covers all of the chicken. Place the bag of chicken in an ice chest or refrigerator and marinate for 4 hours, rolling or otherwise agitating the chicken about every hour for best coverage. Remove the chicken from the marinade and discard the marinade. Pat the chicken dry with paper towels. Season it all over, inside and out, with rub.

Place the chicken in the smoker and cook for 3½ to 4 hours, or until the internal temperature of the thigh or breast registers at least 165°F on a meat thermometer and the juices run clear.

SNAPSHOT OF A CONTEST

Barbeque is all about food, family, fun, and friends, so it's no surprise that barbeque contests have become a popular centerpiece for community festivals.

WHO COOKS IN BARBEQUE CONTESTS?

While at first glance it may appear to be a male-dominated sport, KCBS has many fine female cooks. Lots of teams are made up of family members helping educate the next generation of competition barbequers. There are no racial, gender, or sociological barriers. The only necessary quality is a love of barbeque.

WHO JUDGES THESE COMPETITIONS?

KCBS has certified more than fifteen thousand judges since inception of the CBJ (Certified Barbeque Judge) program. These dedicated folks travel, at their own expense, to contests all over the country to judge world-class barbeque. They use the KCBS circuit as a route map to see the country.

WHO ORGANIZES CONTESTS?

Civic awareness groups use barbeque contests to attract others to their community, to raise money for charity, and to bolster tourism. Some examples of these groups are parks and recreation departments, chambers of commerce, convention and visitors bureaus, and service organizations (Sertoma, Lions, etc.). Other contests are put on by individual charity organizations. There is also a small group of event promoters.

WHO ATTENDS?

Anyone wanting to experience that sense of community, the entertainment, the education, and the chance to sample world-class barbeque. A barbeque contest is culinary tourism at its best.

WHAT IS A KCBS-SANCTIONED CONTEST?

While each has its own signature, a contest is framed by the organizer. The organizer is licensed to use our "system" and provides the venue, prizes, and infrastructure. KCBS provides access to potential teams and judges, as well as the

ARDIE DAVIS—a/k/a REMUS
"Sauce Taster of the Year"

t is universally against health department rules for teams to dispense barbeque to the general public unless they have proper permits, licenses, insurance, and equipment. Most events will have credentialed vendors selling great 'Que. Other events have developed programs like "Buck-a-Bone," People's Choice, and/or tasting kits for sampling.

Buck-a-Bone originated in the days when you could buy a $1 ticket from the contest organizer and exchange it with the vendor for a rib. Both the seller and the contest organizer shared in the profits. The concept survives today, but prices have generally gone up, and the price structure varies from contest to contest.

People's Choice is usually done with tickets and allows people to taste and vote on barbeque. It's not a scientific procedure—it's just for fun. In most cases it's not even the same barbeque the judges are tasting for the main event, but something the teams have cooked up especially for People's Choice. It's still quite an honor to be voted the best by folks attending the competition.

Many contests also issue tasting kits allowing people to sample the barbeque. The local health department still keeps an eye on all of these things, but this way the public can taste some contest-worthy barbeque.

COMPETITION TIP:
To extend the height of your folding table(s), cut 1¾ inches to 2 inches of PVC pipe in about 14-inch sections for a 6- to 8-foot table and 24 inches for the 4-foot tables. Place the legs of the table in one end of each of the pipes. This is a great tip and saves your back!

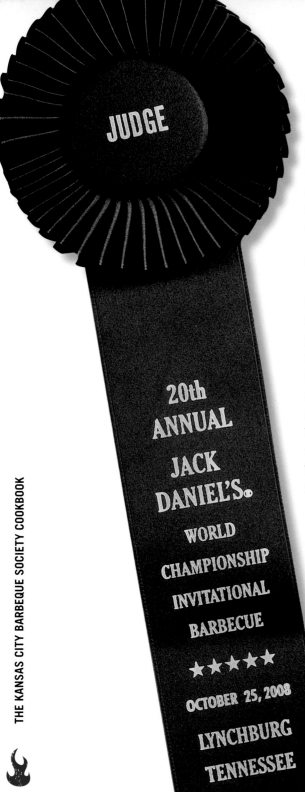

JUDGE

20th ANNUAL JACK DANIEL'S® WORLD CHAMPIONSHIP INVITATIONAL BARBECUE

★★★★★

OCTOBER 25, 2008

LYNCHBURG TENNESSEE

method and personnel for conducting the barbeque contest portion of the event. Picture a community that moves into your community—cooks, judges, contest representatives. KCBS's internal community is largely self-sufficient and self-policing. The teams know the rules, the judges know the procedures, and the Contest Reps meet and greet teams, and conduct the cooks' meeting, judges' meeting, and tabulation of scores. All these components are interdependent and all segments are necessary for a successful contest.

WHAT IS THE KCBS SYSTEM?

Contestants cooking in a KCBS-sanctioned contest are judged in four categories: chicken, pork ribs, pork (butt, shoulder, or picnic ham), and beef brisket. Each entry in each category is scored for appearance, taste, and tenderness, using a scale from 9 (excellent) to 1 (disqualification). Cumulative points for all four categories are used to determine where each team has placed from grand champion on down. Cooks have to compete in one or more of the four main categories, but organizers may also add other categories, such as anything butt, dessert, appetizers, wraps, wings, or something of the organizer's choosing. It's always fun to compete in these extra categories, but they do not count toward grand champion points. One of the fastest-growing categories is kids' 'Qs, which is fostering the next generation of cookers—and some mighty proud parents.

WHEN ARE CONTESTS HELD?

Used to be that contest season was Memorial Day through Labor Day. Now it is year-round. Felda, Forida (go to the edge of the earth and turn left, then go 30 miles farther), starts on New Year's Eve and is judged on New Year's Day. Seriously, people love this contest. January through March, contests are held in the Sunbelt; April opens "season," and it continues through November. There's even a contest in December (Demopolis, Alabama) featuring a boat parade strung with Christmas lights. Anytime is barbeque time!

WHERE CAN I FIND A CONTEST?

The setting could be a park, parking lot, fairground, or around the town square. Any place large enough to

accommodate the cooking teams and the public is acceptable. Music is part of the mix—country and western, rock and roll, bluegrass, blues, jazz, and zydeco work well. Other activities such as a car show, children's activities, a crafts fair, and an art show are often welcome additions to the festivities.

WHY?

It is Americana. Civic awareness and fund-raising are the primary motivations. Showcasing your community and exposing the public to competition barbeque is a natural. Barbeque people enjoy giving back. Organizers love the exposure to the uninitiated and the chance to experience the best 'Que they will ever eat. It is a celebration of barbeque as a food group (the one that was perfected in the USA)—its heritage, its progress (while preserving the heritage), and the premise that we love to feed those we love. Next to funeral food, barbeque is a food bond that is woven into the fabric of America in politics, religion, and society.

In our 25 years, we've sanctioned several thousand events. Have we had hiccups? To be sure. But our 99 percent success rate speaks for itself. We are working hard on the 1 percent! There are other fine sanctioning organizations, and they are friends, but this is our book, so we won't go there. Let us know if we can help.

ONE OF THE FASTEST-GROWING CATEGORIES IS KIDS' 'QS, WHICH IS FOSTERING THE NEXT GENERATION OF COOKERS—AND SOME MIGHTY PROUD PARENTS.

BARBEQUED PORK RIBS: SPARERIBS, ST. LOUIS–STYLE RIBS, LOIN BACK (BABY BACK) RIBS

KCBS contest rules allow spareribs, St. Louis–style ribs, and loin back (baby back) ribs in this category.

When choosing a slab of ribs, first look at the meat coverage over the bones. No bones should be showing through the meat. A bone that is showing through the meat is called a *shiner*. With some cuts of meat, fat is a good thing, adding flavor and moisture. However, with ribs, don't choose slabs with big pockets of fat.

PORK SPARERIBS

Spareribs are the intact rib section removed from the belly of the hog. They may include costal cartilages with or without the brisket removed and the diaphragm trimmed from the edge of the skirt. There are several parts of the sparerib that we need to identify:

1. **FULL SLAB**—Nine to twelve ribs with the breast (or brisket) bone and skirt attached. Ideally, a full slab of spareribs should have at least eleven ribs, but the government says nine or more is acceptable.

2. **BREAST (OR BRISKET) BONE**—The thick bone that runs along the top of the slab of ribs.

3. **SKIRT**—Small flap of meat attached to the bone side of the ribs.

4. **MEMBRANE**—The semitransparent film attached to the bone side of the ribs. It is advisable to remove the membrane before cooking ribs.

To prepare a slab of pork ribs for barbequing, turn the slab, bone side up. Remove the membrane that covers the bones. To do this, insert a table knife or other blunt instrument underneath one edge of the membrane to loosen it. Once you loosen enough to get a good hold on it, grab the membrane and slowly pull it up and away from the meat, working from the top edge of the ribs to the bottom. It may help to use a paper towel to grip the membrane. Once the

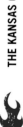

membrane is removed, trim any excess fat. Then you're ready to smoke the ribs.

ST. LOUIS–STYLE PORK SPARERIBS

St. Louis–style ribs originate from pork spareribs. They are prepared by taking a full slab of pork spareribs and removing the breast/brisket bone approximately parallel to the rib side, exposing the gristle on the brisket bone side. The piece that is cut off is what's commonly known as *rib tips.* Then the skirt meat is removed. Cooking the skirt makes a good sampler—or a meal if you have enough of them. Remove the membrane as you would for pork spareribs.

PORK LOIN BACK (BABY BACK) RIBS

The back rib is the section of the pork ribs closest to the spine. Remove the membrane as you would for pork spareribs.

PORK SHOULDER BUTT OR PICNIC

In the early years of KCBS contest rules, any part of the pig could be entered in the pork category. The tenderloin became the cut of choice for most teams. After a lengthy discussion of the pros and cons, the KCBS Board adopted a rule that entries in the pork category would be limited to the whole pork shoulder, the butt, or the picnic.

Between whole shoulder, butt, and picnic, the butt (the top half of the shoulder) is the most popular cut of choice among competition cooks. The first thing to look for in a pork butt is its size. A 7- to 9-pound pork butt is preferable. By rule, it must be at least 5 pounds. The next thing to look for is leanness. Most pork butts have enough fat without buying one with excess fat. Good pork butts are well marbled all the way through. Most barbequers pull pork or chop it, rather than slice it, but all three methods are acceptable for presentation.

The whole shoulder is the next most popular cut in this contest category. When selecting a shoulder, you can choose any size you want, but a 12- to 16-pound shoulder is a good size.

The picnic is the lower half of the whole pork shoulder. Look for leanness when selecting one to cook.

BARBEQUED PORK RIBS
Serves 4 to 6

2 slabs pork ribs, trimmed

¼ cup of your favorite mustard slather (optional)

¼ to ½ cup of your favorite barbeque rub

Use a pastry brush to lightly coat the ribs on the bone side with half of the mustard slather. Sprinkle with half of the rub. Repeat the process on the meat side.

Set up your smoker to cook using indirect heat at 230º to 250ºF. Place the ribs in your smoker, meat side up, and smoke until done, turning every half-time. For pork spareribs (including St. Louis style), that means turning 4 to 6 hours into cooking, turning again 2 to 3 hours later, and turning again 1 to 1½ hours later. For loin back (or baby back) ribs, turn 3 to 4 hours into cooking, again 1½ to 2 hours later, and again 45 minutes to 1 hour later.

How do you know if the ribs are done? Take two side-by-side ribs and pull them apart. If they tear easily, they are done.

PULLED-PORK ADDITIONS

You can serve your competition pork plain or add sauces or spices to flavor it—just make sure they're not puddled or pooled. Here are a couple of things you can add to pulled pork to serve it:

Mix in equal parts beef broth, chicken broth, and apple cider vinegar (all to taste), adding each slowly and blending well, being careful not to make it too soupy. Add some rub to taste.

Mix in about 2 parts barbeque sauce to 1 part apple cider vinegar, adding each slowly and blending well, being careful not to make it too soupy. Add some rub to taste.

BARBEQUED PORK BUTT

Serves 12 to 14

1 (7- to 9-pound) pork butt

1 quart of your favorite brine (optional)

1 cup of your favorite mustard slather (optional)

½ cup of your favorite barbeque rub

Trim any excess fat from the pork butt. If you're brining the butt, use an injection needle to inject the brine into the butt in small doses evenly distributed around the butt. Place the butt in a 1- or 2-gallon resealable plastic bag and place in an ice chest or refrigerator for 6 to 8 hours, turning occasionally. Remove the butt from the brine, rinse it with cold running water, and discard the brine. Pat dry with paper towels.

Coat the bottom and sides of the butt with a light coating of mustard slather; then season with half of the rub. Repeat on the top and both sides, using the same procedure.

Prepare your smoker to cook at 230° to 250°F. Place the butt in the hot smoker, fat side up. Plan on cooking it for 12 to 14 hours, turning every half-time (6 to 7 hours into cooking, 3 to 3½ hours later, and 1½ to 1¾ hours later).

If you are looking for an internal temperature: If slicing the meat, cook it until it registers 185°F on a meat thermometer. If pulling the meat, cook it to 195° to 205°F. Let the meat rest for 10 to 15 minutes before you slice or pull it.

BEEF BRISKET

Beef brisket is regarded by most contest cooks as the most difficult cut of meat to barbeque. It is a tough cut of meat but can be rendered tender and delicious via the slow and low methods of cooking you'll find in this book.

Brisket is the breast of a steer. A whole brisket can be cut into flat and point cuts. Flat cuts have less fat and are usually more expensive than whole briskets. Point cuts are not readily available commercially, so most cooks use whole or flat cuts.

The first thing to look for in beef brisket is the thickness of the flat or blade. The thicker the better. Choose a brisket with an even thickness across the meat, rather than one that is thicker on one end and tapers down to the other side. You also want hard white fat, which tells you that the steer has been fed on grain.

It's also good to wet-age your brisket for 30 to 40 days when you have time to plan ahead. What this means is that you purchase your brisket 30 days before your next contest and keep it in the Cryo-vac bag in your refrigerator. This gives the meat time to relax and makes it more tender.

When you cook a wet-aged brisket, start checking the internal temperature 10 hours into cooking it and check again every hour until you get to an internal temperature of 180°F.

One that's not wet-aged will take longer to cook—12 to 14 hours. The optimum internal temperature for slicing brisket is 185° to 195°F.

BARBEQUED BEEF BRISKET

Serves 18 to 20

1 (10- to 12-pound) certified Angus brisket

½ cup of your favorite mustard slather (optional)

½ cup of your favorite barbeque rub

Trim the fat on the brisket down to ¼ to ⅛ inch. Coat the lean part and the sides of the brisket with a light coating of mustard slather, season with rub, and repeat on the fat side. Don't forget to season the sides of the brisket, too.

Preheat your smoker to 230° to 250°F. Place the brisket in the smoker, fat side up. If your brisket is not wet-aged, plan on cooking it for 12 to 14 hours, turning every half-time. If you're cooking a wet-aged brisket, start checking the internal temperature at 10 hours. The ideal slicing temperature is 185° to 195°F.

GRAND CHAMPION
TAYLORVILLE MAIN STREET
BBQ-BLUES & CRUISE
2009

SHOW ME
YOUR RIBS

Bone
HOT SUCKIN'
Sauce

KINGS
Barbeque Sauce

SMOKEHOUSE
BARBEQUE SAUCE

MOONSHINE

WILBER'S
Barbecue Sauce

APPETIZERS

We don't know who originated the notion that food tidbits served in small portions will perk up your appetite for the main course. Maybe it works at social gatherings of another sort, but when you bite into most appetizers from KCBS members, you could end up eating until you're too full for the main course. If you want our recipes to work as appetizers, you may have to serve them in small quantities and resist making a backup supply. When you're out, you're out.

DELBERT KENNESON

This is called "Level 1 Trauma Salsa" for a reason—it's a lot of heat! Delbert Kenneson loves very hot food, but it also has to be flavorful. He developed this recipe after a little experimentation. It makes a great relish for hogs and sausages and is great on burgers. You can add it to chili or stews, and it is perfect on a chip. It will keep for up to 2 months in the refrigerator, and it gets hotter with age.

DOC K'S LEVEL 1 TRAUMA SALSA

Makes about 4 cups

1 large red onion

1 large green bell pepper

2 poblano chiles

5 large jalapeño chiles

5 habanero chiles

5 serrano chiles

5 Thai chiles

Juice of 1 lime

½ teaspoon kosher or sea salt

1 tablespoon freshly cracked black pepper

1 (28-ounce) can crushed tomatoes

Peel and dice the onion and place it in a food processor. Cut off the cap (the stem end) of the green pepper, remove the veins and seeds, dice it into medium pieces, and place it in a food processor. Trim off the caps of all the chiles and dice them, but do not remove the veins and seeds; add them to the food processor. Add the lime juice and the salt and pepper. Process until minced. Pour the mixture into a large resealable food storage container and add the can of tomatoes. Stir until thoroughly mixed.

Note: *Warning: Try this salsa at your own risk. We haven't tested it for Scoville units, but we know the combination of poblano, jalapeño, habanero, serrano, and Thai chiles in Doc's salsa will go beyond trauma in individuals who are fiery-chile-intolerant. This is a serious combination of fire!*

MANGO SALSA

Makes about 2½ cups

1 cup diced peeled mango

¼ cup diced red onion

1 tablespoon diced seeded
jalapeño chile,
or to taste

½ cup diced tomato

½ cup chopped fresh cilantro

Juice of 1 lime

Salt (optional)

In a medium bowl, combine the mango, onion, jalapeño, tomato, and cilantro. Pour the freshly squeezed lime juice over the top and mix well. If desired, season with a little salt. Refrigerate for 1 to 2 hours before serving.

ARTICHOKE SPREAD

Makes about 3½ cups

1 (14-ounce) can artichoke hearts (packed in water,
not oil), drained and chopped

1 cup grated Asiago cheese

1 to 2 cloves garlic, minced

1 teaspoon fresh lemon juice

½ cup mayonnaise, or more as needed

Salt and freshly ground black pepper

Blend all the ingredients together, adding more mayonnaise if needed to achieve your desired consistency. Refrigerate for at least 1 hour before serving.

LEW MILLER

The combination of mango and jalapeño gives this an interesting sweet-hot flavor. It's great with tortilla chips or on top of bar-bequed chicken.

PAUL SEABROOK

This recipe is a hit wherever Paul takes it. Serve it with your favorite crackers or sliced baguette. Paul says it's also good as a hamburger condiment.

OFFICIAL KCBS BARBEQUE JUDGES OATH

BY ARDIE A. DAVIS,
AKA REMUS POWERS,
PHB

Ardie penned this oath in 1984 for the Diddy-Wa-Diddy National Barbecue Sauce Contest. He adapted it later for barbeque meat-cooking contests and donated it to the Kansas City Barbeque Society (KCBS) in 1989 for use at sanctioned contests. The oath was also given by Remus to judges at the Memphis in May World Championship Barbecue from the late 1980s to the early 1990s. Thousands of judges from across the United States take the oath each year.

I do solemnly swear
To objectively and subjectively evaluate
Each Barbeque Meat
That is presented
To my eyes,
my nose,
my hands,
and my palate.

I accept my duty
To be a [name of contest]* judge,
So that truth,
justice,
excellence in barbeque,
and the American Way of Life,
May be strengthened and preserved forever.
You're on your oath!

* Ardie says this rapidly and makes it too long for most judges to remember and repeat—e.g., "2011 Tenth Annual Harpoon Brewery New England Barbecue Society Championship Barbecue Judge."

DOVIE'S DAUGHTER'S BREAD BOWL BBQ DIP

Serves 10 to 12

1 (1-pound) round loaf whole wheat or multigrain bread

½ pound chopped barbequed pork butt or beef brisket (or ¼ pound of each)

½ pound apple- or hickory-smoked thick-sliced bacon, fried crispy and crumbled

1 (8-ounce) package cream cheese, at room temperature

¾ cup sour cream

½ cup KC Masterpiece Classic Blend (low calorie) or your favorite tomato-based barbeque sauce

1 (4-ounce) can chopped green chiles, drained

5 scallions, chopped

Tortilla or pita chips, for dipping

Prepare your pit to cook with indirect heat at 350°F.

Slice off the top ½ inch of the bread loaf and set it aside to cover the dip later. Scoop the bread from inside the loaf, leaving a ½-inch-thick wall. Save the bread for crumbs or other recipes or feed the birds. Combine the barbequed meat, bacon, cream cheese, sour cream, barbeque sauce, chiles, and scallions. Mix well. Fill the bread bowl with the mixture and top it with the lid. Wrap the bowl in heavy-duty aluminum foil. Bake or roast with indirect heat for 1 hour and 15 minutes. Unwrap the bowl and place it on a serving plate. Discard the foil. Serve the dip with tortilla or pita chips for dipping.

ARDIE A. DAVIS, PHB

Ardie's inspiration for this recipe came from a spiral-bound "Coontz Family Recipes and Memories" book he found in a Waseca, Minnesota, flea market. Patsy Ledgerwood, daughter of Dovie Coontz, submitted the original recipe. Ardie added barbeque ingredients and other tweaks. Warning: Your guests will be tempted to fill up on this dip and chips before the main course is served!

TANA FRENSLEY-SHUPE, PHB

Nostalgic to some, a new idea to others, Tana's cheese ball will be memorable to all. Tana recommends serving it with Wheat Thins or your cracker of choice.

CHEESE BALL
Serves 8 to 10

2 (8-ounce) packages cream cheese, at room temperature

1 (2.25-ounce) jar Armour Star Sliced Dried Beef

1 bunch of scallions, minced

1½ teaspoons Worcestershire sauce

1 teaspoon Accent seasoning, or more or less to taste

Combine the cream cheese, dried beef, scallions, Worcestershire sauce, and Accent seasoning and mix well. Form the mixture into a ball or loaf and chill.

TIM'S HONEY HOT WINGS

Serves 6 to 8

3 pounds chicken wings, cut into sections, tips discarded

1 cup Frank's RedHot sauce or your favorite

1 tablespoon cayenne

Butter spray

1 to 2 cups clover honey

Marinate the wings in Frank's RedHot. If you use a vacuum tumbler, marinate for 20 minutes; otherwise marinate the wings overnight in a resealable plastic bag.

After marinating, lightly and evenly sprinkle both sides of the wings with cayenne.

Prepare a charcoal grill for direct medium heat. Place the wings on the grill; spray liberally with butter spray. Grill for about 5 minutes. Turn the wings over, spray the other side with butter spray, cover the grill, and cook for 3 to 4 minutes, until crispy. Drizzle half of the honey over the wings and grill for about 5 minutes more, or until the wings are done.

Remove the wings from the grill and drizzle the remaining honey over the side not already coated with it.

WENDY AND TIM BOUCHER, FEEDING FRIENDZ BBQ TEAM

This recipe was the Feeding Friendz BBQ Team's winning entry in the "People's Choice Wing" competition at Chillin' Country BBQ State Competition, held in York, Maine. The butter spray gives the wings a crispy skin. The honey is a nice complement to the hot sauce.

RICH AND BUNNY TUTTLE, K CASS BBQ

Rich and Bunny tell us they must give their chicken man, Jeff Seigler, some credit here, although they altered this recipe just a little. He used to cook on their team and did some mighty fine chicken wings. He now has his own team called Ziggys Piggys. If you ever went to the Blue Springs Barbeque Blazeoff in Blue Springs, Missouri, and if you were lucky enough to get there before Rich, Bunny, and Jeff ran out, you got to eat some gooooood wingies! You could serve them with barbeque sauce, blue cheese, or ranch, but Rich and Bunny "garontee" they are better naked!

CHICKEN MAN'S WINGS

About 200 pieces, so it serves a crowd or Paul Kirk

20 pounds chicken wings, tips discarded or saved for stock

1 gallon Louisiana-style hot sauce

1 (13.5-ounce) container Willingham's Cajun Hot Wham Seasoning

Wash and pat dry the chicken wings. Put in a medium cooler or other large container and pour all of the Louisiana hot sauce over the wings. Marinate for at least 2 hours.

Prepare your grill for medium-hot cooking with coals on one side. This will allow you to spin your grate and alternate wings over the heat. Start sprinkling on the seasoning and be liberal with it. Continue turning the grate and turning the wings as they are grilled. The wings will take about 20 minutes. They will appear to be drier, like Memphis dry style.

PINEAPPLE HOT WINGS

Serves 4 to 6, including 2¾ cups rub

ALL-PURPOSE RED RUB

½ cup paprika

½ cup kosher salt

½ cup packed light brown sugar

½ cup granulated garlic

6 tablespoons granulated onion

WINGS

3 pounds chicken wings, tips discarded
or saved for stock

1 (12-ounce) jar Texas Pineapple Habanero Pepper Jelly

2 cups barbeque sauce

Combine all the rub ingredients in a bowl and rub them together with your hands. Store in an airtight plastic or glass container until ready to use. It will keep for up to 6 months if kept away from heat and light.

Set up your grill to cook indirectly at 230° to 250°F. Cut the chicken wings into two pieces at the joint. Put a light coat of the rub on them and put them on the grill on the side away from the fire.

Heat the pepper jelly in a small saucepan over medium heat until it melts, 5 to 7 minutes. After the wings have cooked for about 30 minutes, or until they register 170°F internally, baste them thoroughly with the pepper jelly. Let the baste set for about 10 minutes and then brush lightly with your favorite barbeque sauce. Cook for another 10 minutes to set the glaze.

KELL PHELPS

According to Kell, this is the perfect appetizer. Don't worry—these are not as hot as they sound. If you find they are a bit too spicy, just let them stay on the grill a bit longer after basting them. The longer they cook after basting, the less heat you will taste. You can get Pineapple Habanero Pepper Jelly from Texas Pepper Jelly, texaspepperjelly.com.

BILL MORRIS, AKA BILLY BOB BILLY

If you like your dip good and spicy, this is for you. It will liven up any party. You can use cream cheese instead of the Neufchâtel in this recipe. Neufchâtel has 40 percent less fat. Make this dip volcanic by adding a sliced habanero prior to heating or simply add the habanero prior to serving to add a surprise to some bites. If the peppers are added prior to heating, the heat will spread through all of the dip! Serve it with your favorite chips or pita triangles.

BBQ CHICKEN BUFFALO WING DIP

Serves 6 to 8

2 barbequed chicken breasts or 1 whole barbequed chicken, boned and pulled

1 (8-ounce) package Neufchâtel cheese or cream cheese, at room temperature

1 cup ranch dressing

1½ cups wing sauce

Hot sauce, such as Tabasco, to taste

1 cup thinly sliced celery (about 2 stalks)

8 ounces blue cheese, crumbled

Preheat the oven to 350°F.

Use two forks to shred the chicken breast meat; then coarsely chop it. You want the chicken pieces small enough to be lifted by chips or pita points. Combine the cheese and ranch dressing in a bowl, stirring until smooth. Add the wing sauce, stirring to combine thoroughly, followed by the hot sauce to achieve your desired level of heat. Add the chicken and celery, stirring until fully blended.

Pour the mixture into a 9-inch square baking dish and bake for 15 to 20 minutes, until the surface is bubbly. The dip does not need to be cooked, only heated through. Remove from the oven and allow to cool enough to be eaten. Sprinkle with the crumbled blue cheese just before serving.

KC MASTERPIECE SAUSAGE BALLS

Serves 6 to 8

1 pound bulk seasoned turkey sausage

1 egg, beaten

⅓ cup fresh bread crumbs

1 teaspoon rubbed sage

½ cup KC Masterpiece Hickory Barbecue Sauce

2 tablespoons packed brown sugar

2 tablespoons white vinegar

1 tablespoon soy sauce

In a large bowl, combine the sausage, egg, bread crumbs, and sage. Shape into bite-sized balls. Brown in an ungreased heavy skillet over medium heat. Drain off the excess fat. Mix together the barbeque sauce, brown sugar, vinegar, and soy sauce and add to the skillet. Simmer over low heat for about 20 minutes, stirring occasionally to prevent sticking. Serve hot with toothpicks.

With the last name Davis, and his notoriety in barbeque and barbeque sauce, Ardie is often asked, "Are you the KC Masterpiece guy?" He replies, "No, he's a dear friend, but that's Rich Davis. I'm Poor Davis."

RICH DAVIS

Dr. Rich Davis is a friend, hero, and legend to us and to thousands of KCBS members. Rich gave us this recipe for our previous KCBS cookbook. We like these sausage balls so much that we're giving them an encore.

ROBERT (BBQ BOB) PEPITONE

According to Robert, this recipe was adapted from one called Pig Candy, which has appeared on many Web sites, including www.barbecuebible.com, of which he is a member. The Pig Candy recipe ingredients are bacon, brown sugar, and cayenne. Robert has made this more than once, and since he's a fan of Spam, he gave it a try last year and even added chopped pecans (which weren't in the original recipe). Robert says friends and family love it, and it seems to be a big hit at barbecuebible.com. He even placed second in a contest at Glen Rock Athletic Club in Glen Rock, New Jersey.

SPAM CANDY
Serves 8 to 10

1 (12-ounce) can Spam

1 cup firmly packed brown sugar

¼ teaspoon cayenne

½ cup chopped pecans

Grilled pineapple slices, for serving (optional)

Prepare your smoker with cherry wood. Slice the Spam ¼ inch thick. Combine the brown sugar, cayenne, and pecans. Place the sliced Spam on the grill grate and sprinkle half of the brown sugar mixture on the Spam. Smoke for 1 hour; then flip the Spam slices and sprinkle the remaining sugar mixture on the other side. Smoke for another hour. Serve with grilled pineapple slices.

BURGER ROLLS

Serves 10 to 12

2 pounds ground chuck

1 cup grated cheddar cheese

1 yellow onion, chopped

20 saltine crackers, crushed into crumbs

¼ cup packed brown sugar

1 cup milk

2 tablespoons barbeque sauce, plus more for basting

½ teaspoon celery seeds

¼ teaspoon black pepper

1 teaspoon salt

12 slices bacon

Prepare either a medium-hot grill or a smoker (230° to 250°F).

In a large bowl, combine the ground chuck, cheese, onion, cracker crumbs, brown sugar, milk, barbeque sauce, celery seeds, black pepper, and salt. Use your hands or a heavy spoon to mix well. Divide the mixture into 12 thick, log-shaped rolls. Wrap each roll with bacon, securing the ends with toothpicks.

Place the logs on the grill or smoker and baste with barbeque sauce. Cover the grill or smoker. Grill for 30 to 45 minutes, turning every 10 minutes, until done, or smoke for about 1 hour and 25 minutes, until done, turning less frequently.

TED DENK

Ted made this up one day for a church function. Everybody liked it so much that he's expected to bring out the burger rolls on a regular basis.

DID SHE KNOW WHAT SHE WAS EATING? THE DC JOURNALIST PIG FRY INCIDENT AT THE JACK

In 1992 at the 4th Annual Jack Daniel's World Championship Invitational Barbecue, also known as "The Jack," Steve Holbrook deep-fried some of the most delicious pig testicles, also known as "pig fries," ever enjoyed at a barbeque contest or elsewhere. It was Friday night at the Beaver Castor's booth. People were devouring those fries as quickly as Steve could cook them. When a reporter from the *Washington Post* stopped by, Ardie urged her to "try some pig fries." She did, and she took quite a liking to them. We'll always wonder if she knew what she was eating. Was the joke on her or on us?

ARDIE A. DAVIS, PH8

These lightly smoked deviled eggs add a refreshing difference to this or your own favorite stuffing. The smoke pattern on the egg whites tells your guests, "These deviled eggs are something different!" Ardie gets best results from eggs laid by free-range chickens, sans growth hormones and antibiotics. The yolks are richer in color and flavor than standard supermarket eggs. Eggs that have been refrigerated for a week or two peel better than eggs that are fresher. Have a little extra of the stuffing ingredients available in case you need to adjust the amounts.

SMOKED DEVILED EGGS
Makes 24

12 eggs

⅔ cup canola or olive oil mayonnaise

¼ cup Dijon-style prepared mustard

¼ cup corn relish or pickle relish (sweet or dill)

¼ teaspoon black pepper

Pinch of kosher or sea salt

Pinch of cayenne

¼ cup chopped fresh parsley (curly or flat-leaf), for garnish

Hard-boil the eggs. Cool them in cold water; then drain off the water and refrigerate the eggs (still in their shells) for at least 1 hour or overnight.

Light half a chimney of charcoal briquettes (about 25 briquettes). While they fire up, remove the eggs from the refrigerator and gently roll each egg on a hard surface, creating cracks on the shells. That's where the smoke gets in.

When the fire is ready, place the eggs on a clean, oiled grill grate opposite the fire. Drop ½ cup hardwood chips (your choice; no need to soak in water) directly on the fire, cover your grill, and smoke the eggs for 5 minutes. Remove the eggs, let them cool, and then peel them.

Cut the eggs in half lengthwise and place the yolks in a bowl. Add the filling ingredients and use a table fork to mix until well blended. Add mayo, mustard, or other ingredients as needed for texture and taste.

With a tablespoon, fill the hollow in each egg white with the yolk mixture. Sprinkle with the chopped parsley for garnish.

GRILLED FRESH RAVIOLI

Serves as many as you wish

Fresh ravioli

Olive oil, for brushing

Salt and black pepper

Remove the ravioli from the package, handling them carefully, as they may stick together. Separate the ravioli and brush both sides of each with olive oil. Sprinkle with salt and pepper.

Preheat the grill to cook indirectly on low or medium-low heat. For a charcoal grill, wait until the peak red-hot coals cool to all gray. Place the ravioli on the preheated grill, close the lid, and grill for 5 to 8 minutes. Gently turn the ravioli a few times for super searing as they puff up.

Note: *Judge the initial sear marks to get an indication of how hot you are cooking. If the sear marks are dark to black on the first flip, you are cooking too hot. Turn down the burners or move to a cooler area until the heat is reduced.*

BRAD BARRETT

This is an innovative, easy, and delicious way to cook ravioli, transforming them into a light, crispy side or appetizer. Grilled ravioli is more like a puff pastry than a soggy boiled pasta. Large, fresh, refrigerated ravioli can be purchased in the deli section of most grocery stores. No preboiling is necessary. You can substitute thawed frozen ravioli, but not dried pasta. Any ravioli filling will work! Serve with your favorite dipping sauce, such as marinara.

BELINDA DAVIS

Belinda developed this recipe after a discussion she and her husband, Brad, had at a Chinese restaurant one night. Belinda loves Chinese rangoons, and she wondered what pulled-pork rangoons would taste like. A few weeks later, Belinda and Brad whipped up the following recipe, and it turned out to be really good! Because of package size, you'll need to buy more wrappers than you may need for this recipe, but you'll probably think these are so good you'll want to make another batch soon.

CHUBBS SMOKIN' CHINESE PORK RANGOONS

Makes 40 to 60

1 cup chopped smoked pork butt

1 teaspoon minced scallion

½ (8-ounce) package cream cheese, at room temperature

½ teaspoon steak sauce (Belinda uses Country Bob's)

1 tablespoon minced garlic

1½ tablespoons chopped fresh parsley

1 tablespoon Worcestershire sauce

½ teaspoon soy sauce

½ teaspoon barbeque sauce

Dash of Chinese five-spice powder

1 (1-pound/60-count) package wonton wrappers

1 egg, beaten

Canola oil, for frying

Combine the pork butt, scallion, cream cheese, steak sauce, garlic, parsley, Worcestershire sauce, soy sauce, barbeque sauce, and five-spice powder. Mix well.

Place ½ teaspoon of the mixture in the center of a wonton wrapper; fold the square over to form a triangle. Brush the center with beaten egg. Bring opposite corners together and press gently, so the filling is secure. Repeat with the remaining filling. Once all the rangoons are prepared, heat the oil in a deep-fryer to 365° to 375°F. Fry the rangoons until golden brown—less than 2 minutes. You may want to start with just one wonton and reduce the heat if it cooks too fast. Serve hot.

PEANUT BUTTER JALAPEÑOS

Serves 4 to 6

1 can jalapeños, preferably ones that are already cut in half

Peanut butter (Mike recommends crunchy)

Drain the jalapeños. If they didn't come cut in half, cut them in half. Place the jalapeños on a serving tray and fill each with peanut butter. Enjoy!

MIKE AND CAROL SAWYERS

This recipe was created twenty years ago by Mike's uncle Bill. He was cooking barbeque and decided to make some snacks. With limited items in his kitchen and the barbeque not quite done, these were born. They create quite a conversation piece, especially when you're having a few, shall we say, refreshing beverages. At cook-offs, word gets around about these interesting objects at the Caddo Camp Cookers site. According to Mike, good friends have been met over these curious appetizers.

MONTANA
Big Sky Country
RUBIT BQ
9 200
MONTANA KD086440

Boiled Peanuts—

SOME BARBEQUERS LIKE 'EM. SOME DON'T.

Since his first encounter with boiled peanuts from an outdoor vendor on the banks of the Sewanee River several decades ago, Ardie has been a boiled peanut enthusiast. Carolyn isn't crazy about them, and Paul says they're great with beer. When Ardie has tried sharing boiled peanuts at barbeque events, only about 1 percent of barbequers have accepted a handful, some without much enthusiasm.

We asked Ted and Matt Lee, famous for their boiled peanuts as well as fans of barbeque and all southern foods, for some insights. Here's what they shared with us:

"We know people who like both barbeque and boiled peanuts, but they tend to reside only in the states in which both boiled peanuts *and* barbeque are traditions, which would be South Carolina, Georgia, northern Florida, some precincts of Alabama, and Hawaii (if you count pit-cooked kalua pig as barbeque, of course; boiled peanuts were brought to Hawaii in the 19th century by Chinese laborers. They're a slightly different recipe from those that came to North America from Africa, but that's a whole other story). We'll bet that your 99 percent of barbequers who refuse free boiled peanuts are people for whom boiled peanut culture is unfamiliar. That said, barbeque eaten in conjunction with boiled peanuts —while not unheard of—is not common, even in areas where both foods are consumed with abandon and glee.

I BRAKE FOR BOILED PEANUTS

TO ORDER MAIL $2 TO "BOILED P-NUT PRIDE" PO BOX 315, CHARLESTON, SC 29402 or visit www.boiledpeanuts.com

HOW TO EAT BOILED PEANUTS

Boiled peanuts start fresh and raw. They are boiled in the shell in salted fresh water until tender, usually at least 2 hours. Then they are scooped from the pot and drained. They are usually sold in a brown paper bag. You can also, of course, boil your own.

Shell the boiled peanuts as you do roasted peanuts and discard the shells. They make good compost. Eat and enjoy the way you would roasted peanuts, but expect a different flavor and texture. They are starchy and soft, like raw potato, instead of nutty and crunchy, like circus peanuts.

"In our experience, boiled peanuts are the stuff of ballpark games, fishing trips, stock car races, flea markets, and such. They tend to be eaten with beer or sodas, as a snack, with the shells thrown on the ground. You might find them at an oyster roast potluck or a fish fry. But we've rarely seen them at whole-hog barbeques and the like, and that may be because—strictly from a tasting perspective—while they're both delicious, they just don't go together. They're supremely decadent, insanely rich proteins, and they even have a similar earthy creaminess to them. So eating a handful of boiled peanuts after ingesting a pulled-pork barbeque sandwich would be like having a chaser of heavy cream after a plate of foie gras.

"But it's possible that there's something more fundamental in the distance between boiled peanuts and barbeque—something that points to our very existence. As any hog farmer knows, a peanut-fed hog is the best-tasting pork you'll ever eat. Eating boiled peanuts and pork barbeque in the same bite seems, well . . . it just ain't right, because it begs the question: Are we men, or are we pigs? An awful thought to ponder while gnawing on a snoot or a rib!"

We asked Ted and Matt if they had ever met anyone who liked boiled peanuts but didn't like barbeque. They replied, "Yes. Vegetarians. Believe it or not, we know one or two vegetarians, and they tend to love boiled peanuts, but not barbeque!"

Thanks, Lee brothers!

RONALD LEWIS BUCHHOLZ

Ron hails from Fitchburg, Wisconsin, by way of Milwaukee, and the ingredients in this smoked stuffed jalapeño recipe reflect his heritage and some of his favorite foods. It makes creative use of an empty dozen-count cardboard (not Styrofoam) egg carton with the lid cut off. For a smoky flavor, put ¼ cup unsoaked hardwood chips on the fire before covering the grill.

FIRE IN THE PASTURE!

Makes 12

1 (8-ounce) package cream cheese, at room temperature

¼ cup shredded Wisconsin sharp cheddar cheese

2 tablespoons beer, preferably Schlitz or Spotted Cow

2 teaspoons hot sauce, preferably Wisconsin Badgers

¼ teaspoon black pepper

Pinch of salt

6 slices thick-sliced bacon

12 jalapeño chiles, seeded

Prepare a medium-high grill to cook over indirect heat.

In a large bowl, combine the cream cheese, cheddar cheese, beer, hot sauce, black pepper, and salt. Mix with a table fork until the ingredients are thoroughly combined.

Using a sharp knife on a cutting board, slice a 1-pound package of bacon in half across the grain. Set aside.

Put the cheese mixture in a 1-quart resealable plastic bag. Seal the bag and, with scissors, cut about ¼ inch off one of the bottom corners of the bag.

Cut the lid off an empty cardboard dozen-count egg carton. Place the hollow jalapeños upright in each cup. Squeeze the cheese mixture into each chile. Save any leftover cheese mixture for spreading on crackers and enjoying while the chiles cook.

Cover the top of each stuffed chile with a half-slice of bacon, securing the sides with a plain round wooden toothpick stuck through the bacon and chile. Place the chiles back in the egg carton.

Put the chile-filled egg carton on your grill, opposite the fire, cover the grill, and cook the chiles for 40 to 45 minutes, until the bacon is as done as you like it. The egg carton will absorb the bacon grease; thus no flare-ups.

GRILLED QUESADILLAS

Serves 8

1 teaspoon olive oil

2 large flour tortillas

2 cups shredded Mexican-blend cheese
or mild cheddar

1 cup mild salsa or whatever heat you prefer

Preheat your grill to medium-low to medium direct heat. Brush the olive oil on one side of one tortilla and place the tortilla, oil side down. Sprinkle ½ cup of the cheese on the tortilla. Place the second tortilla on top, creating a sandwich. Spread the salsa on top; then sprinkle the remaining cheese on top of the salsa.

Put the quesadilla on the grill cover, and cook for 3 to 4 minutes. Rotate it a quarter turn and check out the searing on the bottom of the quesadilla. If the searing is dark/black, turn the heat down. Continue cooking until the cheese is melted and the crust turns a nice crispy brown another 4 to 6 minutes. Transfer the quesadilla to a cutting board and cut into 8 slices to serve.

BRAD BARRETT

Quesadillas are fun and easy. The key is the sandwich you create with two flour tortillas and the cheese. You get a firm and crispy crust that is the foundation for whatever you want to put on top.

APPETIZERS

35

PAUL KIRK, PHB

This is an easy and quick appetizer to impress any of your guests.

GRILLED EGGPLANT SANDWICH WITH OLIVE AND SUN-DRIED TOMATO TAPENADE

Serves 4

TAPENADE

4 ounces pitted kalamata olives

4 ounces sun-dried tomatoes (not oil-packed), coarsely chopped

2 tablespoons rinsed capers

1 clove garlic, coarsely chopped

2 tablespoons balsamic vinegar

2 teaspoons extra virgin olive oil

SANDWICHES

8 slices crusty whole-grain bread

1 medium eggplant (about ¾ pound), ends trimmed, thinly sliced crosswise

2 large tomatoes, thinly sliced

½ cup fresh basil leaves, coarsely chopped

Olive oil cooking spray

Preheat a gas grill to medium or prepare a charcoal grill.

In a food processor or blender, combine all the tapenade ingredients and process to a chunky purée, scraping the sides as needed. Set aside.

Spread the tapenade evenly over one side of each slice of bread. Set aside. Place the eggplant slices on the grill and cook until golden brown and tender, 5 to 6 minutes per side. Divide the eggplant slices among 4 slices of bread, arranging the eggplant over the tapenade. Top the eggplant with tomato slices and then sprinkle with chopped basil. Firmly press a second slice of bread on top of each to make sandwiches.

Lightly spray each side of the sandwiches with cooking spray. Grill the sandwiches until the filling is hot and the bread is browned and crisp, turning them carefully with a spatula, 2 to 4 minutes per side. Cut each sandwich in half to serve.

CHEF'S SHRIMP

Makes 16 to 18 large shrimp

1 pound (16- to 18-count) shrimp, peeled
and deveined

3 to 4 jalapeño chiles, julienned

6 slices pepper Jack cheese, cut into thirds

9 slices bacon, halved crosswise

Barbeque sauce, preferably Blues Hog, to taste

Place a shrimp, some chile slices, and a cheese slice on each strip of bacon. Roll everything up and skewer it with a wooden skewer. Place 4 or 5 of these wrapped beauties on each skewer.

Cook for a few minutes over a screaming-hot bed of coals (to cook the bacon quickly without the shrimp getting rubbery). Pull 'em off the coals, place on a plate, and give them a very generous coating of the sauce. Put your feet up, grab whatever beverage you have within reach, and munch down some of the tastiest little jewels that have ever tap-danced on your taste buds!

ROB MULLINS

The Licks (DaHurst, Beezer, LarriLee, and Mullins) actually stole this recipe from a fellow team, Beau Hog BBQ. This is the "treat" they have at midnight, after all of the civilians have left the area and the Licks are left to long, smoke-filled hours of low and slow cooking.

RON SHEWCHUK

Ron is with Butt Shredders. Ron's wife, Kate, found this recipe many years ago in a 1990s collection of recipes from American bistros. Seattle's Enoteca does not exist anymore, but as long as Ron barbeques, he will have this recipe in his repertoire. He likes to keep a few smoked duck halves in the freezer in case they have dinner guests they want to blow away. The original recipe calls for fresh papaya, which is excellent, but Ron says he likes slightly tangier mango as the fruit component.

From *Barbeque Secrets Deluxe!* by Ron Shewchuk (North Vancouver, BC: Whitecap Books, 2009). Reprinted with permission of the author and publisher.

ENOTECA SMOKED DUCK SALAD

Makes 8 appetizer servings or 4 main-course servings

DRESSING

⅔ cup red wine vinegar

½ cup soy sauce

½ cup sugar

¼ cup vegetable oil

¼ cup rice wine vinegar

¼ cup raspberry vinegar

1 tablespoon fresh lime juice

SALAD

1 pound smoked duck or smoked chicken (see Note)

2 whole fresh mangoes

2 (5-ounce) bags fresh baby spinach

½ small purple onion, diced

Freshly ground black pepper

Juice of 1 lime, plus 1 additional lime, quartered, for garnish

1 cup toasted walnuts or pecans, coarsely chopped

To prepare the dressing, bring the red wine vinegar, soy sauce, sugar, and oil to a boil in a medium saucepan over medium heat. Cook the mixture until the sugar is dissolved, 5 to 7 minutes. Stir in the rice wine vinegar, raspberry vinegar, and lime juice and let the dressing cool. This makes enough dressing for 4 salads, but it keeps for at least a few weeks in the refrigerator.

Cut the smoked duck into bite-sized pieces. Peel the mangoes and slice the flesh off the pits; reserve a few slices for garnish. Place the spinach, duck, mango, and onion in a salad bowl. Grind the black pepper over the mixture and pour the lime juice over it. Add the nuts and just enough dressing to coat; toss. (Too much dressing drowns out the other salad fixings.) Garnish the salad with the lime quarters and the reserved mango slices.

Note: *If you are using frozen duck or chicken, thaw it first, heat it up in a 350°F oven, and then let it rest until it's cool enough to handle.*

Hat Pins Rock!

Barbeque contests throughout the network often commemorate their events each year with hat pins, aka lapel pins. These metal mementos show the world that the bearer has been to a contest or was lucky enough to get a pin from a friend. Many people take pride in having a pin for each year of a contest from the beginning to the present.

KC Rib Doctor Guy Simpson sometimes has to remove his hat to give his neck muscles a break. You can imagine what crosses Guy's mind when he hears the words *heavy metal*! Wayne Lohman, Tana Frensley-Shupe, Buddy Richison, Pat Dalton, Bob Lyon, and hundreds of other barbeque cooks and judges also have hat pin collections to die for.

The custom is popular in the chili contest network, too. One of the best-known chiliheads to sport a collection of pins that took up most of the space on his signature top hat was the late Ormly Gumfudgin.

PHIL MORROW

Phil and his wife, Rosemary, compete as AM and PM Smokers. This recipe was prepared at a BBQ contest on the firebox when they didn't bring cups to put the cocktail sauce in to serve individually. You can serve it alone as an appetizer or over pasta, such as angel hair or spaghetti. See Rosemary's Fruit Salad on page 261.

PHIL'S SHRIMP COCKTAIL APPETIZER
Makes about 20 shrimp

1 teaspoon Smokin' Guns Hot BBQ Rub or your favorite dry rub

1 pound (21- to 23-count) shrimp, peeled and deveined

2 tablespoons cocktail sauce

1 tablespoon minced garlic

2 tablespoons butter

Juice of ½ orange or lemon

Sprinkle the rub over the shrimp and let rest for 10 minutes. Mix together the cocktail sauce and garlic and set aside.

Melt the butter in a skillet over medium heat and cook until light brown in color. Add the shrimp and cook, tossing occasionally, for 3 minutes. Add the cocktail sauce and garlic mixture and cook until the cocktail sauce browns slightly. Add the orange or lemon juice just before serving.

INN AT FOX HALL'S CHECKERBOARD CUCUMBER, CREAM CHEESE, AND CHIVE SANDWICHES

Serves 5 to 10

20 very thin slices peeled cucumber

Salt

3 ounces cream cheese, at room temperature

½ teaspoon snipped fresh or dried chives

10 tea-sandwich-sized slices crustless
rye bread

10 tea-sandwich-sized slices crustless
white bread

Sprinkle the cucumbers with salt and set them in a colander to drain
for at least 1 hour.

Stir together the cream cheese and chives in a small bowl. For each
sandwich, spread 1 slice of rye bread with the cream cheese mixture.
Layer 1 slice of white bread with 2 cucumber slices. Cover with
the rye bread slice, cream cheese side down. Cut in half to form 2
triangles.

JENNIFER B. STANLEY

Characters in J. B. Stanley's
murder mystery *Stiffs and Swine*
enjoyed this southern delicacy,
and so will you. Thanks to
Jennifer and her publisher for
giving us permission to reprint
the recipe.

APPETIZERS

RUBEN GOMEZ

Ruben and his wife, Bonnie, call Rio Rancho, New Mexico, home, but their friendship network in the barbeque community is global. Bonnie developed this recipe for a cameo appearance on a TV show, and Ruben has been famous for it ever since! This marriage of freshwater trout with the world's most popular root vegetable will be a big hit at your next party.

SMOKED TROUT– STUFFED POTATOES

Makes 24

12 tiny red potatoes (about 1½ inches in diameter)

¼ cup mayonnaise

¼ cup sour cream

2 tablespoons minced scallion

1 teaspoon snipped fresh dill

¼ teaspoon fresh lemon juice

Pinch of salt

Pinch of black pepper

Dash of hot pepper sauce (optional)

1 cup flaked smoked trout

Fresh dill sprigs, for garnish

Place the potatoes in a saucepan and cover them with water. Bring to a boil, then reduce the heat, cover, and cook for 10 to 15 minutes, until tender. Drain. Cut the potatoes in half horizontally. Cut a thin slice from the bottom of each potato to level it if necessary. Scoop out the pulp with a melon baller, leaving a thick shell.

In a bowl, mash the potato pulp. Stir in the mayonnaise, sour cream, scallion, dill, lemon juice, salt, pepper, and hot sauce, if using. Fold in the trout. Pipe the mixture into the potato shells. Garnish each with dill sprigs.

LOTTA BULL SHRIMP

Makes 10 to 15 shrimp

6 tablespoons Tiger Sauce

1 cup mayonnaise

3 tablespoons Bull Buster Steak Seasoning,
or your own favorite

1 pound (10- to 15-count) shrimp, peeled and deveined

Set up a medium to hot grill.

Mix together the Tiger Sauce, mayonnaise, and steak seasoning. Dip the shrimp in the mixture, then place 5 shrimp on each of 2 or 3 skewers, alternating head to tail and leaving a small space between them.

Place the skewers on the grill and cook until done, 1½ to 2 minutes per side. Do not overcook.

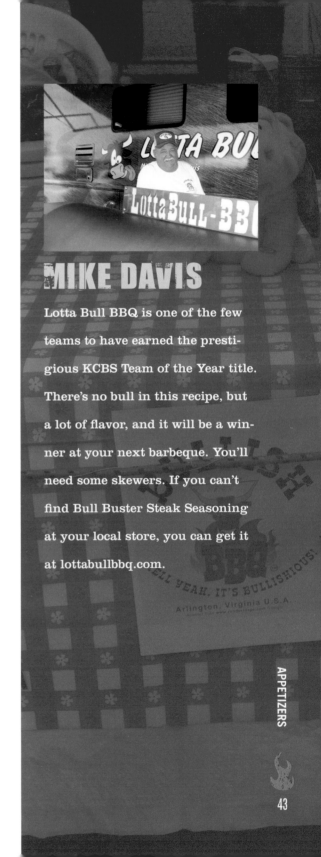

MIKE DAVIS

Lotta Bull BBQ is one of the few teams to have earned the prestigious KCBS Team of the Year title. There's no bull in this recipe, but a lot of flavor, and it will be a winner at your next barbeque. You'll need some skewers. If you can't find Bull Buster Steak Seasoning at your local store, you can get it at lottabullbbq.com.

APPETIZERS

43

BRAD DAVIS

Brad and his wife were doing a local competition and needed some fast and easy food to fix for friends who were dropping by on Friday night. They threw this together, and all the guests said it was really good!

GRILLED PEPPER AND LIME SHRIMP

Serves 4 to 6

Juice of 6 limes (about ¼ cup)

1 cup olive oil

1½ tablespoons freshly ground black pepper

1½ tablespoons Old Bay Seasoning

2 pounds (21- to 25-count) shrimp, peeled and deveined

In a large resealable plastic bag, mix together the lime juice, olive oil, black pepper, and Old Bay Seasoning. Add the shrimp, seal the bag, and marinate in the refrigerator to for 2 to 3 hours, flipping the bag over every hour. Take out the shrimp and reserve the marinade for basting.

Preheat a smoker to the lowest possible temperature (about 150°F) and smoke the shrimp for 30 to 45 minutes. While the shrimp are smoking, pour the marinade into a small pan, bring it to a boil, and boil for 3 minutes. Use as a basting sauce while the shrimp are cooking.

Remove the shrimp from the smoker, place them on skewers, and grill them until fully cooked, 2 to 3 minutes on each side, basting them with the cooked marinade while grilling.

GRILLED OYSTERS WITH ORANGE-WALNUT VINAIGRETTE

Serves 4 to 6

VINAIGRETTE

3 tablespoons French toasted walnut oil

1 tablespoon rice vinegar or champagne vinegar

1 teaspoon finely grated orange zest

1 teaspoon maple syrup

OYSTERS

1 pint shucked large fresh oysters (about a dozen)

Kosher salt and freshly ground black pepper

Neutral-flavored oil like canola or corn oil, for drizzling

1 orange, cut into wedges

Make the vinaigrette by whisking together the walnut oil, vinegar, orange zest, and maple syrup. Set aside.

Drain the oysters and pat them dry with paper towels. Put them on a baking sheet and set them aside.

Prepare your grill for direct high heat, making sure the cooking grate is thoroughly scraped. Season the oysters with salt and pepper and drizzle them with a light coating of oil. Just before you put the oysters on the hot grill, oil the cooking grate using a paper towel dipped in some oil. Carefully place the oysters on the cooking grate, making sure they don't fall through. Grill them for a couple of minutes per side, or until they're just cooked through and the outside edges are a bit charred.

Transfer the oysters to serving plates, top them with a drizzle of the vinaigrette, and garnish with orange wedges.

From *Barbeque Secrets Deluxe!* by Ron Shewchuk (North Vancouver, BC: Whitecap Books, 2009). Reprinted with permission of the author and publisher.

RON SHEWCHUK

Ron's friend Kosta, a fishmonger, suggested this flavor combination, and when Ron tried it, he was astonished at how well the light, refreshing vinaigrette complemented the robust flavor of the grilled oysters.

SIDES

We can't live by meat alone. We've gotta have sides! Basic sides served with barbeque are beans, coleslaw, and potatoes, prepared in a variety of ways. In this chapter you get variations on that three-part medley and then some!

Barbequed beans, pinto beans with jalapeños, white beans, red beans, black-eyed peas, or butter beans pair well with barbeque. From Butt-Kick'n Beans to Maine Baked Beans, Klondike Baked Beans, Baked Green Beans, and even Snail's Not-Baked Beans, we've got this barbeque standby covered with some delicious recipes.

Coleslaw—whether sweet, sour, plain, or pink—is routinely served with barbeque. This pairing harks back to American barbeque's roots with German butchers, who found pit barbeque to be a good way to cook and sell the tougher cuts of meat. Susan Sparr shared her Ramen Noodle Coleslaw recipe with us for this chapter.

The most commonly served potato side in restaurants is fries. Potato side dishes at contests, however, are usually roasted, grilled, or boiled, all with creative combinations of seasonings and other ingredients. Here we've got Guido's Serious Bavarian Potato Salad and Sweet Potato Soufflé, among others.

Greens—especially collard, mustard, or turnip—are less common side dishes nationally, yet very popular in some regions. Salads aren't widely served side dishes either, but we've got a Couscous Salad and, one of our favorites, Corn Bread Salad. And to round it all out, we've got all kinds of corn, Grilled Asparagus, a few spaghetti recipes, and even some breads to fill out your barbeque feast.

The sides here taste great on a stand-alone basis, but of course all are here because they're especially good with barbeque. We're especially fond of Duane Daugherty's Cheesy Scalloped Potatoes on the side, plus Jennifer Stanley's cheese grits and the Spicy Corn Bread from Andy Husbands and Joe Yonan. Then there's Marty's Gaelic Gourmet CAM Onion Bread Pudding. Yum!

Try all of our sides and pick your favorites. And remember to take notes in the margins as to how you tweaked each recipe to fit your own taste.

AL LAWSON

Al's pot of beans never went begging in the early days of the KCBS New Year's party. Back then everyone brought a potluck dish to go with the barbeque cooked on the premises by Al and Bob Lawson, KC Rib Doctor Guy Simpson, Donna McClure, and other KCBS members. You can stretch this recipe to feed more people by adding chopped barbequed beef or pork and a cup or more of your favorite barbeque sauce. Thin with beer if needed.

AL LAWSON'S BARBEQUED BEANS

Serves 25 to 30

¼ pound bacon, diced

1 large yellow onion, diced

4 quarts canned pork and beans

½ cup plus 2 tablespoons Worcestershire sauce

1 teaspoon garlic powder

1 cup barbeque sauce

½ cup packed brown sugar

¾ cup dark molasses

1 tablespoon chili powder

½ teaspoon ground cloves

½ teaspoon ground allspice

2 tablespoons prepared mustard

Sauté the bacon and onion in a skillet over low heat until the onion is wilted and the bacon has rendered some of its fat. In a 6-quart pot, combine the bacon, onion, bacon grease, pork and beans, Worcestershire sauce, garlic powder, barbeque sauce, brown sugar, molasses, chili powder, cloves, allspice, and mustard. Cook over low heat, covered, for 1 hour. Remove the cover and cook for 1½ to 2 hours, stirring often.

SNAIL'S NOT-BAKED BEANS

Serves 24 to 32

½ pound bacon

2 medium to large white onions, chopped

1 green bell pepper, chopped

1 jalapeño chile with seeds and ribs, chopped

4 cups Snail's Simple Sauce (page 228)

1 (8-ounce) can crushed pineapple, with juice

2 cups raisins

2 pounds light brown sugar (about 4 cups packed)

1 (#10) can (12 cups) pork and beans,
fat chunks removed

3 tablespoons Tone's Lemon Pepper (optional)

Barbequed brisket or pork scraps (optional)

¾ cup cornstarch (optional)

In a skillet over medium-high heat, fry the bacon until crisp. When the bacon is cool enough to handle, break it into bits. Sauté the onions and green pepper in the bacon grease over medium heat until tender, 8 to 10 minutes. Add the simple sauce, pineapple, raisins, brown sugar, pork and beans, lemon pepper, meat scraps, and crumbled bacon.

Transfer the mixture to a stockpot and cook over low to medium heat until very warm. If you want thicker beans, dissolve the cornstarch in enough water to form a smooth liquid (about 1 cup) and stir it into the beans. Continue to heat on the stovetop for about another hour at low heat. Do not put the beans in the oven.

JAY "THE SNAIL" VANTUYL

Snail, aka Jay, is known throughout the barbeque network for his great cooking, generosity—he doesn't keep cooking secrets—and artistic skills. If you want a creative sign for your team, Snail's the man to make it. This recipe serves a crowd, but it's so good you won't mind having the extra portions. Snail told us, "Sorry, I don't know a smaller-batch recipe yet!" Snail suggests using a turkey roaster to warm the beans, because the heat is much more controllable and they don't seem to burn as easily.

Grandma Carol Dotterwick of La Crosse, Wisconsin, has made these beans for many years. Grandson Matt told us these beans are frequently requested at family events such as weddings, graduations, and other celebrations. Matt and his wife, Cherish, guarantee these spectacular beans, which they say are even better the next day. They also make a great bean sandwich!

GRANDMA CAROL'S BAKED BEANS

Serves 20 to 24

2 pounds dried navy beans

Leftover ham bone, skin, and bits of ham

1 pound bacon, cut up

1 large yellow onion, diced

1 (8-ounce) can tomato sauce

1 pound brown sugar (about 2 cups packed)

Liquid smoke (optional)

Salt and black pepper

Rinse the beans and soak them overnight in cold water to cover by 2 inches.

The next day, add the ham bone and skin, and cook the beans in the soaking water just until the beans are fork-tender; the time will vary a lot depending on the age of the beans but it could be a couple of hours. Remove the ham skin and bone. When the bone is cool enough to handle, cut any leftover bits of meat from it. Leave enough liquid to cover the beans by about ½ inch. Reserve any additional liquid in case you need it while the beans are baking.

Preheat the oven to 325°F. Add the bacon, onion, tomato sauce, brown sugar, and as much of the leftover bits of ham as you want, plus the ham cut from the bone. If the ham isn't smoke-flavored enough, add a little liquid smoke. Add salt and pepper to taste.

Put the beans in a bean pot or other oven-safe roaster and bake, covered, for 4 to 5 hours, adding the reserved bean liquid as needed to keep the beans moist during baking.

BARBEQUE:
America's Cuisine

Who among us would throw rocks at a hot, steamed wiener slathered with mustard, grilled onions, and sauerkraut, folded into a warm, spongy bun from a New York City street vendor? Not us!

We wonder, however, what's the deal about wieners filled with finely ground meat, offal, and cereal being dubbed "The All-American Food"?

Although the so-called "hot dog" has its merits—tasty, fast, cheap, easy, and full of good memories for generations of Americans—it is by no means America's true cuisine.

Admittedly, we haven't accomplished it yet, but we're serious about the KCBS mission statement, "We want barbeque to be recognized as America's Cuisine." There are other respectable contenders—hot dogs, chili, apple pie, Brunswick stew, burgoo, hamburgers, and fried chicken, among them—but barbeque earns the title hands down.

Can you imagine the earliest Americans—indigenous natives, explorers, and colonists—sitting around a campfire eating hot dogs, hamburgers, fried chicken, chili, and apple pie? How about those same Americans chomping on barbequed wild turkey legs, squirrel, rabbit, fish, and wild boar ribs? Hail to America's Cuisine!

99¢
THE ALL AMERICAN MEAL
HOTDOG & A COKE
99¢

RON HARWELL, PhB

Ron Harwell, aka Sheepdog, knows the KCBS ropes. From CBJ (Certified BBQ Judging) Instructor to Contest Rep, Table Captain, or any other important job that needs to be done, Ron's there to do it. As a holder of the PhB degree, Ron can also discuss the finer points of philosophical issues related to barbeque. And don't get him started talking about his favorite football team, the University of Alabama Crimson Tide, unless you have a lot of time on your hands.

OLD-FASHIONED STOVETOP BEANS FROM SHEEPDOG'S KITCHEN

Serves 12 to 16

½ pound thick-sliced bacon, diced, or pulled pork, ground beef, or other favorite meat

1 large Vidalia onion, diced

1 medium green bell pepper, diced

2 (15.8-ounce) cans Bush's Great Northern beans

1 (15-ounce) can Bush's black beans

2 (4.5-ounce) cans chopped green chiles

1 (4-ounce) can diced jalapeño chiles

½ cup prepared yellow mustard

½ cup ketchup

½ cup maple syrup or ½ cup packed brown sugar

1 cup barbeque sauce, preferably Smokers Wild

In a large skillet over medium heat, brown the bacon. Remove it from the pan and set it aside. Add the onion and green pepper to the bacon grease and sauté until tender, 8 to 10 minutes.

Combine the beans, chiles, mustard, ketchup, maple syrup, and barbeque sauce in a large pot. Add the bacon and the sautéed onion and green pepper and mix thoroughly. Cook over medium heat until the contents are thoroughly warmed.

MAINE BAKED BEANS

Serves 6 to 8

1 pound dried State of Maine yellow eye beans
(or navy beans)

1 teaspoon baking soda

Dash of salt

¼ teaspoon black pepper

1 teaspoon dry mustard

½ cup dark molasses

¼ cup firmly packed brown sugar

2 cups boiling water

1 medium onion, peeled and quartered

¼ pound meaty salt pork

In a large pot, completely cover the beans with water and soak them overnight. In the morning, add the baking soda and parboil the beans in the same water over high heat, uncovered, for about 10 minutes. Skim off the foam. Drain the beans, but don't rinse them.

Preheat the oven to 300°F or prepare your smoker (230° to 250°F). In a bowl, combine the salt, pepper, dry mustard, molasses, brown sugar, and 2 cups boiling water. Stir the mixture into the beans.

Place the onion quarters in the bottom of a bean pot or Dutch oven. Pour the bean mixture over the onion and top with the scored salt pork. Cover the pot and bake or smoke for 4 to 6 hours. Watch closely, adding water as needed to keep the beans moist.

RICK CRAWFORD, JAW BREAKER BBQ

Rick promises this recipe is better than commercial baked beans. It's a traditional New England recipe passed down in his family from one generation to the next. He told us, "It's great at chowders and lobster boils, but new to BBQ," and these beans do seem like they would go great with any barbeque meal. Some might ask what the heck is the baking soda for. It creates the scum, which directly reduces the gas later on!

GUY SIMPSON

There is a lot of barbeque history behind this recipe. The original was published in *Woman's Day* magazine in March of 1987 and has been tweaked over the years. It's a surefire hit at parties and catering events.

K.C. RIB DOCTOR'S BAKED BEANS

Makes about 6 cups

1 cup diced sliced bacon (about ½ pound)

1 large onion, diced (about 1 cup)

1 large red bell pepper, diced (about 1 cup)

1 cup packed dark brown sugar

1 cup tomato-based barbeque sauce

⅓ cup real maple syrup

3 (28-ounce) cans pork and beans, preferably Bush's Original

Chopped brisket burnt ends, as desired

Preheat the oven to 400°F. Fry the bacon in a heavy skillet over medium heat until lightly browned. Add the onion and red pepper and cook for 3 minutes, until the vegetables are tender-crisp. Stir in the brown sugar, barbeque sauce, and maple syrup. Put the beans in a 12 by 6 by 3-inch foil pan. Add the bacon mixture and burnt ends; stir to mix.

Loosely cover with a sheet of foil. Place the beans in the oven and bake for 40 to 60 minutes, stirring 3 times.

If you're going to cook the beans in your smoker, preheat it to 230°F and cook uncovered for about 4 hours, stirring 3 to 4 times, adding barbeque sauce or liquid if the beans get too dry.

WAYNE'S BEANS

Serves 8 to 10

½ pound bacon, cut into ½-inch-long pieces

1 medium yellow onion, diced

3 (15-ounce) cans pork and beans, drained

¼ cup packed brown sugar

¼ teaspoon cayenne

1 teaspoon prepared yellow mustard

¼ cup dark molasses

¼ teaspoon ground ginger

¼ teaspoon ground cumin

½ cup barbeque sauce

1 or 2 jalapeño chiles, seeded and chopped

Preheat the oven to 350°F. In a large skillet over medium heat, fry the bacon until rendered but not crisp. Add the onion and cook until soft, 8 to 10 minutes. Transfer the bacon and onion to a bean pot and add the pork and beans, brown sugar, cayenne, mustard, molasses, ginger, cumin, barbeque sauce, and chiles. Bake, uncovered, for 1 hour.

You could also cook the beans in a slow cooker for 3 hours, but Jody says, "That's not how Dad cooks them."

JODY CARTER

Jody's dad, Wayne, received a bean recipe years ago from a distant relative of a distant relative. He changed it a bit, added some personal touches, and made it a family favorite. Jody is honored to share this recipe with KCBS!

DENNIS LANG

Dennis said he thinks he first got a form of this recipe from the *Kansas City Star* several years ago. He told us, "The present form barely resembles the original." "Why a vegetarian recipe in a BBQ cookbook?" you might ask. His reply: "With all of the meat that you usually find at a family picnic, maybe our bodies could use a break on the side dish." Dennis also allows, "Of course, you could always add your favorite sausage to the mix!"

VEGETARIAN SLOW COOKER RED BEANS AND RICE

Serves 8 to 10

1 pound dried red kidney beans

2 tablespoons cooking oil

2 cups chopped yellow onion

1 cup chopped green bell pepper

1 to 2 jalapeño chiles (optional)

1 teaspoon liquid smoke

2 tablespoons minced garlic

2 teaspoons dry mustard

2 teaspoons salt

½ teaspoon cayenne

2 teaspoons ground ginger

1 bay leaf

1 teaspoon ground cumin

1 teaspoon garlic powder

1 teaspoon onion powder

1 teaspoon dried oregano

1 teaspoon black pepper

1 teaspoon dried thyme

7 cups chicken broth or 4 to 5 chicken bouillon cubes dissolved in 7 cups water

1 to 2 cups white rice, prepared according to package directions

In a large pot, cover the kidney beans with water and soak them overnight.

Heat the oil in a large skillet over medium heat and sauté the onion and green pepper for 5 minutes, until tender. Drain the water from the beans and place them in a slow cooker. Add the cooked onion and green pepper, the chiles, all the seasonings, and the broth. Mix well. Add enough water to cover the mixture and cook on high for 4 to 5 hours, until the beans are tender.

To serve, pour the bean mixture over the prepared rice.

KLONDIKE BAKED BEANS

Serves 14 to 16

2 pounds dried navy beans

About 2 quarts chicken broth or water (enough to cover the beans)

2 bay leaves, crumbled

1 bunch of parsley, chopped

6 celery stalks, chopped

5 cloves garlic, crushed

1 tablespoon dried oregano

1 tablespoon chili powder

6 whole cloves

1 tablespoon salt

1 pound lean unsliced bacon, cubed

6 large tomatoes, chopped

1 (6-ounce) can tomato paste

3 large yellow onions, chopped

3 large yellow onions, diced

2 cups molasses

1 cup sherry

2 pounds ham hock meat, chopped (optional)

2 pounds pulled pork (optional)

2 pounds brisket (optional)

2 pounds sausage (optional)

½ pound thinly sliced bacon

Place the beans in a large pot, add enough cold water to cover them by several inches, and soak them overnight. The next morning, drain the beans and add enough chicken broth or water to cover the beans by 2 inches, then add the bay leaves, parsley, celery, garlic, oregano, chili powder, cloves, and salt. Simmer over medium-low heat for approximately 1½ hours, or until the skin breaks on a bean when you blow on it. Drain and reserve the liquid. Place the beans in a large bean pot or earthenware casserole and add the cubed bacon.

Preheat the oven to 250°F. Put a few cups of the reserved bean liquid into a separate pot and bring to a simmer over medium heat. Add the tomatoes, tomato paste, and onions and heat, stirring occasionally, until the mixture is hot and the tomato paste is thoroughly mixed in. Add the molasses and sherry and reheat. Pour the mixture over the beans in the bean pot. Add the ham, pork, brisket, and/or sausage.

Bake the beans for 6 hours. Check after 2 and 4 hours to see if there is enough liquid, and stir; if not, add some of the remaining bean liquid. After 1 more hour (5 hours into the bake) again check the liquid and cover the top of the beans with the sliced bacon. Cover and continue cooking for 1 hour. Remove the lid and place the beans under the broiler for 3 to 5 minutes, until the bacon is crisp.

GORDON HUBBELL

According to Gordon, "These beans will make you fall over happy! And they're a great accompaniment to all kinds of barbeque." He adds, "Most people who taste these beans rate them far, far superior to the fast kind." By "fast kind" he means canned beans.

BUTT-KICK'N BEANS

Serves 6 to 8

1 pound dried pinto beans

Salt

5 slices bacon

½ pound leftover smoked pork butt, chopped

1 medium yellow onion, chopped

Barbeque sauce, preferably tomato-based

The day before you plan to serve the beans, rinse and sort the dried beans, discarding any bad ones and rocks. Place the beans in a deep pan or bowl and add water to cover them by 3 or 4 inches. Set aside to soak for at least 12 hours.

Before cooking, rinse the beans a second time; then drain them in a colander. In a large, heavy, deep pan (a Dutch oven works well), add the beans and enough water to cover by about 2 inches. Add a couple of pinches of salt. Bring to a rapid boil, reduce the heat so the mixture simmers slowly, cover, and cook until the beans begin to soften, usually 1 to 2 hours. Meanwhile, fry the bacon until crisp and then chop into medium pieces.

Thoroughly drain the water from the beans and add the meats, chopped onion, and enough sauce to wet but not cover or soak the beans. Stir to combine thoroughly and cook for about 30 minutes to blend the flavors.

GREEN BEAN CASSEROLE

Serves 12 to 14

8 tablespoons (1 stick) butter

1 small onion, grated

2 (4-ounce) cans mushrooms, preferably stems and pieces

¼ cup all-purpose flour

2 cups milk

¾ pound cheddar cheese, grated (about 3 cups)

Dash of Tabasco sauce

2 teaspoons soy sauce

½ teaspoon black pepper

1 teaspoon salt

3 (14.5-ounce) cans French-style green beans

1 (5-ounce) can sliced water chestnuts

1 (2.8-ounce) can fried onions, crumbled

Preheat the oven to 350°F and butter a 9 by 13-inch casserole dish.

In a large pot over medium-high heat, melt the butter. Add the onion and mushrooms and sauté for 5 minutes, or until the onion is translucent. Add the flour and stir. Blend in the milk and cook, stirring constantly, until thick and smooth. Add the cheese, Tabasco, soy sauce, pepper, and salt and simmer, stirring, until the cheese is melted. Add the green beans and water chestnuts, mix well, and then turn the mixture out into the prepared casserole dish. Bake for 10 minutes. Sprinkle the top with crumbled onions and bake for 10 minutes more, or until the casserole is bubbling and the onions are golden brown.

SANDY HARNISCH

This recipe was donated by Sandy Harnisch, a longtime friend of Don Przybyla. Don returned home from a Memorial Day barbeque with Sandy and Bill. As they always do after they have their fill of very great food, they sat around talking at the table. Don told her that as soon as he got her recipe, he sent it off for this cookbook. Then Sandy told Don a little story about her aunt. When she had relatives over, she would tell them, "Don't eat this. It's terrible," and nobody would eat it. Then toward the end of dinner she would help herself to whatever was left. When she piled a helping of this casserole on her plate and everyone asked her why, she replied, "If I didn't tell you it was bad, you wouldn't leave anything for me."

SIDES

SHARON OXLEY

This recipe has been modified from an original by the Barefoot Contessa and is served at Uncle Mike's BBQ in Wanaka, New Zealand.

COUSCOUS SALAD

Serves 4 to 6

1½ cups couscous

2 tablespoons unsalted butter

1½ cups boiling water

½ cup yogurt

¼ cup good-quality extra virgin olive oil

1 teaspoon white wine vinegar

2 teaspoons mild curry powder

½ teaspoon ground turmeric

2 teaspoons salt, plus more to taste

1 teaspoon freshly ground black pepper, plus more to taste

½ cup finely diced carrot

½ cup diced red bell pepper

½ cup minced fresh cilantro

½ cup golden raisins

¼ cup slivered blanched almonds, toasted

¼ cup finely diced scallion

½ cup finely diced red onion

Place the couscous in a medium bowl or shallow pan. Melt the butter in the boiling water and pour it over the couscous. Cover tightly and allow the couscous to soak for 5 minutes. Fluff with a fork.

Whisk together the yogurt, olive oil, vinegar, curry, turmeric, salt, and pepper. Pour over the fluffed couscous and mix well with a fork. Add the carrot, red pepper, cilantro, raisins, almonds, scallion, and red onion. Mix well and season to taste. Serve at room temperature.

RAMEN NOODLE COLESLAW

Serves 6 to 8

SLAW

1 (16-ounce) package slaw mix

4 scallions, chopped

¼ cup toasted sliced almonds

2 tablespoons sesame seeds or sunflower seeds

1 package chicken-flavored ramen noodles,
uncooked and noodles crushed

DRESSING

2 tablespoons sugar

1 teaspoon salt

½ cup vegetable oil

½ teaspoon black pepper

3 tablespoons rice vinegar, regular or sweet

1 packet chicken seasoning from the
ramen noodle package

Combine all the slaw ingredients in a large bowl and blend well. Combine the dressing ingredients in a jar with a tight-fitting lid and shake well to mix. Pour the dressing over the slaw mixture and toss to coat. Serve immediately.

SUSAN SPARR

Susan, from McKinney, Texas, gave us this recipe, which goes great with barbeque. It's standard fare when she and her husband, Brad, host the Gun Club.

SIDES

PAUL KIRK, PHB

This features a surprising combination of apple and raisins mixed with mayonnaise and honey. It really complements your barbeque.

CREAMY COLESLAW WITH APPLE AND RAISINS

Serves 4

SLAW

1 medium carrot, diced

⅓ cup minced red onion

½ cup minced red or green bell pepper

2 scallions, diced

3 cups thinly sliced white or red cabbage

⅓ cup diced unpeeled apple

⅓ cup raisins

DRESSING

¼ cup light mayonnaise

2 tablespoons yogurt

2 tablespoons fresh lemon juice

1½ teaspoons clover honey

Salt and black pepper

In a serving bowl, combine all the slaw ingredients.

In a small bowl, stir together the dressing ingredients, mixing well. Pour over the salad and toss gently to combine.

CABBAGE AND CORN SLAW

Serves 6 to 8

SLAW

5 cups shredded green cabbage

1 cup shredded red cabbage

2 cups cooked corn kernels

½ cup diced red onion

¼ cup diced yellow bell pepper

¼ cup grated carrot

DRESSING

⅓ cup white wine vinegar

⅓ cup canola oil

¼ cup sugar

1 to 2 tablespoons seeded and minced jalapeño chile

Salt and freshly ground black pepper

In a large bowl, combine the slaw ingredients. Chill for 1 to 2 hours. Put the dressing ingredients in a small jar with a tight-fitting lid. Screw on the lid and shake well to combine. Pour the dressing over the cabbage mixture just before serving and toss to coat.

ERIC ABRAHAM

Here's a creative twist on a classic favorite from Eric Abraham, ceramic artist and proprietor of the world-famous Flying Pig Studio in Lucas, Kansas. When he isn't busy in his studio or flying pigs over the Garden of Eden and other Lucas attractions, Eric likes to chow down on a platter of pork barbeque with a frosty bottle of Kansas City's Boulevard Wheat. Eric recommends the dry-cured bacon from Brant's Meat Market in downtown Lucas. He told us, "One pound fries up with only about two or three tablespoons of grease."

FLYING PIG BLT SALAD

Serves 2 as a main dish or 4 as a side salad

2 (1-pound) round whole wheat or multigrain bread loaves

1 pound applewood-, maple-, or hickory-smoked bacon

1 cup canola or olive oil mayonnaise

¼ cup buttermilk

1 teaspoon Worcestershire sauce

1 teaspoon fresh lemon juice

1 teaspoon finely grated lemon zest

2 tablespoons crumbled blue or Gorgonzola cheese (optional)

1 (12-ounce) bag shredded iceberg lettuce

2 medium ripe red tomatoes, chopped

½ sweet onion, chopped (optional)

½ cup bread crumbs from the bread bowl or ½ cup panko crumbs

Slice the top 1 inch off each bread loaf. Scoop the bread from inside the loaf, leaving a 1-inch-thick wall. Save the leftover bread for crumbs, for other recipes, or to feed the birds.

Fry the bacon until almost crisp. Set it aside to cool and drain on paper towels. Reserve 1 tablespoon of the bacon grease.

In a medium bowl, whisk together the mayonnaise, buttermilk, Worcestershire, lemon juice, lemon zest, and reserved bacon grease until smooth. For a surprise complement, add the blue cheese.

Chop the bacon or cut the strips in half and form bacon curls by twisting each half around the tines of a table fork.

Put the lettuce in a large bowl and toss with the dressing until well coated. Add the bacon, tomatoes, and chopped onion and toss again. Fill each bread bowl with the salad. Garnish with the bread crumbs and serve immediately.

FIELD OF DREAMS SALAD

Serves 8 to 10

SALAD

1 head Romaine lettuce, torn into pieces

1 head red-tip lettuce, torn into pieces

½ medium sweet onion, sliced or chopped

1 strawberry, sliced

4 ounces feta cheese, crumbled

DRESSING

2 tablespoons white vinegar

2 tablespoons balsamic vinegar

½ cup olive oil

¼ cup sugar or Splenda

Dash of salt and black pepper

Mix all of the salad ingredients together and toss to mix. Whisk all of the dressing ingredients together, pour the dressing over the salad, and toss to coat.

MIKE AND THERESA LAKE

This is a special salad that Mike and Theresa serve to the volunteers and cooks who come in early for the Illinois State Barbeque Championships in Shannon, Illinois. They named it the "Field of Dreams Salad" because the Shannon cook-off site, which is held on two adjoining baseball diamonds that are surrounded by cornfields most years, is referred to as barbeque's Field of Dreams.

DECATUR, ALABAMA

CAROLYN McLEMORE, BIG BOB GIBSON BAR-B-Q

When Carolyn McLemore fixes this at Big Bob Gibson's, it's a real crowd pleaser. You can use self-rising cornmeal, but if you do, do not add the baking soda and baking powder.

CORN BREAD SALAD

Serves 10 to 12

CORN BREAD

1 tablespoon vegetable oil

3 cups buttermilk

2 eggs

1 cup yellow cornmeal

1 teaspoon baking soda

1 teaspoon baking powder

1 teaspoon salt

1 (4-ounce) can chopped green chiles

SALAD

1 (1-ounce) package ranch-style dressing mix

1 (8-ounce) container sour cream

1 cup mayonnaise

3 large tomatoes, chopped

½ cup chopped green bell pepper

½ cup chopped scallion

2 (16-ounce) cans pinto beans, drained

2 cups shredded cheddar cheese

1½ cups cooked and crumbled bacon

1 (15-ounce) can corn, drained

Preheat the oven to 425°F. Coat a cast-iron skillet with the vegetable oil and heat it in the oven. Mix the buttermilk and eggs in a bowl; then add the cornmeal, baking soda, baking powder, salt, and chiles, stirring briskly. Pour the batter into the hot skillet. Bake for 15 minutes, or until lightly browned. Cool completely, then crumble.

To make the salad, whisk together the ranch dressing mix, sour cream, and mayonnaise and set aside. Combine the tomatoes, green pepper, and scallion to form a salsa and set aside. Put half of the crumbled corn bread into the bottom of a large serving bowl. Top with 1 can of the pinto beans. Follow with half of the salsa, half of the cheese, half of the bacon, half of the corn, and half of the dressing mixture. Repeat the layers, starting with the rest of the corn bread and ending with the rest of the dressing mixture. Cover and chill for at least 2 hours before serving.

3 X WESTERN DRESSING

Makes about ½ gallon

4 (12-ounce) cans tomato paste

1 cup honey (optional, but best)

1 cup canola oil

1 cup olive oil

1 cup water

¼ cup white vinegar

¼ cup prepared mustard

1 cup Splenda, or more if you don't use the honey

1 tablespoon paprika, or more to taste

1 tablespoon sodium-free salt (potassium chloride)

1 tablespoon instant coffee granules

In a medium saucepan, combine all of the ingredients, mix well, and bring to a boil over medium-high heat. Reduce the heat to medium-low and simmer for 20 minutes. Cover the pan and let the dressing cool to room temperature; then refrigerate for at least an hour before serving. Pour the mixture into a tightly sealed container and shake well before using.

KEN MISHOE

Ken told us, "I eat way too much dressing on my salad, so I thought I should come up with a healthier equivalent of my favorite: Western Dressing." He also suggested that you play with this recipe to suit your own taste. This recipe makes plenty of dressing. You can freeze the extra in airtight freezer bags and thaw it as needed.

GUIDO MEINDL

Guido Meindl, saucemeister extraordinaire, and his wife, Cathy Sue, pull out all the stops for the annual Fourth of July party at their home in Pasadena, California. Besides heavenly slabs slathered with Guido's Serious Sauce—now an heirloom collector's item since Guido recently ceased production—guests chow down on Bavarian Potato Salad and a cornucopia of other culinary delights. Who needs the Rose Parade when Guido and Cathy roll out the welcome mat for the Fourth? Guido says, "All you need now are thirty slabs of baby back ribs, three kegs of beer, the Purple Ground Hogs western band from Bakersfield, and a good woman!"

GUIDO'S SERIOUS BAVARIAN POTATO SALAD

Serves 40 to 50

10 pounds White Rose potatoes, unpeeled

1 large red onion, thinly sliced

½ cup olive oil (virgin if you can find it!)

1 cup red wine vinegar

¼ cup salt, plus more to taste

2 tablespoons coarsely ground black pepper, plus more to taste

1 tablespoon caraway seeds

5 slices smoked bacon

1 bunch of parsley

Scrub the potatoes, place them in a large pot, cover with water, and bring the potatoes to a boil over medium-high heat. Boil for about 30 minutes. Check the pot occasionally, and when the first crack appears on the skin of a potato, remove the pot from the heat. Drain off the hot water, fill the pot with cold water, and let sit for 5 minutes. Drain off the water and peel the potatoes with a sharp knife. Just catch a piece of the broken skin and peel—it's easy. The potatoes will still be a bit hot, so Guido says to just blow on your potato hand!

Cut the potatoes in half lengthwise, then cut into a bit less than ¼-inch slices (no chunks, please!) and place them in a very large bowl. Add the onion to the bowl.

In a 1-pint measuring cup, combine the olive oil, vinegar, salt, pepper, and caraway seeds. Stir well and let the mixture sit while you prepare the rest of the ingredients.

Cook the bacon until crisp, transfer it to a rack or a paper-towel-lined plate, let cool, and crumble it into small pieces. Keep the rendered fat.

Remove the parsley leaves from the stems of the bunches and set them aside.

In a very large bowl, combine the potatoes and dressing and mix well. Cover and refrigerate for 4 hours (or preferably overnight) before serving.

Just before serving, add the bacon bits and some of the bacon fat (if you like). Taste and add more salt and pepper if necessary. Sprinkle the parsley over the top of the salad and serve.

BAKED GREEN BEANS

Serves 8 to 10

3 (14.5-ounce) cans green beans

1 cup ketchup

1 cup packed brown sugar

1 medium yellow onion, diced

6 slices bacon, diced

Preheat the oven to 275°F. In a 2-quart casserole dish, combine the beans, ketchup, brown sugar, onion, and bacon and mix well. Cover and bake for 4 hours.

KARI LUKE

This simple bean recipe has been entered into the bean category at a lot of contests and has done very well. This also works great in your smoker (230° to 250°F) for 3½ to 4 hours.

PERRY SKRUKRUD

When Minnesota Perry and his wife, Cheri, aren't indulging in the pleasures of life on the shores of Lake Hubert, Minnesota, they enjoy road tripping and sampling local cuisine. This recipe was obviously inspired by some adventures in North Carolina. Serve it in small portions as a side or larger portions for a meal in itself.

CAROLINA SMASHED POTATO PIG BUTT BAKE

Serves 4 to 6

2 pounds small (B-size) red potatoes

½ cup apple cider vinegar

½ teaspoon hot red pepper flakes

1 tablespoon black pepper

1 teaspoon salt

4 tablespoons (½ stick) unsalted butter

3 tablespoons corn bread crumbs

½ pound chopped barbequed pork butt

1 (16-ounce) container cottage cheese

½ pound sharp cheddar cheese, shredded (about 2 cups)

½ pound hickory- or applewood-smoked bacon, fried crispy and crumbled

Place the potatoes in a large pot and add enough water to cover them. Add the vinegar, red pepper flakes, black pepper, and salt. Bring the potatoes to a boil over high heat and boil until tender but not mushy, 10 to 15 minutes. Remove the potatoes from the water, set them aside to cool, and discard the water. When the potatoes have cooled, use the bottom of a drinking glass or jar to smash each potato flat.

Preheat the oven or your pit to 300°F. Use the butter to grease a 9 by 13-inch ovenproof glass or ceramic dish. Sprinkle half of the corn bread crumbs on the bottom of the pan. Place half of the smashed potatoes in a layer on top of the crumbs. Top the potatoes with half of the pork butt. Add another layer of corn bread crumbs, then another layer of smashed potatoes, then a layer of cottage cheese, followed by the rest of the pork butt. Top with the cheddar cheese and crumbled bacon. Bake uncovered for 30 minutes.

GRILLED CHEESY POTATOES

Serves 4

3 cups cubed red potatoes

5 tablespoons water

1½ cups cubed processed cheese, such as Velveeta

1 large yellow onion, diced

1 tablespoon Worcestershire sauce

½ teaspoon sea salt

1 large clove garlic, pressed

¼ teaspoon black pepper

2 to 4 tablespoons butter

Prepare a grill for medium heat. Place the potatoes and 3 tablespoons of the water in a microwave-safe bowl. Cover and microwave on high for 3 to 4 minutes, until almost tender; drain.

In a large bowl, combine the cheese and onion. Stir in the potatoes. Transfer to a double thickness of greased heavy-duty aluminum foil (about 18 inches square).

Combine the Worcestershire sauce, salt, garlic, pepper, and remaining 2 tablespoons water; sprinkle over the potatoes. Dot with the butter.

Fold the foil around the potato mixture and seal tightly. Grill, covered, for 8 to 10 minutes, or until the potatoes are tender and the cheese is melted. When serving, open the foil carefully to allow steam to escape.

PAUL KIRK, PHB

Yes, Paul does occasionally cook in foil. Here's the proof.

SIDES

DUANE DAUGHERTY

This is an all-American potato dish. Everyone who has tried this dish has liked it. This recipe is a keeper. Duane uses his own homemade sauce, Doggity-Style, but you can use your own favorite. This goes great with barbeque!

CHEESY SCALLOPED POTATOES

Serves 4 to 6

2 pounds small (B-size) red potatoes, unpeeled

⅓ cup tomato-based barbeque sauce

1 pound thick-sliced applewood- or hickory-smoked bacon

1 teaspoon ground cumin

Salt and black pepper

1 medium sweet onion, quartered and thinly sliced

8 ounces sharp cheddar cheese, grated (about 2 cups)

½ cup skim milk

2 tablespoons mixed chopped fresh cilantro and chives, for garnish (optional)

Preheat your oven or pit to 400°F.

Wash the potatoes and slice them about ⅛ inch thick. Rinse them in ice water and pat them dry. Toss them in the barbeque sauce and marinate for an hour or so.

In a large skillet over medium heat, cook the bacon until almost crispy. Transfer all but 1 slice to a rack or a paper-towel-lined plate to cool. Fry the remaining strip until crispy and add it to the plate. When cool, chop the less-crispy bacon into small pieces and reserve the crispy slice for garnish.

Use the bacon grease to coat a deep 9 by 13-inch ovenproof glass or ceramic casserole dish. Cover the bottom with half of the potatoes. Sprinkle with half of the cumin, and then season with salt and pepper. Add a layer of onions, then the chopped bacon, and half of the cheese. Add the rest of the potatoes, sprinkle with the rest of the cumin, and add more salt and pepper. Level the mixture with a spatula. Pour the milk over the top.

Cover and bake for 1 hour and 15 minutes. Remove the cover and sprinkle the remaining cheese on top. Bake for another 20 minutes, or until the top is almost brown. Garnish with the reserved crisp bacon, cilantro, and chives. Serve hot or cold.

SWEET POTATO SOUFFLÉ

Serves 10 to 12

6 cups mashed sweet potatoes

2 cups granulated sugar

1 teaspoon salt

2 teaspoons vanilla extract

4 eggs, beaten

10⅔ tablespoons butter, melted

1 cup sweetened condensed milk

TOPPING

2 cups packed brown sugar

⅔ cup granulated sugar

1 cup chopped pecans

10⅔ tablespoons butter, softened

Preheat the oven to 350°F. Grease a 9 by 13-inch pan. In a large bowl, mix the sweet potatoes, granulated sugar, salt, vanilla, eggs, butter, and sweetened condensed milk. Pour the mixture into the prepared pan. In a medium bowl, mix together the topping ingredients and sprinkle over the soufflé. Bake for 40 minutes, or until golden brown.

DAWN ENDRIJAITIS

This is a rich, sweet, delicious way to serve sweet potatoes.

SIDES

MARTY LYNCH

Not to be confused with the annual Gaelic Gourmet events in Boston since the year 2000, Marty Lynch and Kevin O'Grady's Gaelic Gourmet BBQ Team has been burning sticks and wowing barbeque judges since the early 1980s. When Marty gave Ardie a taste of CAM Onions at the 2008 Great American Barbecue, Ardie said, "You've gotta give me your recipe for the next KCBS cookbook!" Marty gladly obliged. He adapted this from Rick Browne's Oz Onion Pudding in Rick's *Grilling America* book (2003). Rick gave us permission to share this version, tweaked by Carolyn Wells, Amy Winn, and Marty Lynch—hence the CAM acronym.

MARTY'S GAELIC GOURMET CAM ONION BREAD PUDDING

Serves 6

8 tablespoons (1 stick) butter

1 tablespoon olive oil

8 cups thinly sliced Vidalia or Texas Sweet onions

¼ cup dry vermouth (optional)

1 clove garlic, crushed

6 cups French bread in 1-inch chunks

6 cups grated Emmenthaler or Swiss cheese

3 eggs

1½ cups half-and-half

1 teaspoon sea salt or kosher salt, or to taste

Freshly ground black pepper

Preheat a gas grill to 400° to 500°F or a charcoal grill until hot. Melt half of the butter with the olive oil in a cast-iron skillet on the grill. Add the onions, cover the skillet, and move it to a cooler zone to simmer for 15 minutes.

Uncover the skillet, move it to a medium-heat zone, and stir occasionally until the onions caramelize, about 20 minutes. Add the vermouth and garlic and continue heating until the liquid evaporates, stirring constantly for 10 to 15 minutes. Remove the onion mixture from the skillet and transfer it to a large bowl.

Clean the skillet; then spray the sides and bottom with nonstick cooking spray. Add the bread and stir well. Spread the onion mixture in the pan. Melt the remaining butter and pour it over the bread and onion mixture. Sprinkle the cheese on top.

In a medium bowl, beat the eggs slightly and add the half-and-half and salt and pepper. Pour this mixture over the bread, onion, and cheese mixture. Use a spatula to lift the bread to make sure the liquid is infused throughout. Place the skillet on the grill. Using the indirect heat method, cook for 30 to 40 minutes, until puffed and golden brown. When the pudding is done, remove it from the grill, cut it into large triangles, and serve.

Note *from Marty: When I cook the onions, 15 minutes is enough time. I never caramelize onions. I find the Emmenthaler will cancel any additional caramel flavor, but it might make a more dramatic presentation. "Live to BBQ! BBQ to Live!"*

GRAPE SALAD
Serves 8 to 10

2 to 3 pounds seedless green or red grapes

1 (8-ounce) container sour cream

1 (8-ounce) package cream cheese, at room temperature

½ cup granulated sugar

1 teaspoon vanilla extract

3 to 4 tablespoons packed brown sugar

1½ cups chopped pecans

In a large bowl, mix together the grapes, sour cream, cream cheese, granulated sugar, and vanilla. In a small bowl, mix together the brown sugar and pecans and sprinkle over the grape mixture. Chill for at least 1 hour before serving.

TANA FRENSLEY-SHUPE, PHB

You may think this side is sweet enough to serve as dessert. True, but we find it's a great complement to barbequed brisket, smoked salmon, or smoked chicken. Tana tells us it's best to use really sweet grapes.

SIDES

HOW TO GRILL
Vegetables

- Many vegetables grill well, but some aren't cut out for it, especially those high in water content. Cucumbers don't make the grade, nor does celery, lettuce, or most leafy vegetables. Vegetables that do work well on a grill are asparagus, eggplant, onions, and even cabbage. All of the pepper family grill well, as do summer squash.

- Cooking times will vary according to your choice of vegetables. Be sure to keep a close watch, though, as vegetables are generally more delicate than meats and other grillables. A touch of smoke greatly enhances vegetables, but charred lumps of carbon won't be a hit with anyone.

BELL PEPPERS: Halve and stem the peppers, then remove the seeds. Grill for 3 to 5 minutes, skin side down, turning when grill marks appear.

CARROTS: Cook whole for 3 to 5 minutes on each side, then cover and cook over moderate heat until tender.

CORN WITHOUT HUSK: Cook whole for 5 to 7 minutes on each side, until lightly browned on all sides.

CORN IN HUSK: Before cooking, soak the ears in water for 20 to 30 minutes. Cook whole for 15 to 20 minutes on each side.

MUSHROOMS: Cook whole with stems removed for 2 to 4 minutes on each side. Cook top side down, turning when grill marks appear.

ONIONS: Cook halved for 5 to 7 minutes. Start with the cut side down, then turn when that side is fully browned.

POTATOES: Cut in half lengthwise and cook for 2 to 4 minutes cut side down. Cook until grill marks appear.

SUMMER SQUASH: Halve lengthwise or slice 1 inch thick for skewers. Cook, cut side down, for 4 to 5 minutes, until grill marks appear.

SWEET POTATOES: Halve lengthwise and place, cut side down, on the grill. Cook for 6 to 8 minutes, until grill marks appear.

TOMATOES: Cut large tomatoes into quarters. Cut plum tomatoes in half lengthwise. You also can grill cherry tomatoes. Cook for 2 to 4 minutes, turning when grill marks appear.

ZUCCHINI/YELLOW SQUASH: Cut in half lengthwise and cook, cut side down, for 3 to 5 minutes. Squash cook quickly, so watch closely.

BASIC GRILLED CORN ON THE COB

Fresh corn on the cob, in husks

1 to 2 tablespoons butter per ear

Salt and black pepper

Let the corn in husks soak in a pot of water for 1 hour. Pull down the husks (but don't remove them) and remove the silks. Brush each ear with butter and sprinkle with salt and pepper. Pull the husks back up around the ears. Place the corn on a gas grill over medium heat or on a charcoal grill 4 to 6 inches from medium coals. Grill for 20 to 30 minutes, turning the ears halfway through the cooking time.

PAUL KIRK, PHB

Corn is one of the best summer foods of all time. The best way to butter a cooked ear of corn is to load up a piece of bread with butter, wrap the corn in it like a blanket, and roll. Discard the bread. When you cook corn on the grill in the husk, if the husks start to burn, don't worry. Have a spray bottle of water handy to spray the flame.

SIDES

77

MIKE DAVIS

We know two Mike Davises in the barbeque network. One owns and operates the acclaimed Whole Hog Café in Little Rock, Arkansas. The other Mike Davis and his wife, Debbie, from Oklahoma, routinely bring home trophies, ribbons, and prize money from the most competitive barbeque contests in the country. Their team name is Lotta Bull BBQ. Their talent is quality food. You'll get a taste of Mike and Debbie's magic with your first bite of this corn on the cob.

FRESH CORN ON THE COB

Serves 4 to 6

4 to 6 ears fresh corn on the cob, in husks

½ cup mayonnaise

¼ cup freshly grated Parmesan cheese

¼ cup crumbled crisp-cooked bacon

Preheat the oven to 350°F. Soak the ears of corn in water for 30 minutes; drain off the water, then place them in the oven directly on the racks for 45 minutes. Pull the husks and remove the silks, then put the corn on a medium-hot grill. Once the ears have grill marks, use a brush to apply mayonnaise to each ear. Mix the Parmesan cheese and bacon bits together on a plate. Roll the corn through the mixture and serve immediately.

GRILLED CORN WITH ROASTED ANAHEIM PEPPERS IN FOIL

Serves 4

4 Anaheim peppers

4 ears corn, shucked

4 tablespoons (½ stick) unsalted butter, softened

Salt and fresh-cracked black peppercorns

Roast the peppers on your grill until sufficiently blackened, place them in a resealable plastic bag, seal it shut, and leave it for about 10 minutes. Transfer the peppers to a clean work surface and remove the outer skin. Cut down the length of one side of a pepper and open it up. Remove the stem, seeds, and any ribs from inside and repeat the procedure with the remaining peppers. Dice the peppers and divide into 4 piles.

Cut two pieces of heavy-duty aluminum foil big enough to wrap around the corn with room enough for some peppers on top. Place a buttered piece of corn in the center and top with one of the piles of diced peppers. Spread them over the corn and season the whole thing with the salt and pepper. Wrap tightly and repeat with the remaining ingredients.

Prepare the grill for medium heat. Grill the corn for 20 to 25 minutes, turning frequently, and serve at once. The corn will have a wonderful flavor.

PAUL KIRK, PHB

This is a deliciously spicy alternative to grilled corn on the cob. Paul notes that when he is having steak with this, he likes to dump the cooked peppers on top of the steak. You can also cut the corn from the cob and blend with the chopped peppers and add some halved cherry tomatoes and a squirt of lime juice for a wonderful corn salsa for grilled chicken breast.

SIDES

DANIELLE DIMOVSKI

Spices can turn everyday vegetables into extraordinary side dishes. This recipe takes corn to a new level.

DIVA Q CHIPOTLE LIME CORN

Serves 8 to 12

2 tablespoons grated lime zest

2 teaspoons salt

1 teaspoon lemon pepper

1 teaspoon garlic pepper

½ teaspoon ground dried chipotle chile

1 dozen ears corn, shucked

10⅔ tablespoons butter

1 lime, cut into wedges

Preheat the grill to 325°F. Diva Q recommends hickory, oak, apple, or pecan pellets.

In a small bowl, combine the zest, salt, lemon pepper, garlic pepper, and chipotle powder. Cut 3 large sheets of aluminum foil and place 4 ears of corn on each. Liberally sprinkle the corn with a third of the spice mixture. Divide the butter among the ears of corn.

Fold and crimp the foil to make tightly sealed packets, place them on the grill for 15 minutes, and then flip them over and grill for another 15 minutes.

Remove the corn from the packets, making sure to drizzle butter over all of the cobs. Serve with lime wedges.

DIVA Q HOMESTYLE ROASTED CREAM CORN

Serves 4 to 6

8 ears corn, roasted and cooled

8 tablespoons (1 stick) butter

½ cup all-purpose flour

2 to 3 cups milk

½ cup finely minced shallot

1 tablespoon sugar

¼ teaspoon freshly grated nutmeg

1 to 2 teaspoons salt

1 to 2 teaspoons white pepper

Cut the corn off the cobs and set it aside.

Melt the butter in a medium saucepan over medium heat. Add the flour and cook for a few minutes, stirring constantly, until the butter and flour come together well.

Whisk in 2 cups of the milk ½ cup at a time until the mixture gets thick and bubbly.

Do not stop whisking or the flour will stick.

Add the corn, shallot, sugar, nutmeg, and salt and pepper to taste; mix well to coat the corn kernels. Add more milk (or a little more butter) if the mixture is too thick for you. Continue cooking until the mixture is heated through. It does not need to come to a boil. Adjust the seasonings, if necessary, before serving.

DANIELLE DIMOVSKI

This is a great use for leftover corn. It's good hot or cold and a great complement to a medium-rare steak.

GORDON HUBBELL

Gordon says asparagus used to grow wild in the yard when he was a kid, but now he pays a pretty steep price for good spears at the grocery store. Whether you are lucky enough to get it from the garden or have to shell out for it, it makes great grill fodder! Fresh asparagus has a fruity, subtle flavor that proper grilling amplifies nicely. Thus, minimal spicing is recommended. One bunch (1 pound) of asparagus and about ⅓ cup of olive oil will make about 4 servings.

GRILLED ASPARAGUS

Serves as many as you need

Fresh asparagus

Good-quality extra virgin olive oil

Salt and black pepper

Rinse the asparagus spears in cold water, then dry them on a paper towel. Cut off the woody blunt ends (usually about an inch or so will be enough). Place the spears in a square baking dish and douse them with the olive oil. Sprinkle lightly with salt and black pepper. Mix to spread the oil, salt, and black pepper evenly over the spears. This can be done several hours ahead if you're planning on grilling a bunch of stuff and you need extra time.

Medium heat works best because there's no point in going for much in the way of grill marks and the fatter spears can take a while over the heat.

Unlike parts of the unwieldy onion, it is easy to protect your precious asparagus from succumbing to the coals. Simply place the spears at a 90-degree angle to the grill grate. Be vigilant! The minute you let one get to about 45 degrees, it will assume a mind of its own and dive in, making a little nasty smoke in the process. Asparagus is suicidal by nature.

Asparagus is done when the spears are softened through but not terminally limp. Store grilled asparagus, covered, in the warming oven for as long as you need to (well, within reason, anyway). If you have leftovers, and that is uncommon, you can even nuke them in the microwave without damaging their molecular structure.

GRILLED
BBQ ASPARAGUS

Serves 4

1 cup water

1 pound asparagus, trimmed

¼ cup barbeque sauce

Set up a grill for medium heat. Soak about 16 wooden skewers in cold water for at least 30 minutes. In a large skillet over medium-high heat, bring the water to a boil and add the asparagus. Cover and cook for 4 to 6 minutes, until almost tender; drain and pat dry. Cool slightly.

Thread several asparagus spears onto two parallel soaked wooden skewers. Repeat. Grill, uncovered, over medium heat for 2 minutes, turning once. Baste with barbeque sauce. Grill for 2 minutes longer, turning and basting once more.

PAUL KIRK, PHB

This is great with steaks,

hamburgers, or pork chops.

PAUL KIRK, PHB

Broccoli is one of Paul's least-favorite vegetables, but he loves it when it's grilled.

GRILLED BROCCOLI

Serves 6

6 cups fresh broccoli florets

2½ tablespoons fresh lemon juice

2 tablespoons olive oil

¼ teaspoon sea salt

¼ teaspoon freshly ground black pepper

¾ cup freshly grated Parmesan cheese

Place the broccoli in a large bowl. Combine the lemon juice, oil, salt, and pepper; drizzle over the broccoli and toss to coat. Let stand for 30 minutes.

Coat the grill rack with cooking spray before starting the grill. Prepare the grill for medium indirect heat. Toss the broccoli, then drain off the marinade.

Place the Parmesan cheese in a large resealable plastic bag. Add the broccoli, a few pieces at a time, and shake to coat.

Grill the broccoli, covered, for 8 to 10 minutes on each side, until crisp-tender.

GRILLED VIDALIA ONIONS

Serves 6 to 8

6 medium to large Vidalia onions

6 tablespoons butter

Salt and black pepper

Prepare your grill with medium-hot coals.

Peel the onions, cut a cross on top of each one, add 1 tablespoon butter to each, and then add salt and black pepper to taste. Wrap each onion in aluminum foil and cook until soft, 45 minutes to 1½ hours.

LEW MILLER

We can't quite picture Kansas City Lew standing out in a Vidalia, Georgia, field of onions, harvesting a few for this recipe. Fortunately the sweet gem of root vegetables is available nationwide. As Lew's recipe shows, Vidalia onions are so tasty they don't need a lot of seasonings.

SIDES

85

PAUL KIRK, PHB

Don't tell anyone, but this recipe came from Duke.

COUNTRY-STYLE BBQ ONIONS

Serves 8

8 medium Vidalia onions

1 can Bush's Best Country Style Baked Beans or your favorite

¼ cup packed dark brown sugar

½ cup barbeque sauce

4 tablespoons (½ stick) butter, cut into 8 pieces, at room temperature

4 slices bacon, cooked and cut into 8 (2-inch) pieces

Freshly ground black pepper

Prepare the grill to cook with indirect heat at 350ºF. Peel the onions. Carefully hollow out the onions, leaving two or three layers and the base intact. Chop the onion pieces you hollowed out and mix them with the baked beans, brown sugar, and barbeque sauce. Spoon the mixture into the onions and top with the butter and bacon. Sprinkle with black pepper. Grill the onions using indirect heat for 40 minutes to an hour, or until golden brown and tender.

STUFFED GRILLED ONIONS

Serves 6

6 large (8-ounce) yellow onions

2 cups Stove Top stuffing mix, any flavor

⅔ cup chicken broth

¼ pound mild or hot Italian sausage

To prepare the onions for stuffing, leave the outer skin on the onions and rinse them. Trim off the root ends to make flat bottoms. Cut the tops off and reserve them. Hollow out the centers of the onions, leaving two or three outer layers intact; save the centers for another use.

In a medium mixing bowl, soak the stuffing mix in the chicken broth, turning to coat until the broth is completely absorbed. Add the sausage and toss gently to mix well. Fill the onions with equal amounts of the sausage mixture. Place the tops on the onions.

Place each onion upright in the center of a piece of heavy-duty aluminum foil; bring up the edges and seal, leaving a little space for the expansion of steam.

Place the foil onion packets upright in the center of the cooking grate; cook for 2 hours, or until very tender. Remove the onions from the foil and discard the outermost skin. Serve the stuffed onions with the juices from the foil packets.

PAUL KIRK, PHB

These can be served as a side or a meal in themselves.

PAUL KIRK, PH8

People don't often grill tomatoes, but they're delicious!

GRILLED CHERRY TOMATOES

Serves 4 to 6

2 pints cherry tomatoes, halved

3 tablespoons unsalted butter

2 cloves garlic, pressed

½ teaspoon dried oregano

½ teaspoon black pepper

Preheat the grill to medium.

Place the tomatoes on a double thickness of heavy-duty aluminum foil (about 24 by 12 inches). In a skillet over medium heat, melt the butter and sauté the garlic, oregano, and black pepper for about 2 minutes. Pour over the tomatoes. Fold the foil around the tomatoes and seal tightly. Grill, covered, over medium heat for 8 to 10 minutes, until the tomatoes are heated through, turning once. When serving, open the foil carefully to allow steam to escape.

I DIDN'T CLAW MY WAY TO THE TOP OF THE FOOD CHAIN TO BECOME A VEGETARIAN.

GRILLED GARLIC TOMATOES

Serves 4

¼ cup mayonnaise

3 tablespoons freshly grated Parmesan cheese

2 tablespoons seasoned dried bread crumbs

1 large clove garlic, pressed

1 teaspoon fresh lemon juice

2 large tomatoes, cut in half crosswise

Preheat the grill to high.

Cut two 12-inch squares of Reynolds Wrap Non-Stick Aluminum Foil and layer them with the dull side up to form a double thickness. Place the foil sheets on a baking sheet and set them aside.

Combine the mayonnaise, Parmesan, bread crumbs, garlic, and lemon juice. Spread the mixture evenly on the cut side of each tomato half. Arrange the tomatoes on the foil sheets. Slide the foil sheets onto the grill.

Cover the grill and cook for 12 to 15 minutes, or until the tops of the tomatoes are browned. Slide the foil sheets from the grill onto the baking sheet and serve hot.

PAUL KIRK, PHB

These are great on their own, or on a BLT, in a salad, or on a bruschetta. You'll need some Reynolds Wrap Non-Stick Aluminum Foil for this. It works best for keeping the tomatoes from sticking.

LEW MILLER

About 2 cups of the sauce or dressing marinade will cover a lot of vegetables.

MARINATED GRILLED VEGETABLES

Serves as many as you need

Your favorite grilling vegetables, such as zucchini, yellow squash, eggplant, and red onion

Teriyaki sauce or Wishbone Italian dressing

Grated Parmesan cheese, for serving

Salt and black pepper

Slice the vegetables ½ inch thick. Marinate them for 2 to 3 hours in teriyaki sauce or Wishbone dressing in a large resealable plastic bag in the refrigerator, tossing the bag occasionally to coat the vegetables. Grill in a grill basket until dark in color, being careful not to overcook. To serve, sprinkle the vegetables with Parmesan cheese, salt, and black pepper.

GRILLED VEGETABLE MEDLEY

Serves 8

1 pound asparagus, trimmed

1 each red, yellow, and green bell pepper, julienned

1 cup sliced fresh mushrooms

1 medium tomato, chopped

1 medium onion, sliced

1 (2¼-ounce) can sliced ripe olives, drained

2 cloves garlic, minced

2 tablespoons olive oil

1 teaspoon minced fresh parsley

½ teaspoon salt

½ teaspoon black pepper

¼ teaspoon lemon pepper

¼ teaspoon dried dill weed

Set up a grill for indirect cooking at medium heat. In a disposable foil pan, combine the vegetables, olives, and garlic; drizzle with olive oil and toss to coat. Sprinkle with parsley, salt, black pepper, lemon pepper, and dill; toss to coat.

Grill, covered, for 20 to 25 minutes, or until the vegetables are crisp-tender, stirring occasionally.

PAUL KIRK, PHB

This colorful veggie recipe happened by accident. One evening, Paul didn't have room on the grill for all the things he wanted to prepare, so he threw two of the dishes together and came up with this medley. It goes great with any grilled meat.

RED LACES

As told by William E. "Billy Bones" Wall:

We started a team ritual quite by accident in 1986. I needed new shoelaces for my grease-soaked, sauce-soaked tenny runners. The only option was a vendor near the barbeque site who specialized in glitzy shoelaces for the "younger crowd." Being desperate, I bought a fine pair of red shoelaces. When I returned, my wife pointed out they were of the nature that would invite comments such as "Geez! Those are REALLY red!" or "You've got to be kidding!" I never thought shoelaces would exact such utterances from friends!?!? So . . . my natural bravado (usually seen only when I'm backed to the wall) cried out, "Leave me alone," but I really found myself explaining that none but the best barbequers were allowed to wear red shoelaces and that the condition of my shoes proved that I had earned the right to wear the "incredibly beautiful" scarlet laces—badge of the proud and the few.

Eventually I won a few folks to my way of thinking (mostly among the younger folks), and red laces were being displayed proudly at all occasions where barbeque was discussed or practiced. Eventually all members of the Billy Bones BBQ Team earned their red laces, and they are much sought after to this day.

Reprinted with permission from the *National Barbecue News*, April 2005

GRILLED GARDEN VEGGIES

Serves 8

2 tablespoons olive oil

1 small yellow onion, chopped

2 garlic cloves, minced

1 teaspoon dried rosemary, crushed

2 small zucchini, sliced ¼ to ½ inch thick

2 small yellow summer squash, sliced ¼ to ½ inch thick

½ pound medium mushrooms, quartered

1 large tomato, diced

¾ teaspoon salt

¼ teaspoon black pepper

Prepare a grill for medium heat. Drizzle 1 tablespoon of the oil over a double thickness of heavy-duty aluminum foil (about 24 by 12 inches). Combine the onion, garlic, and ½ teaspoon of the rosemary; spoon the mixture over the foil. Top with the zucchini, yellow squash, mushrooms, and tomato; drizzle with the remaining oil. Sprinkle with the salt, pepper, and remaining rosemary.

Fold the foil around the vegetables and seal tightly. Grill, covered, for 15 to 20 minutes, until tender. When serving, open the foil carefully to allow steam to escape.

PAUL KIRK, PHB

Even die-hard carnivores like this meat-free recipe. It's great as a side or a meal in itself.

PAUL KIRK, PHB

No, Paul isn't suddenly becoming a vegetarian, but he does like these veggies.

GRILLED SUMMER VEGETABLES

Serves 4

1 small zucchini, sliced ½ inch thick on the bias

1 small yellow squash, sliced ½ inch thick on the bias

1 medium onion, sliced ½ inch thick

1 red, green, or yellow bell pepper, cut into 2-inch pieces

2 plum tomatoes, quartered

4 ounces fresh button or shiitake mushrooms, cut or whole

Italian dressing or teriyaki sauce, for marinating

Prepare the grill for high heat. Combine all the vegetables in a bowl. Toss with the dressing or teriyaki sauce. Marinate for 5 to 10 minutes. Grill on a vegetable grill topper or in a fish basket for 5 to 10 minutes. Serve immediately.

GRILLED GREEK-STYLE ZUCCHINI

Serves 6

4 small zucchini, thinly sliced

1 medium tomato, seeded and chopped

¼ cup pitted ripe olives, halved

2 tablespoons chopped scallion

4 teaspoons olive or canola oil

2 teaspoons fresh lemon juice

½ teaspoon dried oregano

½ teaspoon garlic salt

¼ teaspoon black pepper

2 tablespoons freshly grated Parmesan cheese

Prepare a grill for medium heat. In a bowl, combine the zucchini, tomato, olives, and scallion. Combine the oil, lemon juice, oregano, garlic salt, and pepper; pour over the vegetables and toss to coat. Place on a double thickness of heavy-duty aluminum foil (about 23 by 18 inches). Fold the foil around the vegetables and seal tightly. Grill, covered, for 10 to 15 minutes, until the vegetables are tender. Open the packet carefully to avoid being burned by the steam. Sprinkle with Parmesan cheese and serve at once.

PAUL KIRK, PHB

These are good as a side or a topping for pizza. Check out the pizza recipes on pages 185 to 195.

SIDES

WAYNE LOHMAN

Here is Wayne's variation of the famous recipe from Neely's Bar-B-Que Restaurant in Wayne's hometown, Memphis, Tennessee. Ask any two Memphians where to get the best barbeque spaghetti in town and you could start an animated argument. There is no argument, however, that this Memphis classic is delicious!

MEMPHIS-STYLE BARBEQUE SPAGHETTI

Serves 6 to 8

2 tablespoons olive oil

¾ cup chopped green bell pepper

1 cup chopped yellow onion

1 clove garlic, chopped

1 (1.5-ounce) package Lawry's Original Style Spaghetti Sauce Spices & Seasonings, prepared according to package instructions

2 (16-ounce) bottles of your favorite Memphis-style barbeque sauce, such as Neely's

2 pounds smoked pork, pulled or chopped

1½ pounds cooked spaghetti (8 to 10 ounces dried)

In a large pot, heat the oil over medium heat. Add the green pepper, onion, and garlic and sauté for 8 to 9 minutes, stirring frequently, until tender. Add the prepared spaghetti sauce. Bring it to a boil; then reduce the heat and add both bottles of barbeque sauce and the pulled pork. Cover and cook over low heat for 1 hour. Serve the sauce over the prepared spaghetti.

BEST SPAGHETTI SAUCE EVER

Serves 8 to 10

2 pounds Italian sausage, bulk or links, casings removed

1 small yellow onion

3 tablespoons pressed garlic

1 (28-ounce) can diced tomatoes, with juice

2 (6-ounce) cans tomato paste

2 (15-ounce) cans tomato sauce

2 cups water

1 tablespoon minced fresh basil

2 teaspoons dried parsley

1 tablespoon packed brown sugar

1 teaspoon salt

½ teaspoon hot red pepper flakes

¼ teaspoon black pepper

In a large pot over medium-high heat, brown the Italian sausage with the onion and garlic. Add the tomatoes with their juice, tomato paste, tomato sauce, and water. Mix well. Add the basil, parsley, brown sugar, salt, red pepper, and black pepper. Bring to a boil, reduce the heat, and simmer for at least 1 hour before serving over cooked spaghetti.

DAWN ENDRIJAITIS

Dawn concocted this recipe after searching for a great sauce recipe for months. After trying numerous recipes found on the Web, she decided just to make her own. The tasty result is right here.

SHARI GEORGE

On those rare occasions when you don't feel like eating barbeque, Shari's spicy pasta sauce on angel hair is a refreshing option.

MRS. G'S SPICY PASTA SAUCE

Serves 6

2 tablespoons olive oil

1½ pounds lean ground beef

½ cup minced garlic (1 to 2 heads)

½ cup minced onion

¼ cup minced celery

3 jalapeño chiles, seeded and minced

2 tablespoons minced fresh rosemary

2 tablespoons minced fresh thyme

8 large fresh basil leaves, minced

1 (29-ounce) can tomato sauce

1 tablespoon dried oregano

1 tablespoon garlic salt

1 tablespoon Garlic Garni (see Note)

1 teaspoon black pepper

¾ pound angel hair or other favorite pasta, cooked according to package directions

Heat the olive oil in a medium pot over medium-high heat. Add the ground beef, garlic, onion, and celery and stir until thoroughly cooked, 10 to 15 minutes. Add the jalapeños, rosemary, thyme, and basil and mix well. Stir in the tomato sauce, oregano, garlic salt, Garlic Garni, and black pepper. Simmer for 30 minutes, stirring occasionally. Serve over the cooked pasta.

Note: *Garlic Garni is a garlic seasoning sold by Garlic Festival Foods (garlicfestival.com).*

BBQ SPAGHETTI PIE

Serves 6 to 8

1 (10-ounce) package dried spaghetti

1½ pounds chopped barbequed pork butt

1 (16-ounce) can or jar traditional spaghetti sauce

1 (16-ounce) bottle Memphis-style barbeque sauce

Dash of kosher salt (Phil notes, "Like the T-shirts of Jubon's BBQ Team say, 'At least the salt is kosher'")

2 extra-large eggs, beaten

¼ cup grated Parmesan cheese

½ pound mozzarella cheese, grated (about 2 cups)

2 tablespoons Rendezvous Famous Seasoning or mild chili powder

6 to 8 deep-fried battered onion rings, preferably from Leonard's Pit Barbecue in Memphis

Preheat the oven or your pit to 350°F. Grease a 9 by 13-inch glass or ceramic baking dish.

Break the spaghetti in half and boil it in salted water until al dente. Drain and set aside.

Combine the meat, spaghetti sauce, barbeque sauce, and salt in a large saucepan and simmer for 5 minutes.

Combine the cooked spaghetti, eggs, and Parmesan cheese and mix well. Spread the mixture evenly in the prepared dish. Pour the sauce mixture on top of the spaghetti mixture and spread it evenly. Cover the dish with heavy-duty aluminum foil and bake for 25 minutes. Remove the foil and sprinkle the mozzarella cheese on top, followed by the dry seasonings. Bake for another 5 minutes, uncovered, until the cheese melts. Garnish each serving with an onion ring.

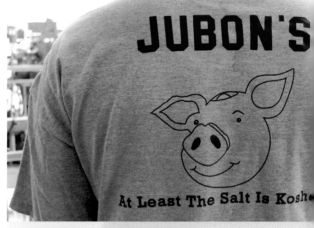

PHIL LITMAN

We don't know of any Memphis restaurants that serve this pie, but it is clearly inspired by Phil's many adventures in Memphis during the world championship barbeque contest. Way to go, Phil!

JENNIFER B. STANLEY

Fox Hall is a fictional bed and breakfast in Jennifer Stanley's mystery novel *Stiffs and Swine*, in which a famous pitmaster is found murdered. He wasn't murdered at Fox Hall, but these grits are to die for!

FOX HALL'S CHEESE GRITS

Serves 8 to 10

6 cups water

1½ cups quick-cooking grits

6 tablespoons butter

1 pound extra-sharp cheddar cheese, grated (about 4 cups)

2 teaspoons seasoning salt

1 tablespoon Worcestershire sauce

½ teaspoon Tabasco sauce, or more or less to taste

2 teaspoons salt

3 eggs, well beaten

Paprika, for garnish (optional)

Preheat the oven to 350°F. Lightly grease a 9 by 13-inch baking dish.

In a medium saucepan over medium-high heat, bring the water to a boil. Stir in the grits. Reduce the heat to low. Cover and cook for 5 to 6 minutes, stirring occasionally. Mix in the butter, cheese, seasoning salt, Worcestershire, Tabasco, and salt. Continue cooking for 5 minutes, or until the cheese is melted. Remove from the heat, cool slightly, and fold in the eggs. Pour into the prepared baking dish and bake for 1 hour, or until the top is lightly browned. Garnish with paprika before serving.

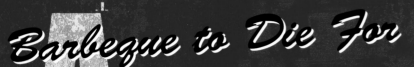

Although barbeque gets frequent mention in works of fiction, it is seldom front and center. Fannie Flagg's *Fried Green Tomatoes at the Whistle Stop Café* (1987)—the Sweeney Todd of barbeque fiction—comes to mind, plus a few other entertaining mysteries.

In *The Revenge of the Barbeque Queens* (1997), Kansas City's beloved Lou Jane Temple populates her engaging story with characters that remind us of people we have met in the competition barbeque network. She gives a whole new meaning to the concept of getting "sauced."

Gerald Duff's *Memphis Ribs* (1999) skillfully uses the annual Memphis in May barbeque and some excursions to the Mississippi Delta to tell a spicy story of greed, murder, power, and barbeque that entertains and makes you hungry enough to take the next plane to Memphis.

J. B. Stanley's *Stiffs and Swine* (2008) features the murder of a barbeque legend known as "The Pitmaster" at a Virginia Hog Fest. J. B. told us that the KCBS was of tremendous value to her in doing research for the book. She and publisher Midnight Ink/Llewellyn Publications kindly gave us permission to reprint some of the recipes from *Stiffs and Swine* in this book.

Tryon, North Carolina, one of our favorite contest sites, is the locale for Gene Davis's mystery, *Murder at the Blue Ridge Barbecue Festival* (2008).

Janet Evanovich's *Finger Lickin' Fifteen* (2009) opens with a Food Channel barbeque sauce celebrity chef losing his head. It ends when the decapitating perpetrators are captured at a New Jersey barbeque contest. Gases—propane and methane—figure prominently in the plot. In the end, real charcoal and hardwoods fuel the barbeque and a "methane emission" foils the crooks.

JOHN ROSS, PHB

John, a former KCBS board member, can fill any role needed at a sanctioned contest—from Rep to Table Captain and beyond. He is also a sought-after Certified Barbeque Judge (CBJ) instructor and holds a PhB degree. Besides barbeque, John's culinary passion is bread making. He wrote down this recipe and the Garlic Parmesan Bread recipe that follows for us one day at Johnny's Barbecue in Mission, Kansas, during our "First Wednesday" informal barbeque lunch group (you're invited) while we ate barbeque ribs, chicken and beef.

BARBEQUE BREAD

Makes 1 loaf

2¼ teaspoons instant yeast

¾ cup water

½ cup barbeque sauce

2 tablespoons butter, melted and cooled

3 cups bread flour

2 tablespoons sugar

1½ teaspoons salt

Add all the ingredients to your bread machine in the order recommended by the manufacturer. After 10 minutes of kneading, add enough water or flour to achieve a tacky dough ball. Bake according to the bread machine manufacturer's instructions.

Note: *You could also bake the bread in the oven. Preheat the oven to 350°F and grease a loaf pan. Dissolve the yeast in the water; then combine the yeast mixture, barbeque sauce, and butter. Add the flour, sugar, and salt and mix until well combined. Knead on a lightly floured surface for 10 minutes; then place the dough in the prepared pan and bake in the oven for 30 to 35 minutes, until the internal temperature of the bread reaches 190° to 200°F.*

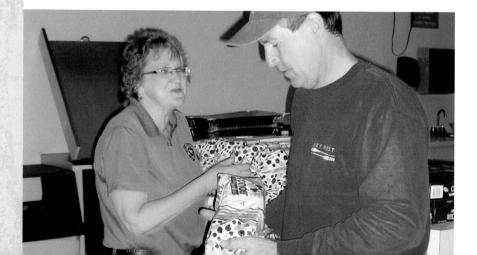

GARLIC PARMESAN BREAD

Makes 1 loaf

1 cup water

2 tablespoons butter, melted and cooled

2½ teaspoons instant yeast

2 cups bread flour

1 cup whole wheat flour

¼ cup nonfat dry milk

2 tablespoons sugar

1½ teaspoons salt

½ to 1 teaspoon granulated garlic

Add all the ingredients to your bread machine in the order recommended by the manufacturer. After 10 minutes of kneading, add water or flour as needed to achieve a tacky dough ball. Bake according to the bread machine manufacturer's instructions.

Note: *You could also bake the bread in the oven. Preheat the oven to 350°F and grease a loaf pan. Dissolve the yeast in the water, then combine the yeast mixture and butter. Add the flours, dry milk, sugar, salt, and granulated garlic and mix until well combined. Knead for 10 minutes on a lightly floured surface; then place the dough in the prepared pan and bake in the oven for 30 to 35 minutes, until the internal temperature of the bread reaches 190° to 200°F.*

JOHN ROSS, PHB

We especially like this bread with barbequed chicken. It is also a great alternative to a bun on John's favorite nonbarbeque sandwich at Johnny's, the deep-fried tenderloin sandwich. Make it open-face, get a knife and fork, and dig in!

ANDY HUSBANDS AND JOE YONAN

Corn bread is great with barbeque and the spiciness of this one takes it to new heights. Thanks to Andy and Joe for giving us permission to reprint it here.

SPICY CORN BREAD

Serves 8

3½ cups all-purpose flour

2 cups cornmeal

2½ tablespoons baking powder

1 tablespoon salt

¼ cup cumin seeds, toasted and ground

½ tablespoon ground cinnamon

1 teaspoon cayenne

½ cup chopped fresh chives

8 tablespoons (1 stick) butter, softened

1 cup sugar

2 eggs

2 cups buttermilk

2 cups fresh corn kernels (from about 4 large ears)

Preheat the oven to 450°F. Grease a 10-inch cast-iron skillet with canola or corn oil.

In a large bowl, combine the flour, cornmeal, baking powder, salt, cumin seeds, cinnamon, cayenne, and chives; mix well.

In another large mixing bowl, cream the butter and sugar until light and fluffy. Add the eggs, one at a time, blending well after each addition. Stir in the buttermilk. Fold in the dry ingredients in 3 batches, then fold in the corn.

Pour the batter into the prepared pan and bake until it begins to brown and a skewer inserted near the center comes out clean, 30 to 40 minutes. Let cool in the pan for 10 minutes. Turn out and serve hot.

CORNY CHEESE CHILE PEPPER BISCUITS

Makes about 30

1 (¼-ounce) package active dry yeast

¼ cup warm water

2⅔ cups all-purpose flour

2 tablespoons sugar (optional)

1½ teaspoons baking powder

½ teaspoon baking soda

½ teaspoon kosher salt

½ cup lard or shortening

½ to 1 cup buttermilk

1 (15.25-ounce) can whole kernel creamed corn, with juices

1 (4-ounce) can diced green chiles, drained

4 ounces sharp cheddar cheese, shredded (about 1 cup)

4 tablespoons (½ stick) unsalted butter, melted

Preheat the oven to 450°F. Lightly grease 2 baking sheets.

In a small bowl, dissolve the yeast in the warm water and let it sit for 5 minutes.

Meanwhile, in a large bowl, whisk together the flour, sugar, baking powder, baking soda, and salt; cut in the shortening with a pastry cutter or two forks until the mixture is crumbly. Add the yeast mixture, ½ cup of the buttermilk, the corn, chiles, and cheese. Stir until a moist dough forms, adding more buttermilk if necessary. Lightly flour a work surface and gently knead the dough for 10 minutes.

Roll out the dough to ½-inch thickness. Use a 2-inch biscuit cutter or a table knife to cut the biscuits into 2-inch rounds.

Put the biscuits on the prepared baking sheets and brush the tops with the melted butter. Bake for 10 to 12 minutes, until golden brown, rotating the baking sheets halfway through the baking time.

MONTE JONES

Monte Jones, aka Biscuits O'Bryan, a retired Episcopal priest and acclaimed cowboy storyteller, lives with his wife, Virginia, at their I O Everybody Ranch in San Angelo, Texas. His alter ego, Biscuits O'Bryan, is a chuck wagon cook who is ready to spin a tall tale at the drop of a Stetson. We met Monte when he judged on three occasions at The Jack, where he regaled fellow judges with tall tales, jokes, and his infectious sense of humor. He seemed the perfect source for a good biscuit recipe. Biscuits prefers his biscuits without sugar; same goes for his corn bread. He was making a batch of pear honey when we last contacted him. He said, "It is wonderful on homemade hot biscuits." (That recipe is on page 277.) We especially appreciated the following recipe when Biscuits told us, "I don't really make biscuits from a recipe. I just dump stuff together, and it ends up being delicious baking powder biscuits." Biscuits has published several volumes of his stories, plus a book about his "errant childhood," *Biscuits O'Bryan, Texas Storyteller* (2005).

BAR·B·Q
PITAS
CHICKEN
PORK
SAUSAGE

"Professor Holmes
HA
CORBIN, KY.

JACK DANIEL'S
OLD TIME
Quality
Tennessee
SOUR MASH
WHISKEY
Old
No. 7
BRAND
DISTILLED &
BOTTLED BY
JACK DANIEL DISTILLERY
LYNCHBURG (POP. 361) TN USA
EST. & REG. IN 1866

WHISKEY

BUNG
TOSS

BUTT
Bowling

FOLLOW US TO A GREAT BBQ EVENT!

PRESENTED BY THE KANSAS CITY BARBEQUE SOCIETY AND THESE PROUD SPONSORS

Chipotle   KINGSFORD   Scott SHOP TOWELS   TUMS   weber

MEET KCBS PROS   LEARN BBQ TIPS   SAMPLE T

KCBS
KANSAS CITY
BARBEQUE
SOCIETY

THE GREAT AMERICAN B.

ANYTHING BUTT

In contest lingo, "anything butt" means any meat dish that isn't in a sanctioned category. Although "but" would be the correct spelling to fit the meaning, in barbeque vernacular another "t" is added.

Here's where the rules and regs go out the window. Although "anything butt" doesn't count toward annual team score totals to qualify for Team of the Year, wins in this category are coveted. Here's where the creative culinary juices shine!

Judges are ambivalent and hesitant about some of the "mystery dishes" put before them—especially when dishes are labeled "roadkill." Could be alligator tail, rattlesnake, octopus, shark, catfish, guinea pig, armadillo, venison, kangaroo, ostrich, raccoon, opossum, or anything else but pork ribs, pork butt, chicken, or beef brisket. More often than not, however, teams enter dishes that are easily recognized by judges and are crafted to net a blue ribbon or first-place trophy.

In this chapter, we've loosened the rules even further. A few of these dishes aren't barbequed or even grilled. Some are breakfast foods that teams serve in the morning before a competition. Others are just-plain good, barbequed or not. You'll find a few exotic dishes—venison meat loaf, elk, and beef tongue, for example—but for the most part our contributors played it safe with a delicious variety of dishes that will resonate with fussy palates inside or outside the judging compound.

RICK BROWNE, PHB

When Rick got the assignment to team up with Jack Bettridge in the mid-1990s to embark upon "a pilgrimage in search of America's best barbeque," an immensely popular book of color photos, engaging text, and recipes, *Barbecue America* (1999), was the result. Since then, Rick has gone on to produce a series of *Barbecue America* TV shows on PBS, and has racked up several more books on barbeque and grilling. Rick's world tour in search of the best barbeque is one of his latest ventures. Like most of us, Rick is ever mindful of his roots. This basic cedar-plank salmon recipe harkens from Rick's roots in the Pacific Northwest. Regardless of your roots, if you like salmon, you'll love the results you get from this recipe.

RICK BROWNE'S CEDAR-PLANK SALMON

Serves 4 to 6

1 (2½-pound) fresh salmon fillet, skin on

1 tablespoon plus 1 teaspoon balsamic vinegar

1 tablespoon ground ginger

1 tablespoon garlic powder

2 tablespoons packed brown sugar

2 tablespoons chopped scallion, green part only

¼ cup extra virgin olive oil

Sea salt or kosher salt and freshly ground black pepper

¼ cup fresh raspberries

1 cup water

1 teaspoon granulated sugar

Soak an untreated cedar shingle or plank large enough to hold the salmon fillet in warm water for at least 4 hours, ideally overnight.

Place the salmon in a shallow baking dish. In a mixing bowl, combine 1 tablespoon of the vinegar, the ginger, garlic powder, brown sugar, and scallion; pour the mixture over the salmon. Let stand for 30 minutes, turning the fish once or twice.

Preheat a charcoal or gas grill to 500°F. Fill a spray bottle with water to douse flare-ups.

Remove the salmon from the marinade and drain, discarding the marinade. Remove the plank from the water and brush it with the olive oil. Place the salmon, skin side down, on the plank; season with salt and pepper. Transfer the plank to the grill rack over direct heat. Close the lid and cook for 20 to 25 minutes, basting two or three times, until the fish is cooked: white fat will bubble to the surface, the edges will just start to turn brown, and the center will be medium-rare. Near the end of cooking, the plank may flare up around the edges. This is OK; spray with water to douse flames and continue cooking.

Meanwhile, in a mixing bowl, combine the raspberries with the water, the remaining teaspoon of balsamic vinegar, and the granulated sugar; let stand until the salmon is cooked. Remove the plank from the grill and place it on a serving tray. Drain the raspberries, sprinkle them over the fish, and serve.

RON SHEWCHUK

This is one of Ron's signature recipes. He's cooked it scores of times over the last few years, won awards with it, and people often comment, "This is the best salmon I've ever eaten." The sweet, woody flavor of the Jack Daniel's and maple syrup complements the richness of the salmon and the aroma of the cedar in this West Coast dish. Ron likes to present it on the plank and then serve it on a bed of field greens tossed with some French walnut oil, kosher salt, and toasted pumpkin seeds.

CEDAR-PLANKED SALMON WITH WHISKEY-MAPLE GLAZE

Serves 6 to 8

WHISKEY-MAPLE GLAZE

½ cup Jack Daniel's Tennessee Whiskey

1 cup maple syrup

1 teaspoon hot red pepper flakes

1 tablespoon butter, at room temperature

SALMON

1 (3-pound) whole wild Pacific salmon fillet, skin on

Kosher salt and freshly ground black pepper

1 teaspoon granulated onion or onion powder

2 lemons, halved

Fresh parsley sprigs, for garnish

1 tablespoon minced fresh flat-leaf parsley

Soak an untreated cedar shingle or plank large enough to hold the salmon fillet in warm water for at least 1 hour or overnight.

Make the glaze by combining the whiskey and maple syrup in a small saucepan. Bring the mixture to a low boil and reduce it by about half, until you have a thick syrup that coats the back of a spoon. Add the hot red pepper flakes and butter and stir the sauce until just combined. Set it aside and keep it warm on the stovetop.

Season the skinless side of the salmon with salt, pepper, and granulated onion. Let the salmon sit at room temperature for 10 to 15 minutes, until the rub is moistened.

While the salmon is sitting, preheat the grill to medium-high for 5 to 10 minutes, or until the chamber temperature rises above 500°F. Fill a spray bottle with water to douse flare-ups. Rinse the soaked plank and place it on the cooking grate. Cover the grill and heat the plank for 4 to 5 minutes, or until it starts to throw off a bit of smoke and crackles lightly. Reduce the heat to medium-low. Season the plank with salt and place the salmon, skin side down, on the plank.

Cover the grill and cook the salmon for 15 to 20 minutes, until the fish has an internal temperature of 135°F. Check it periodically to make sure the plank doesn't catch fire and spray the burning edges with water if it does, making sure to close the lid afterward.

When the salmon is done, squeeze half a lemon along its length and carefully transfer it, plank and all, to a platter. Garnish it with parsley sprigs and the remaining lemon, cut into slices. Drizzle a spoonful of the sauce over each portion as you serve it, and sprinkle it with a little chopped parsley.

From *Barbeque Secrets Deluxe!* by Ron Shewchuk (North Vancouver, BC: Whitecap Books, 2009). Reprinted with permission of the author and publisher.

TYPES OF SALMON

RON SHEWCHUK

For North American consumers, there are basically five kinds of salmon on the market.

CHINOOK: Also known as *spring* or *king salmon,* this is my favorite fish, with firm flesh, good fat content, and exceptional flavor. The most exotic and delicious of all salmon is the white spring or white king, which has a light pink, almost ivory-colored flesh. I think it's best for plank cooking because it's the largest of the salmon species, which means you can often get 4- or 5-pound fillets, or even larger. At its freshest, spring salmon has flesh so firm and flavorful it reminds me of lobster meat.

SOCKEYE: Sockeye has a bright red-orange color and rich, tasty flesh. It's a smaller breed, with fillets in the 2- to 3-pound range. It's tasty but easy to overcook on the plank because of its small size.

COHO: This is the feistiest of the West Coast game fish, renowned for its habit of leaping out of the water while being reeled in. If you can get wild coho, buy it and try it. It's really succulent, and sometimes you can get fairly big fillets.

CHUM: Leaner and lighter in color than its cousins, the chum is delicious but milder in flavor than the bigger species.

PINK: I love fresh pink salmon, although it's not as good for plank cooking as some other kinds because it's the smallest and leanest of the salmon species. But it has a delicate flavor and light-colored flesh that make it excellent for panfrying or quick roasting.

From *Barbeque Secrets Deluxe!* by Ron Shewchuk (North Vancouver, BC: Whitecap Books, 2009). Reprinted with permission of the author and publisher.

MICHIGAN UP PINE WOODS FISH BOIL

Serves a whole clan

First, set an iron scalding pot on a hot fire. Pine knots and splits make the hottest fire. Fill with boiling water, maybe five or six gallons to start. Be sure to have a holey metal basket with appropriate iron rings settled into the iron pot. It'll ease the lifting burden later.

Set the "camp kids" to cuttin' a notch in the redskins (potatoes)— maybe a bushel. Add a "pinch" o' salt, about 3 pounds kosher. This is to bring up the boiling action, not necessarily for flavoring. That notch in the potatoes ensures they are properly seasoned. Give the potatoes 20 to 30 minutes to cook. Add another "pinch" of kosher salt, about 3 more pounds. Add the white fish fillets; about a bushel will be just right. Once the fat from the fish is rising to the top, it's proper to skim the water a few times. We toss a bit of kerosene onto the fire during this time to keep the fire hot and the fat floating to the top. This final cook may take only 10 to 12 more minutes for fish to be properly done. Now it's time to add a pint and a half of kerosene to the fire one last time. If added to the fire properly, the fish pot will boil over, unleashing the last of the floating fish fat particles and catching fire in a rather dramatic fashion when the fat hits the fire. After the flames have died down a bit, it is time to run a sturdy pole through those "handy iron loops" on the fish basket and pull it from the remaining broth, to be served with heaps o' corn bread and great piles of fresh coleslaw. Your favorite brew should accompany this feast, and be sure to top it all off with Michigan's famous red tart cherry pie and heaps of ice cream.

WILLIAM E. "BILLY BONES" WALL

It ain't all BBQ in Michigan. Billy Bones's favorite ritual with fire is a fish boil. It was originally conceived as a cheap way to feed lumbermen after a hard day felling white pine. Billy's grandparents were camp cooks in the Seney/Shingleton area of the Upper Peninsula of Michigan. Grandpa got this one right from the Finnish boys in camp.

GRILLED AHI TUNA STEAKS

Serves 2

½ teaspoon dark sesame oil

2 (6- to 10-ounce) ahi tuna steaks, 1 inch thick

½ teaspoon ground ginger

Freshly ground black pepper

Sea salt

Romaine lettuce, for serving

Light Asian sesame and ginger vinaigrette, for serving

Prepare your grill for high heat. Apply the sesame oil to all sides of the steaks. Sprinkle on the ginger, pepper, and salt. Place the steaks directly over the coals and cook for about 2 minutes on each side. It is very easy to overcook, so be careful. Remove from the grill and carefully separate with a fork. The fish should flake naturally. Serve on a bed of romaine lettuce drizzled with Asian vinaigrette.

RICH AND BUNNY TUTTLE, K CASS BBQ

Rich came up with this recipe when he and Bunny were experimenting with tuna steaks. "It's very simple and quick," Rich told us, "and the Asian flair complemented the steaks very well." Ahi tuna is sometimes called yellowfin tuna. You can find Asian vinaigrette at your local grocers.

SASHIMI AHI TUNA WITH MAUI ONION DRESSING

Serves 4 to 6

½ Maui onion, finely diced

¼ cup soy sauce

¾ teaspoon rice wine vinegar or sushi vinegar

2 tablespoons water

Dash of shichimi (Japanese red pepper flakes) or cayenne

¼ cup extra virgin olive oil

16 to 24 ounces sashimi-grade ahi tuna (about 2 rectangular blocks of yellowfin tuna)

Dash of black pepper

Kosher salt

Daikon sprouts or alfalfa sprouts, for serving

Combine the onion, soy sauce, vinegar, water, and shichimi and let the mixture sit in the refrigerator for at least an hour before using.

Put the olive oil in a 1-gallon resealable plastic bag, add the tuna steaks, and marinate overnight (this will soften the tuna).

Place a skillet on the stove over medium-high heat. Sprinkle the black pepper and kosher salt on the tuna. Sear the tuna in the hot pan for about 30 seconds on each side.

Slice the tuna into pencil-thick slices. Pour the dressing on a flat plate and arrange the ahi slices around the plate. Garnish with some Daikon sprouts and serve.

HARRY SOO

Harry's team, "Slap Yo' Daddy," made a huge splash when he and teammate Mark Tung entered their second year of competition in 2009 with limited competition experience. Taking first place in all four sanctioned meat categories in four different KCBS sanctioned contests is rare for any team, let alone a new team. After those victories in California, they competed at the Great American Barbecue in Kansas City and took Reserve Grand Champion. As Kathleen McIntosh reported in the *National Barbecue News*, these men "are hot! They are on fire! They are also very smart when it comes to BBQ." Since tuna is said to be a "brain food," don't be surprised if you're feeling smarter after preparing and eating this Slap Yo' Daddy–style tuna.

115

WENDY AND TIM BOUCHER, FEEDING FRIENDZ BBQ TEAM

The Feeding Friendz BBQ Team lives in Deerfield, New Hampshire. A love of cooking sparked their interest in BBQ, and eventually these frustrated back-yard barbequers decided they needed to expand. Cooking for two was not an option (for Tim), so they started regularly sending invitations to all of their friends. After attending a couple of local contests and speaking with some teams, they were hooked, and of course Feeding Friendz was a natural team name! They are now in their fifth season of competing—practicing all year long and still feeding all of their friends. This recipe was their winning entry in the Iron Chef competition at Chillin' Country BBQ State Competition, held in York, Maine. You can add more oysters if you like; it's nine here because that's all they were given for the Iron Chef competition.

OYSTERS "THERMIDOR"

Serves 3 to 6

OYSTERS

6 puff pastry shells

9 oysters in the shell

6 ears corn, shucked

2 tablespoons olive oil

Salt and black pepper

1 medium red bell pepper

½ cup drained canned sliced mushrooms

WHITE SAUCE

1 (1-ounce) package white sauce (béchamel) mix

8 tablespoons (1 stick) butter

1¾ cups half-and-half

1 teaspoon dry mustard

Chopped fresh chives, for garnish

Prepare a charcoal grill for indirect cooking. Place the puff pastry shells on a perforated grilling sheet pan, put them on the grill, cover, and grill until the shells turn golden brown, 7 to 10 minutes. Remove from the grill and set aside.

Rub the corn all over with the olive oil and season with salt and pepper to taste. Grill the corn on all sides until cooked, 2 to 3 minutes per side. Remove the corn and set aside until cool enough to handle. Cut the corn from the cobs and set aside.

Rub oil all over the pepper and grill until charred all over. Place in a paper or resealable plastic bag; seal and let rest for about 15 minutes. Remove the pepper from the bag, peel off the skin, seed and mince, and set aside.

Remove 3 of the grilled oysters carefully from the shells and mince. Put the minced oysters and all the oyster liquor in a small saucepan; add all the white sauce ingredients. Cook over medium heat until thickened, 5 to 7 minutes. Add the mushrooms, corn, red pepper, and remaining whole oysters. Blend well, being careful not to break up the oysters, and heat just until warmed through, about 1 minute. Divide the mixture among the puff pastry shells, making sure each serving includes a whole oyster. Garnish with chives.

DENNYMIKE'S SHEPHERD'S PIE

Serves 8 to 10

5 pounds potatoes

2 cups milk

8 tablespoons (1 stick) plus
1 tablespoon butter

Salt and black pepper

1 large yellow onion, chopped

2½ pounds ground chuck or good-
quality ground beef

3 tablespoons Cow Bell Hell or
your favorite rub

2 (16-ounce) cans cream-style
corn

1 (16-ounce) can whole kernel
corn, drained

Peel the potatoes, dice them, and place them in a large stockpot. Add water to cover and bring to a boil over medium-high heat. Cook until the potatoes are fork-tender, 10 to 15 minutes depending on size. Meanwhile, warm the milk.

Drain the potatoes and add the stick of butter and half of the warmed milk. Whip with an electric mixer on medium speed until the butter and milk are incorporated. Whip in the rest of the milk, if needed to achieve the desired texture, and season to taste with salt and pepper. Set aside.

Preheat the oven to 375°F. Melt the remaining tablespoon of butter in a skillet over medium-high heat. Add the onion and cook until translucent, 2 to 3 minutes. Add the ground beef and 2½ tablespoons of the Cow Bell Hell and brown the meat until no red remains. Drain off the liquid. Reserve ½ cup of the meat mixture to sprinkle on top.

Place the rest of the meat mixture in a 10 by 14-inch baking pan. Mix the cans of corn together in a bowl and spread the corn evenly over the meat mixture. Spread the mashed potatoes evenly over the corn. Sprinkle with the reserved meat mixture, then sprinkle the remaining 1½ teaspoons Cow Bell Hell evenly over the top. Bake for 30 to 45 minutes, until bubbling.

DENNYMIKE SHERMAN

DennyMike gave us this recipe,

with special thanks to his mother,

Rita Sherman. Cow Bell Hell

is one of four barbeque rubs

DennyMike markets.

PAUL KIRK, PHB

This recipe was inspired by one of Ardie's Excellent Adventures with friends Ron Buchholz and Bill Herman, in Madison, Wisconsin. We're talking meat, potatoes, and pastry, not burlesque. Smoky Jon Olson has put Madison on the barbeque map with his Smoky Jon's #1 Bar-B-Q, and Myles Allen—proprietor of Myles Teddywedgers Cornish Pasty—has made Madison as famous for pasties as for cheese, beer, brats, and Badgers. We asked them to team up for a special barbeque pasty recipe, but they didn't get around to it, so we asked Chef Paul Kirk to do the job. We love the result!

BARBEQUE PASTY

Serves 6 to 8

CRUST

3 cups all-purpose flour

1 teaspoon salt

½ cup solid white vegetable shortening

FILLING

6 thick slices bacon

1 medium yellow onion, diced

1 tablespoon sugar

2 medium potatoes, cooked, peeled, and diced

1 pound barbequed brisket point, diced

1 pound barbequed pork butt, diced

Salt and black pepper

Barbeque sauce, for serving (optional)

Mix the flour and salt together and use a pastry cutter or two knives to cut in the shortening until it has the texture of cornmeal. Add water (1 to 2 tablespoons) until the mix is doughlike (it's best to err on the side of dryness, although if you get it too wet you can always add flour). Wrap the dough tightly in plastic wrap and refrigerate it for about 30 minutes while you prepare the filling.

In a skillet over medium-high heat, fry the bacon until crisp. Place it on paper towels to cool. Do not drain the grease. Add the onion and sugar to the skillet and sauté until caramelized, 3 to 5 minutes. Use a slotted spoon to remove the onion from the grease and drain on paper towels. Discard the grease.

Crumble the bacon and place it in a large bowl. Add the caramelized onion, diced potatoes, brisket, and pork butt and mix well. Season with the salt and pepper to taste.

Preheat the oven to 450°F. Roll out the crust on a lightly floured surface as you would a pie crust, only more oblong than round. Put the filling on one half of the crust. Dip your finger in some water and make a line of moisture around the filling. Flip the other half of the crust over the filling and press it down over the line of moist dough; crimp the edges. Poke the crust four times or so with a fork and place it on an ungreased baking sheet.

Bake for 20 minutes, reduce the heat to 350°F, and bake for another 20 minutes. Cool for at least 15 minutes on the sheet before eating. Slice and serve with your favorite barbeque sauce, butter, or whatever turns you on.

BILLY BONES ON PASTIES

When we asked Billy Bones for a good pasty recipe, he shared this with us instead: "My favorite place for pasties has been Letho's on Route 2, a few miles west of St. Ignace, Michigan. It was the first stop for Dad and my uncles after taking the ferry north across the straits to deer hunt in the Upper Peninsula of Michigan. I am talking 1949–1955. Letho's rather simple but very original recipe is published online." The big sign outside Letho's says, "The only original—since 1947."

BILL HERMAN, CBJ

When KCBS Certified BBQ Judge Bill Herman isn't traveling the country judging barbeque in Kansas City; Lynchburg, Tennessee; Windsor, Vermont; and elsewhere, he serves as the town administrator of Auburn, New Hampshire. Bill, an active member of the American Academy of Certified Public Managers, is a former president of the organization. He is also a Tennessee Squire, and he knows his way around the kitchen as well as the barbeque pit. Bill's hearty stromboli is a great way to put barbeque leftovers to good use. Or for a traditional stromboli, use ¾ pound sliced deli meat, such as salami or ham, and cheese, such as Muenster.

HEARTY STROMBOLI

Serves 6 as a main course or 12 as a snack

1 (10-ounce) package refrigerated pizza crust, at room temperature

2 tablespoons prepared hearty brown mustard

½ pound barbequed pulled pork or sliced brisket

¼ pound sliced Muenster or provolone cheese

1 egg, beaten

1 teaspoon sesame seeds

Preheat the oven to 425°F. Roll the pizza dough into a 13 by 10-inch rectangle. Spread the mustard on the dough. Arrange the meat and cheese on top, leaving a 1-inch border. Fold the long edges of the dough over the filling, overlapping sides. Pinch the long edge of the dough to seal. Pinch the ends together and tuck them under the dough. Place on a greased baking sheet. Cut slits in the top of the dough. Brush with the beaten egg and sprinkle with the sesame seeds. Bake for 15 minutes, or until golden. Cool on a rack. Cut into slices to serve.

NEW YORK STRIP STEAK SANDWICH

Serves 4

MARINADE

¾ cup plus 1 teaspoon peanut oil

5 cloves roasted garlic

1¼ teaspoons turbinado sugar

4 (10-ounce) New York strip steaks

4 tablespoons (½ stick) butter

1 medium red onion, sliced

2 jalapeño chiles, stemmed, seeded, and cut into strips

2 tablespoons beef stock

4 large fresh hoagie rolls, sliced in half and buttered

Slices of your cheese of choice, for serving (Stuart recommends New York state cheese)

Kosher salt and freshly ground black pepper

STUART CARPENTER

This recipe calls for New York strip steaks. To be accurate, being from Kansas City, we prefer Kansas City strips to New York strips, though in reality they are the same cut. Your favorite steak will work just fine. Make sure you use real cheese, not processed cheese.

Whisk together ¾ cup of the peanut oil, the roasted garlic, and the sugar until blended. Place the steaks in a resealable plastic bag, pour in the marinade, seal the bag, and shake to coat the meat. Marinate in the refrigerator for 4 to 24 hours. Remove and drain the steaks 30 minutes before cooking.

Heat the remaining teaspoon of peanut oil and 2 tablespoons of the butter in a large, heavy skillet over high heat. Add the red onion, reduce the heat to medium, and sauté until the onion begins to caramelize, about 5 minutes. Add the jalapeños and cook for 1 minute. Remove and reserve the onion and chiles.

To cook the steaks, heat the remaining 2 tablespoons butter in the skillet over high heat until foaming. Add the steaks to the skillet and sear each side, 2 to 3 minutes. Add the beef stock and continue cooking for 5 to 7 minutes, until you reach your desired doneness. Pour the pan sauce over the steaks just before serving.

Alternatively, you can cook the steaks on a grill over high heat for 5 to 7 minutes, until done.

To serve, slice the steaks thinly across the grain, place on the buttered hoagie rolls, and top with the onions, jalapeños, and cheese. Season to taste with salt and black pepper. Slice into halves or thirds.

THE KC RIB DOCTOR'S
MEMPHIS IN MAY
ROADKILL STORY

Guy Simpson, the KC Rib Doctor, can match tall tales with anyone on the barbeque contest circuit. We hope he has recorded his many tales, as they would make a fun and memorable book.

One of our favorite Rib Doctor performances was at the 9th Annual Memphis in May World Championship Barbecue Cooking Contest (MIM) in 1986. Team Kansas City, fresh from winning the World Cup in Lisdoonvarna, Ireland, had been invited to compete in Memphis. Team members Paul Kirk, Ronaldo Camargo, and Karen Putnam formed a Memphis-bound KC convoy with Dick Mais (aka the King of Kansas City Barbeque), Mark Henry, Jim "Putter" Putnam, and Ardie A. Davis.

Somewhere between St. Louis and Cape Girardeau a tire on one of the pit trailers blew out. The convoy stopped roadside to replace the tire, which was raggedy to say the least, and totally beyond repair. Before the KC BBQ Baron could toss the tire, Guy said, "Hold off! Let's take it with us. I've got an idea." The Baron found room for the tire in the back of Dick's "Green Monster" pickup, and the convoy drove on all night to Memphis.

Friday is the "Anything Butt" contest at MIM. Guy was in charge of Team Kansas City's entry, which that day was grilled beef tenderloin with a sweet raspberry-jalapeño sauce and fresh raspberry garnish. It was a beautiful thing to behold, with a knockout flavor.

When the onsite judges arrived at Team Kansas City's booth, the KC Rib Doctor was ready with a story. "Welcome, Judges, to Team Kansas City," Guy greeted them. "Today we are serving you a mysterious meat that is so flavorful we wish we could find more of it and put a patent on it. How we found this meat is almost as intriguing as the meat itself."

Guy, with the raggedy blowout tire in hand, proceeded to tell the judges about how the tire met its demise. "On a very dark highway between St. Louis and Cape Girardeau," he said, "we hit something that

sheared the tire down to the steel lining. It was a dark and scary night," he continued, in a quiet voice, eyes wide, face animated. "When we finally managed to stop our rig, we saw that we had hit a varmint and shredded the hide off it. Being good barbequers—"if

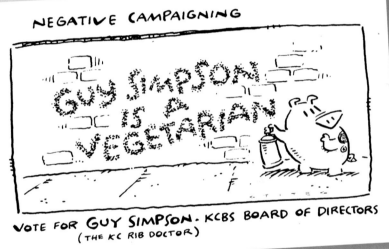

NEGATIVE CAMPAIGNING

GUY SIMPSON IS A VEGETARIAN

VOTE FOR GUY SIMPSON - KCBS BOARD OF DIRECTORS
(THE KC RIB DOCTOR)

it moves, we can grill it"—we threw it in the cooler and went on to Memphis. And, not wanting to waste the mystery meat, we cooked it here for you today. We of course tried it first, and we liked it so much it was, frankly, hard to part with for judging."

The judges must have liked the story and the meat. Team Kansas City got a first-place blue ribbon. Guy has kept the blue ribbon and the old frayed tire as a souvenir of that great award.

BRAZILIAN BARBEQUE RECIPES

JEREMY RAVENSHAW FOWLER

Brazil's ethnic mix of Portuguese, African, Italian, Spanish, German, and Asian cultures has created a national cooking style marked by distinct regional differences. The gaucho, or cowboy, has traditionally made dishes with sun- or salt-dried meats and churrasco, a meal of wood-grilled fresh meats. Jeremy Ravenshaw Fowler offered this version of Brazilian barbeque.

CHURRASCO (BRAZILIAN BARBEQUE)

Churrasco (pronounced shoo-RAS-koo) was the traditional food of the gauchos when they first imported cattle to southern Brazil from around 1530. Today's churrascarias (restaurants where meats are still cooked over barbeque coals using a spit or long sword-type skewer) now seldom use hollowed-out pits in the ground. Other countries give this method different names—kleftico in Greece or peat cookery in Ireland, for example.

Many home cooks now have their own brick-built oddity surrounded by tiles and use gas, charcoal, or lump wood. This means that traditional dishes can be replicated at home much more easily than before.

Churrasco usually features beef, lamb, veal, or ribs. The meat is cooked a good distance away from the fire. It takes longer to cook, but pieces can be cut off the outside and eaten as they cook—a method also used in India, Greece, Mexico, and other countries. This makes barbeque a more protracted event rather than an all-at-once meal.

BEEF TENDERLOIN CHURRASCO

Serves 4

1 cup extra virgin olive oil

2 tablespoons white vinegar

1½ cups hot chile sauce or jalapeño relish, plus some for serving

4 cloves garlic, crushed

3 ounces beer, preferably Brazilian Brahma

Salt and black pepper, preferably smoked salt and freshly cracked black pepper

1 large bunch of curly parsley, minced

2 pounds center-cut beef tenderloin

In a medium bowl, whisk together the oil, vinegar, chile sauce, garlic, beer, and salt and pepper to taste. Reserve some parsley to sprinkle over the finished dish; then add the rest to the bowl.

With a very sharp knife, remove any slivers of skin from the meat and cut into the length of the tenderloin to a depth of about ¼ inch. Now turn the knife blade 90 degrees and continue to slice a layer ¼ inch thick, going all the way around the circumference of the tenderloin and cutting deeper to make a larger and larger ¼-inch-thick slab. Keep cutting until you get to the center of the meat. Open the meat up flat; it's a bit like opening a jelly roll. You should end up with a ¼-inch-thick flat rectangle.

Reserve some of the marinade for basting. Place the meat in a large resealable plastic bag, pour in the rest of the marinade, and allow it to infuse the meat for at least 2 hours in the refrigerator.

Cut the meat into widths that will fit onto skewers. A clever variant could be to use a sharp knife to make two lengthwise cuts down to 1 inch from the thickest end of the meat, effectively making three equal-width strands still connected at the top. Then plait the strands and pin them at the bottom with a toothpick. Thread the meat lengthwise through the skewer.

Grill over a very hot fire to your desired doneness, basting with marinade. A slow fire will dry tenderloin churrasco, unlike tougher cuts of meat. Season to taste and serve with more chile sauce, garnished with the remaining parsley.

ANYTHING BUTT

LEE AND KELLI CHO DAVIS

This dish is always popular when Lee and Kelli and their son, Elliott, host gatherings of family, friends, and business associates. The Korean term for it is *bulgogi*. *Bul* means "fire"; *gogi* means "meat." Thus it is meat grilled by fire. Kelli told us the marinade for this dish is basically the same marinade she and Lee use for *kalbi*, or beef short ribs. Since the rib meat is thicker, she doubles the quantity and marinates the ribs overnight.

Serve this with rice or noodles and coleslaw or kimchi. Kelli presents the *bulgogi* on a bed of butter lettuce leaves. Guests have the option of wrapping meat servings in a lettuce leaf. Sometimes she combines the meat with noodles—a good way to serve more people with less meat.

KOREAN FIRE MEAT

Serves 4

2 tablespoons sugar, or to taste (Kelli says "more is always better")

½ cup good-quality soy sauce, or to taste

½ cup cola or any carbonated soda

1 or 2 scallions, cut into 2-inch pieces

1 medium onion, thinly sliced or minced

1 tablespoon dark sesame oil

1 tablespoon toasted sesame seeds (optional)

1 teaspoon black pepper

2 to 3 cloves garlic, crushed

2 pounds thinly sliced sirloin steak (see Note)

Combine the sugar, soy sauce, cola, scallions, onion, sesame oil, sesame seeds, pepper, and garlic in a nonreactive saucepan. Simmer gently over medium heat until the sugar is dissolved. Add more sugar or soy sauce to taste. Set aside to cool to room temperature.

Separate the sirloin slices and place them in a flat glass or plastic container; cover the meat with marinade. Cover and marinate overnight in the refrigerator for at least 2 hours. Since the meat is thin, 2 hours is sufficient.

Prepare the grill for medium-hot cooking. Grill the meat strips for about 5 minutes total, turning once. On rare occasions when you don't have access to a grill or you don't feel like grilling, the meat can be sautéed in a cast-iron skillet or wok.

Note: *If your butcher is unwilling to slice the meat paper-thin, find a Korean grocer that sells the steak already sliced. Likewise for the thin-sliced beef short ribs. Another option is to freeze the meat and, with a very sharp knife, cut it while still frozen but slightly thawed into thin strips.*

Tip: *Use a grill topper or aluminum foil on top of the grill grate to avoid losing the meat to the fire. The thin strips will fall through your grill grate.*

OLE RAY'S MEAT LOAF

Serves 8 to 10

2 pounds ground chuck

½ large yellow onion, chopped

2 celery stalks, chopped

½ green bell pepper, chopped

1 tablespoon chopped garlic

1 cup bread crumbs, fresh or dried

1 egg, beaten

Salt and black pepper

¼ cup Ole Ray's Kentucky Red Bourbon or
Apple/Cinnamon Barbeque Sauce, plus more for topping

Preheat the oven to 350°F or set up your smoker to cook indirectly (230° to 250°F).

In a large bowl, mix all the ingredients together with your hands or a stiff spoon. Place the mixture into a loaf pan or baking dish. Spread more barbeque sauce on top and bake, covered, in the oven for 1 hour to 1 hour and 15 minutes, until done; or in the smoker for 2 to 2½ hours; or until the internal temperature of the meat registers 165°F.

RAY GREENE

In his Pitmaster classes, Paul Kirk says, "If you've never made sausage, raise your hand." Most hands go up. Paul then says, "Now raise your hand if you've ever made meat loaf." All hands go up. "If you've made meat loaf, you've made sausage." Ground meat combined with seasonings and other ingredients is the essence of sausage—be it link or loaf. Loafs are called "phatties" in barbeque jargon. This meat loaf recipe from Ray Greene doesn't care what you call it as long as you make it for dinner.

DR. HOWARD L. TAYLOR

Howard told us that he has enjoyed meat loaf, especially in sandwiches, since the first several decades of his life. One thing about traditional meat loaf bothered him, however, and that was "the loss of meat flavor from milk, bread, and eggs." Those three fillers and binders were disturbing, "especially when considering meat loaf to be smoked or barbequed." Howard had a meat loaf epiphany of sorts when he spent ten years in the Middle East. There he discovered Greek ground lamb and beef dishes using wine and other Middle Eastern ingredients, with, he told us, "much higher spice levels, and broth instead of milk, and rice instead of bread." When he returned to the United States,

continued on page 129

BBQ (SMOKED) MEAT LOAF

Serves 8 to 10

2 to 3 tablespoons hickory-smoked bacon drippings

1 cup diced red onion

3 cloves garlic, minced

1 teaspoon paprika, preferably smoked

2 chipotle chiles in adobo, seeded and chopped, sauce reserved

¾ cup beef broth

2 teaspoons unflavored gelatin powder

2 large eggs, lightly beaten

2 teaspoons balsamic or red wine vinegar

2 tablespoons Worcestershire sauce

2 teaspoons Tabasco or other hot sauce, or to taste (optional)

2 teaspoons salt

1 teaspoon black pepper

2 teaspoons cumin seeds, toasted and ground, or ground cumin

1 to 2 teaspoons chili powder or hot sauce (optional)

1 teaspoon minced fresh oregano or ground coriander (optional)

1 teaspoon coarsely chopped fresh thyme

2 tablespoons minced fresh cilantro

2 tablespoons brown sugar, or to taste (optional)

2 pounds 80 to 85% lean ground chuck

1 cup cracker crumbs, preferably whole wheat Ritz, or as needed

1 cup barbeque sauce, smoky or regular, for serving (optional)

Heat the bacon drippings in a large skillet over medium heat. Add the onion and cook until lightly browned, 5 to 8 minutes. Pour off all but 1 tablespoon of the fat. Add the garlic, paprika, and chipotle chiles and sauté for 1 more minute. Add ¼ cup of the beef broth and stir to deglaze the pan. Remove from the heat, sprinkle in the gelatin, and stir. Let the mixture sit for 5 minutes to cool.

In a bowl, combine the eggs, remaining ½ cup of beef broth, vinegar, and Worcestershire. Add hot sauce to taste. Stir. Add the salt, black pepper, cumin, chili powder, oregano, and thyme and stir. Add the cilantro leaves, brown sugar, and onion mixture to the bowl. Mix well. Add the ground beef and mix well with a stiff spoon or by hand. Mix in enough cracker crumbs to make the mixture slightly stiff. Form the meat into one large loaf or 6 to 8 small loaves, kabobs (logs), or patties.

A water smoker is recommended but not essential. Wrap the smoker grills (racks) in aluminum foil. Punch many 2- or 3-inch-diameter holes in the foil. For a larger, more square loaf, punch holes in the bottom and sides of an aluminum foil loaf pan and put the loaf in it. Place racks or pans over a water pan or drip pan in the smoker. Leave some clearance. Preheat the smoker to 215° to 250°F. Place the meat loaves on the foil.

Bake until the internal temperature reaches 165°F in the center. Depending on the loaf size and smoker temperature, this could take 45 minutes to 4 hours. As an option, the meat loaf can be basted with a glaze of your choice and cooked for 5 to 10 minutes more.

Remove the loaves and let them rest for 10 to 15 minutes before serving. Slice and serve with warm barbeque sauce on the side.

Howard found several meat loaf recipes calling for consommé, or beef broth and gelatin. This, at last, was meat loaf worthy of barbeque. Howard recommends smoking meat loaf on a flat piece of aluminum foil or in a pan with holes in it so the liquids can drain out and the smoke can get in. For a spicier (piquant) flavor, Howard says, "use more hot sauce and chili powder." This meat loaf is great served with barbeque sauce or mushroom gravy or topped with cheddar or pepper Jack cheese. The leftover meat loaf can also be refrigerated and used a day or two later for a main dish or in sandwiches.

DENNYMIKE SHERMAN

DennyMike is a very outgoing, dynamic, larger-than-life guy and a big supporter of barbeque events. This is his version of "It's Not Your Mother's Meat Loaf Recipe" from thatsmyhome.com. You can get some of his Cow Bell Hell rub at dennymikes.com.

DENNYMIKE'S MEAT LOAF

Serves 8 to 10

2 whole bay leaves

1 heaping tablespoon plus 1 teaspoon Cow Bell Hell or your favorite rub

1 teaspoon ground cumin

4 tablespoons (½ stick) butter

1 cup chopped yellow onion

⅔ cup chopped celery

¾ cup chopped green bell pepper

⅓ cup chopped scallion

1 small jalapeño chile, minced

8 cloves garlic, minced

6 to 8 shakes hot sauce, or to taste

1 tablespoon plus 2 teaspoons Worcestershire sauce

⅓ cup milk

⅓ cup ketchup

2½ pounds ground beef

1 pound sweet Italian sausage

1 pound hot Italian sausage

3 eggs, lightly beaten

1½ cups very fine dry bread crumbs with Italian seasoning

In a small bowl, combine the bay leaves, Cow Bell Hell, and cumin and set aside. Melt the butter in large sauté pan over medium heat. Add the onion, celery, bell pepper, jalapeño, scallion, jalapeño, garlic, hot sauce, Worcestershire, and bay leaf mixture. Sauté for 5 to 6 minutes, stirring occasionally. The mixture will begin sticking to the bottom of the pan, so scrape the bottom as you stir. Add the milk and ketchup and continue cooking for about 2 minutes, stirring constantly. Remove from the heat and allow the mixture to cool to room temperature. Remove the bay leaves.

In a large bowl, combine the ground beef, sausage, eggs, cooked vegetable mixture, and bread crumbs. Mix thoroughly by hand.

To bake the meat loaf in the oven: Preheat the oven to 350°F. Shape the mixture into a loaf and place it in the middle of a 12 by 16-inch baking pan. Bake for 30 minutes, increase the temperature to 400°F, and continue cooking until done, 30 to 45 minutes longer.

To cook in the smoker: DennyMike recommends a Traeger pellet smoker model #075. Place on a perforated grilling tray or mesh baking rack to allow smoke underneath. Bring the smoker to 350° to 375°F and cook for 30 minutes, reduce the temperature to 180°F, and cook for 1½ hours. Bring the temperature back to 300°F, brush on your favorite barbeque sauce (DennyMike likes Sweet 'n Spicy), and cook for 15 to 30 minutes, or until done.

SOUP BURGERS

Serves 4

1 pound ground beef

1 teaspoon salt

1 teaspoon black pepper

1 teaspoon garlic powder

1 tablespoon beef bouillon granules

Prepare a medium-hot charcoal grill. In a large bowl, mix together the ground beef, salt, black pepper, garlic powder, and beef bouillon granules. Form the mixture into 4 patties.

Place the patties on the grill, cover, and cook for 5 to 6 minutes per side for medium-rare, or longer if desired.

WAYNE NELSON

This makes a better burger, and the recipe is easy. The bouillon uses the juices of the meat to make soup in the burger.

ANYTHING BUTT

STEVE HOLBROOK

Paul met Steve years ago when Paul was looking for someone to build a trailer-drawn barbeque pit. Paul said he'd trade catering services for Steve's services and Steve said, "No, but how about if you teach me to barbeque?" It was a done deal. Steve's favorite way to eat beef tongue is to slice it very thin, crosswise of the lick, spread mustard on some bread, add dill pickles, the sliced tongue, some really good horseradish, and some provolone cheese, and then grill it like a grilled cheese sandwich.

BEEF TONGUE

1 beef tongue

Place the tongue in a stockpot and cover it with water. Bring it to a boil, cover the pot, and reduce the heat to a medium boil for 3 to 4 hours until fork tender, depending on the size of the tongue. After boiling, drop the tongue into cold water to shock it. When the tongue is cool enough to handle, pull the skin off and trim the bone and cartilage from the root.

At this point it can be seasoned as barbeque and smoked (230° to 250°F) for 1 to 1½ hours. Or it can be glazed with honey mustard and enjoyed.

NEW YORK STATE SPIEDIES

Serves 6 to 8

1½ cups extra virgin olive oil

½ cup hot garlic oil

1 tablespoon dried oregano

3 cloves garlic, crushed

1 large sprig fresh mint

1 tablespoon fresh rosemary leaves

2 teaspoons salt

1 teaspoon freshly cracked black pepper

1 cup red wine vinegar

2 pounds boneless pork, lamb, beef, venison, or chicken, cut into 1½-inch cubes

Fresh Italian bread, thickly sliced

Combine the olive oil, garlic oil, oregano, garlic, mint, rosemary, salt, pepper, and vinegar in a 1-gallon resealable plastic bag. Mix well. If desired, you can reserve some of the marinade before you add the meat and drizzle it on the spiedies before serving. Add the meat and toss to coat evenly. Refrigerate for 24 hours. Soak about 8 wooden skewers in cold water overnight or for at least a couple of hours or use metal skewers.

Remove the meat from the marinade, place the marinade in a medium saucepan, and bring it to a boil over medium-high heat. Boil for 3 to 5 minutes; then set it aside to cool.

Place 4 to 5 pieces of marinated meat each on the drained skewers or metal skewers. Grill on a hot grill, basting often with the marinade, until done. Serve hot on fresh Italian bread, drizzled with the reserved marinade, if desired.

STUART CARPENTER

Stuart has followed the barbeque trail from New York to deep into Texas and learned a lot on the way.

JOHN MARKUS AND NICOLE DAVENPORT

According to John, "I once had a boss from Philadelphia who, in addition to teaching me how to aim for truth in writing comedy, enlightened me in the ways of the hoagie and Philly cheesesteak. What's more, he astonished me with his capacity to ingest a large one of each, only to walk onstage moments later in front of an audience of thousands, mustering the energy to keep 'em laughing for hours. After ingesting the same meal, my immediate activity was to take a long nap." Thus this recipe is dedicated to Bill, for giving John the wisdom to recognize both what's funny and what's tasty.

continued on page 135

SMOKED PHILLY CHEESESTEAK

Serves 6

1 (3- to 4-pound) ribeye roast

3 bell peppers—1 red and 2 green or 1 green and 2 red

Salt and black pepper

2 medium Vidalia onions

3 tablespoons olive oil

6 soft French rolls

½ pound provolone cheese, thinly sliced (24 slices)

Cheez Whiz, for serving

Days before the contest, prepare your pit to smoke with two chunks of hickory at 350°F. While waiting, indoors or out, sear the ribeye over high heat on all sides. Place the meat in the smoker for 15 minutes. Remove it, wrap it tightly, and place it in the freezer.

A day before the contest, take the frozen meat hunk to a butcher who has a deli meat slicer and have the butcher slice the frozen roast paper-thin onto butcher paper. You should be able to read a magazine through the meat. Refrigerate the meat until the day before the contest.

The evening before you plan to serve the meat, load the firebox and burn the wood/charcoal until it forms angry embers.

Seed the bell peppers and slice them into thin strips. Season them with salt and pepper and set them aside. Do the same with the Vidalia onions. Place a seasoned 12-inch cast-iron skillet directly on the coals. After 5 minutes, pour the olive oil into the skillet. When a wisp of white smoke rises, add the sliced peppers and onion and sauté until caramelized; don't take them off a moment sooner! Transfer the peppers and onion to a plate and set aside. Scrape the brown bits off the bottom of the skillet; then cook the ribeye slices in the skillet in batches, browning them on both sides and cooking them to medium-well.

Slice open the rolls and place them cut side down on the grill; grill for 2 to 3 minutes to toast them. Remove the rolls and place 4 slices of provolone on one side and a Cheez Whiz smear on the other. Add 4 slices of beef, then heap some sautéed veggies on top. Close bun. Eat. Have another.

John, along with Central Pork West co-pitmaster Nicole Davenport, added a barbeque twist to this favorite, a ritual on the eve of every KCBS contest. John notes, "There's extra prep in pulling this off, but your stomach will be so grateful, it'll do whatever it can to help your brain pull down at least a Reserve Grand Championship." John adds, "And thank Bill for it."

DANIELLE DIMOVSKI

Diva Q likes to serve this beef with smashed red potatoes and steamed veggies.

DIVA Q BBQ ROULADEN

Serves 9 to 18

2¼ pounds beef top round

¾ cup Dijon mustard

1 to 2 teaspoons garlic pepper

6 whole dill pickles, sliced lengthwise into thirds

1 large red onion, thinly sliced

1 pound bacon, cooked and drained

2 tablespoons olive oil

6 ounces white button mushrooms, sliced

Salt and black pepper

4 to 6 cups beef stock, jus, or gravy of your preference

Preheat the grill to 275°F. Slice the meat into 18 very thin rectangles. Spread each slice with Dijon mustard to coat it completely; then sprinkle with the garlic pepper. At one end of the beef, place a slice of pickle and 1 or 2 onion slices (you'll have more than you need for the 18 beef rolls). Now you can either add a slice of cooked bacon or use the bacon at the end, crumbled into the gravy. Roll the bundle tightly, securing it with two toothpicks.

Place all the meat rolls on the grill for 10 minutes. Turn over the meat rolls and grill for another 10 minutes.

Meanwhile, preheat the oven to 300°F. Heat the olive oil in a large skillet over medium heat and sauté the remaining onions and the mushrooms. Season with salt and pepper and sauté for 5 to 7 minutes, until tender.

Remove the meat from the grill and transfer it to an ovenproof container with a lid. Cover the meat with the sautéed onions and mushrooms and the stock. If you didn't add the bacon to the bundles, crumble it and add it now. Bake for 2 hours, until the meat is fully tender. Remove the toothpicks before serving.

Note: *Instead of baking the meat and onion mixture, you can cook it, covered, in your grill or smoker over indirect heat for the same amount of time.*

ARKANSAS BBQ NACHOS

Serves 8 to 10

CHEESE SAUCE

1 pound processed cheese, preferably Velveeta

½ pound cheddar cheese, shredded (about 2 cups)

½ pound Monterey Jack cheese, shredded (about 2 cups)

1 (14-ounce) can diced tomatoes with green chiles, preferably Rotel

1 jalapeño chile, finely diced, seeded if you want it milder

NACHOS

1 (24-ounce) bag tortilla chips, warmed in the oven

1 to 2 pounds barbequed pork shoulder, shredded

TOPPINGS

Barbeque sauce

Barbeque rub

Minced scallions

Diced tomatoes

Chopped fresh cilantro

Cut the processed cheese into large cubes and place them in a microwave-safe bowl. Add the shredded cheeses, canned tomatoes with chiles, and jalapeño. Microwave, covered, on high until the cheese is completely melted, about 1 minute.

Arrange the heated chips on individual plates or bowls. Cover the chips with the pork shoulder. Top sparingly with your favorite barbeque sauce; then smother with the cheese sauce. Top with barbeque rub, scallions, tomatoes, and cilantro to taste. Serve immediately.

BRAD DAVIS

In Arkansas, the hog is worshipped. I'm not just talking about the domesticated hog we all know and enjoy, but also the wild razorback variety. Many autumn Arkansas Saturdays are spent eating pork BBQ and cheering on the Arkansas Razorbacks. One of the treats that many Razorback fans enjoy in Donald W. Reynolds Razorback Stadium is barbeque nachos. The following recipe is the Davis family version. Oh, by the way, it will be just as good rooting for your own team on Saturdays in the fall. Enjoy!

PHILLIP L. DELL

Phillip Dell of Sin City Chefs believes that one of the most requested recipes stems from the question "What do I do with leftover barbeque?" Well, folks, Phillip has an answer your family or guests will truly enjoy. Every week he has the pleasure of cooking for a big "family" of law clerks and attorneys. One day during lunch someone requested enchiladas for the following week. After a few brief thoughts, he came up with this one, and it is now one of the most requested items on the menu! These enchiladas go perfectly with spicy black beans and grilled corn.

BBQ ENCHILADAS

Serves 6 to 8

1 tablespoon olive oil, or more as needed

¼ cup diced yellow onion

¼ cup diced green bell pepper

1 to 2 cloves garlic, minced

½ pound bulk chicken, beef, or pork chorizo sausage

¼ pound soft garlic herb cheese (such as Boursin or Alouette)

1 cup chicken broth

1 pound pulled smoked chicken, beef, pork, or a mixture

1 tablespoon barbeque rub/ seasoning, or to taste

Hot pepper sauce

6 to 8 flour or corn tortillas

1 cup roasted tomatillo chile sauce (such as Trader Joe's), plus more for topping, if desired

1 cup shredded Mexican-blend cheese

Chopped fresh cilantro, for garnish

Diced tomato, for garnish

Preheat the grill to 350°F. Lightly grease a heatproof oblong baking dish that will hold the enchiladas snugly.

Heat the olive oil in a deep skillet. Add the onion and sauté until translucent, 3 to 4 minutes. Add the green pepper and garlic and continue cooking for 2 to 3 minutes, adding more olive oil if necessary to prevent sticking. Add the chorizo and cook until brown, breaking it up as it cooks. It should be a crumbly mixture. Add the garlic herb cheese and broth and stir to combine. Cook until the cheese has melted. Add the pulled meat and season to taste with the rub and hot pepper sauce. Stir to combine and remove from the heat.

Place a few tortillas in front of you and fill the middle of each one with the meat mixture. Roll the tortillas over the meat; then place them seam side down in the prepared dish. Once you have filled all the tortillas, pour some of the roasted tomatillo sauce over the middle of the enchiladas. Top each end that is not covered in sauce with the shredded cheese.

Place the dish on the preheated grill and cook, covered, for 20 to 30 minutes, until the cheese is bubbling and golden around the edges. Allow the enchiladas to rest for a few minutes before digging in. Garnish with chopped cilantro and diced tomato.

Notes: *If using anything other than chicken for the meat, Phillip really enjoys using roasted pepper garlic herb cheese. If there isn't any available, you can make it simply by blending the garlic herb cheese and some roasted peppers in a food processor until smooth.*

To add some authentic flair, after pulling the enchiladas from the grill, sprinkle cotija cheese or queso fresco cheese on top.

FOOD FOR THOUGHT
by Craig Meathead Goldwyn, AmazingRibs.com

The three greatest food educators and cookbook authors of the last century lived far longer than the designers of the two most famous diets of the last century (Robert Atkins, who died at age 73, and Nathan Pritikin, who died at age 70):

- Julia Child, died at 92
- James Beard, 82
- Craig Claiborne, 80

DANIELLE DIMOVSKI

Diva Q takes barbeque to new heights with this recipe. The Asian marinade flavors complement the classic American sage–corn bread stuffing flavors.

DIVA Q EAST MEETS WEST PORK LOIN

Serves 6 to 8

MARINADE

½ cup red wine

¼ cup red wine vinegar

¼ cup ketchup

¼ cup hoisin sauce

2 tablespoons soy sauce

3 cloves garlic, minced

½ cup packed brown sugar

1 teaspoon Chinese five-spice powder

1 teaspoon ground ginger

½ teaspoon salt

½ teaspoon black pepper

PORK LOIN

1 (3-pound) boneless pork loin

STUFFING

2 tablespoons butter

1 onion, finely minced

Handful of chives, minced

1 teaspoon rubbed sage

½ teaspoon salt

½ teaspoon black pepper

4 cups crumbled corn bread

1 egg

2 tablespoons to ⅓ cup chicken stock

Whisk together all the marinade ingredients. Place the meat in a large bowl, cover with the marinade, cover the bowl, and let the pork rest in the refrigerator overnight.

To make the stuffing, melt the butter in a large sauté pan over medium heat and add the onion. Sauté until translucent, 2 to 3 minutes. Add the chives, sage, salt, and pepper. Mix in the corn bread, egg, and enough chicken stock to make the stuffing easy to spread. Stuff the meat with the stuffing.

Prepare your smoker to cook at 230° to 250°F and smoke until the internal temperature registers 155°F on a meat thermometer, 1 to 1½ hours. Remove the meat from the smoker, loosely tent it with aluminum foil, and allow it to rest for 15 to 25 minutes before carving and serving.

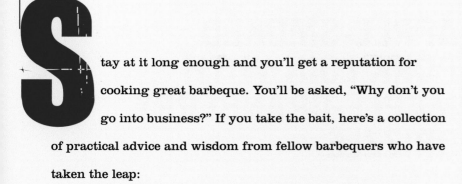

BEST BBQ CATERING AND RESTAURANT TIPS

Stay at it long enough and you'll get a reputation for cooking great barbeque. You'll be asked, "Why don't you go into business?" If you take the bait, here's a collection of practical advice and wisdom from fellow barbequers who have taken the leap:

- Apprentice with a successful caterer. Hands-on experience will expose you to hundreds of catering details you'd have to learn the hard way if you started out on your own without prior experience. You'll also find out if you're cut out for this kind of business. Go outside your planned service area when volunteering for apprenticeships, unless you know a local caterer who doesn't mind adding a competitor to the neighborhood.

- Many successful barbeque restaurants today started as catering businesses. Consider catering before you leap into a full-scale restaurant operation.

- Never forget the importance of word-of-mouth advertising. Do a great job and you can count on free advertising to ten times the number of satisfied diners you've served. Do a lousy job and the word on you will likewise get out.

- Figure out early on if you are going to prepare all foods from your home-based kitchen and pit or whether you're going to take your cooker and kitchen to the catered event—or some of both.

- Establish your maximum limits early on. If two hundred or two thousand is your max, say so in your advertising. Larger groups won't waste your time or theirs if they know your limits up front.

There is, of course, much more to learn and do before you go into business. We can assure you that putting in many hours of research and hands-on experience will serve you well when you take the leap!

MIKE STINES, PHB

This recipe combines a marinated pork loin with smoky applewood and a sweet-tart sauce. Mike suggests serving it with garlic smashed potatoes and sautéed green beans with caraway. The Maple-Cranberry Drizzle goes well with smoked or roasted pork loin or smoked or roasted chicken. The recipe here yields about a cup, and it will keep, covered and refrigerated, for 1 week.

APPLE-SMOKED PORK LOIN WITH MAPLE-CRANBERRY DRIZZLE

Serves 4

MARINADE

1½ cups apple cider

1 cup apple cider vinegar

¾ cup dark molasses

½ cup reduced-sodium soy sauce

½ cup ketchup

½ cup packed light brown sugar

1 tablespoon hot sauce

APPLE-SMOKED PORK LOIN

1 (2½- to 3-pound) center-cut pork loin

MAPLE-CRANBERRY DRIZZLE

1 cup pure Vermont grade B maple syrup

½ cup dried cranberries

¼ cup fresh lemon juice

2 tablespoons reduced-sodium soy sauce

1 tablespoon ground ginger

1½ teaspoons minced garlic

In a bowl large enough to hold the pork, combine all the marinade ingredients. Add the pork and cover with plastic wrap. Refrigerate for at least 3 hours or overnight, turning the pork occasionally.

Remove the pork from the marinade and let it sit at room temperature. Meanwhile, soak 3 cups of applewood chips in warm water for at least 30 minutes. Bring the marinade to a boil in a medium saucepan over medium heat and simmer for 5 minutes. Keep the marinade warm for use as a basting sauce during cooking.

Preheat a smoker to 225°F. If using a covered grill, arrange the coals on two sides at the bottom of the grill and place a disposable foil pan between the piles. When the coals are covered with ashes, sprinkle a handful of drained applewood chips over the coals. When the chips begin to smoke, place the pork on the cooking rack over the drip pan.

Cover the smoker or grill and smoke/cook the roast, adding more coals and wood chips as needed, for 2 to 2½ hours, until the roast has an internal temperature of 155°F, basting with the reserved marinade every 45 minutes.

While the meat is cooking, combine the drizzle ingredients in a 2½-quart saucepan and bring them to a simmer over medium heat. Reduce the heat to medium-low and continue simmering until the glaze is reduced by about half, about 20 minutes.

Remove the roast from the grill/smoker, tent with foil, and allow the roast to rest for 10 minutes before slicing. Spoon the Maple-Cranberry Drizzle over the slices and serve.

CY-CONE

Serves 1

3 ounces smoked beans	About ⅓ pound pulled pork
1 waffle cone	Barbeque sauce, for serving
3 ounces coleslaw	Bacon bits, for garnish

Put the beans in the bottom third of the waffle cone, then top with the slaw, and finally an ice-cream scoop full of pulled pork for the "ice cream." Drizzle with barbeque sauce, sprinkle with bacon bits, and enjoy.

MIKE TUCKER

This is a true barbeque original from the Hawgeyes BBQ team of Ankeny, Iowa.

ANNE REHNSTROHM

Anne, of the Great Pork BarbeQlossal fame, kicks up an elegant roast by giving it a glaze of hot pepper jelly. She likes to serve it with her cilantro pesto pasta salad and jalapeño-cheddar corn bread. For an elegant dinner atmosphere, she also suggests serving this with a dry Riesling or Sauvignon Blanc wine.

GRILLED PORK ROAST WITH PEPPER JELLY GLAZE

Serves 8

1 (2-pound) boneless pork loin roast

MARINADE

½ cup apple juice

½ cup apple cider vinegar

½ cup hot pepper jelly

GLAZE

⅓ cup hot pepper jelly

2 tablespoons apple cider vinegar

Place the pork in a large resealable plastic bag. Heat the marinade ingredients together over medium heat until the jelly melts, then pour the mixture over the pork in the bag. Seal the bag tightly and refrigerate for 12 to 24 hours.

Prepare a medium-hot grill. Remove the pork from the marinade and discard the marinade. Place the pork roast on the grill over a drip pan and close the grill hood. Grill for 30 to 45 minutes (about 20 minutes per pound), until the internal temperature on a meat thermometer reads 150°F.

While the meat is cooking, stir together the glaze ingredients. During the last 10 minutes of cooking, coat the roast with the glaze. Remove the roast from the heat and let it rest until the internal temperature reaches 160°F, about 10 minutes.

DIVA Q STANDING STUFFED PORK ROAST

Serves 6 to 8

2 tablespoons butter

1 pound andouille sausage, finely diced

½ medium red onion, minced

1 leek, the white and the tender greens only, minced

1 red bell pepper, minced

2 cups crumbled corn bread

1 tablespoon rubbed sage

1 teaspoon salt

1 teaspoon black pepper

½ cup minced fresh parsley

3 cloves garlic, minced

2 tablespoons Cajun-style rub

1 (6- to 8-bone) pork rib roast

½ cup honey mustard sauce

Preheat the grill to 275°F. Diva Q recommends pellets—your choice of hickory, oak, pecan, apple, or cherry.

In a large skillet over medium heat, melt the butter. Add the sausage, onion, leek, and red pepper and sauté until the onion and leek are soft, 7 to 8 minutes. Add the corn bread, sage, salt, pepper, parsley, garlic, and half the Cajun rub and mix well. Remove the mixture from the heat and let it cool completely.

Ask your butcher to open the pork roast out so you can use a meat mallet to flatten it into a rectangle. Season the pork on both sides with the remaining Cajun rub. Spread the sausage filling out onto the pork, covering the entire rectangle. Roll the pork together tightly toward the bones and secure using butcher's twine or silicone loops.

Grill for about 2½ hours, or until the internal temperature is 145°F on a meat thermometer. During the last few minutes of cooking, glaze with the honey mustard sauce. Let rest for 15 minutes before serving.

DANIELLE DIMOVSKI

Danielle Dimovski, known in barbeque circles as Diva Q, is a bright star of 'Que from the frozen white north.

ANYTHING BUTT

STUART CARPENTER

This is one of Stu's old standby recipes. He has entered it in nine contests and it has placed in all but one.

PORK CHOPS WITH FRESH PEACH CHUTNEY

Serves 4

¼ cup sugar

¼ cup apple cider vinegar

1 small yellow onion, minced

¼ cup raisins

Ground cinnamon, for dusting, plus 1 teaspoon for the chutney

1 teaspoon ground ginger

3 medium peaches, peeled, pitted, and sliced

¼ cup peach brandy

4 pork chops, each 1 to 1½ inches thick

Salt and freshly ground black pepper

Prepare a grill for medium-hot cooking.

Meanwhile, combine the sugar, vinegar, onion, raisins, 1 teaspoon cinnamon, and the ginger in a saucepan. Cook, covered, on the grill or side burner, stirring often until the onions are transparent and the raisins are plump. Add the peaches and peach brandy and cook for 3 more minutes. Remove the pan from the heat and set it aside.

Season the pork chops with salt and pepper, then dust them with cinnamon. Grill for 5 to 7 minutes, or until they reach your desired doneness, turning once.

Place one-sixth of the peach chutney on each of four plates. Top each plate with a pork chop, drizzle with the remaining chutney, and serve immediately.

WOOD-GRILLED PHILIPPINE PORK STEAKS WITH PINEAPPLE-TANGERINE GLAZE

Serves 6

2 pounds pork steaks, cut ½ inch thick (see Note)

PINEAPPLE TANGERINE GLAZE

⅔ cup tangerine juice

⅓ cup crushed pineapple

⅓ cup soy sauce

3 cloves garlic

1 small piece fresh ginger, sliced

¼ teaspoon hot red pepper flakes

Place the pork steaks in a large resealable plastic bag.

To make the glaze, combine all the glaze ingredients and pour half of the glaze over the pork. Close the bag and refrigerate for at least 30 minutes and up to 2 hours. Reserve the other half for basting the pork while it cooks.

Prepare a medium-hot indirect fire in your grill. Place the wood on the fire side of the grill. Karen and Judith suggest oak, apple, or orange.

Remove the pork steaks from the bag and discard the used glaze. Grill the pork steaks directly over the fire for about 2 minutes per side. Move them to the indirect side of the grill and baste with the reserved glaze. The steaks may be overlapped. Close the lid and cook indirectly for 30 to 45 minutes, basting with the glaze and moving the steaks around on the grill for even heat.

Note: *Karen and Judith recommend thin-cut pork steaks or chops.*

KAREN ADLER, PHB, AND JUDITH FERTIG, PHB

BBQ Queens Judith and Karen formed an all women's barbeque team in 1995 to respond to a men-versus-women challenge issued by a Kansas City radio station. The BBQ Queens lost to the men that year, but won in later years. Their barbeque sauce, "Love Potion for the Swine," was sold to benefit local charities. They have co-authored six barbeque books—and counting—and teach cooking classes and travel the country spreading barbeque goodwill.

ANYTHING BUTT

CRAIG "MEATHEAD" GOLDWYN, AMAZINGRIBS.COM

Craig promises that if you follow this recipe, you can make dizzyingly delicious Chinatown *char siu* ribs at home in the oven or on the grill. That makes them a great choice for the winter, when you've got a hankering for ribs and the smoker is snowed in.

Many Chinese restaurants use spareribs that are chopped into 3- to 4-inch riblets. If you want, your butcher can make you riblets with a band saw. Craig likes baby backs for this recipe because they are a bit meatier. You can also substitute 4 pounds of pork loin for the ribs if you wish.

continued on page 149

THE KANSAS CITY BARBEQUE SOCIETY COOKBOOK

CHINATOWN CHAR SIU BARBEQUE RIBS OR PORK

Serves 4 to 8, including 1½ cups marinade

MARINADE

½ cup hoisin sauce

½ cup brandy, rum, or bourbon

¼ cup honey

¼ cup soy sauce

2 tablespoons dark sesame oil

2 tablespoons hot sauce, such as Asian chile sauce or Tabasco

2 tablespoons ground ginger or minced fresh ginger

2 teaspoons garlic powder or minced fresh garlic

2 teaspoons Chinese five-spice powder

2 tablespoons onion powder

2 teaspoons red food coloring

RIBS

2 slabs baby back ribs, cut in half lengthwise through all the bones

¼ cup honey or *char siu* sauce

Chopped fresh chives, for garnish

Combine the marinade ingredients in a bowl and whisk thoroughly. Place the meat in a resealable plastic bag (you may need more than one), add the marinade, seal tightly, and toss to coat. Refrigerate for at least 3 hours or overnight.

Heat your cooker to 300°F. (You can also use an indoor oven. Just place the ribs on a wire grate over a pan or on a broiler pan.) If you are using a gas grill, turn off one or two burners and place the meat over the cool burners. If you are using a charcoal grill, set it up by banking the coals against one side for indirect cooking. Remove the ribs from the marinade and cook for about 1 hour; then paint the bone side of the ribs with a coat of the honey or *char siu* sauce. Cook for 10 minutes, underside up; then turn meat side up, paint with more honey or *char siu* sauce, and cook for another 10 minutes. Remove the ribs, let them sit for 5 minutes, cut them into individual ribs, and serve hot, garnished with chopped fresh chives.

The booze is important for the marinade because it helps penetrate the meat, and even if you're a teetotaler, don't worry—there isn't any measurable alcohol in the ribs. If you must skip it, use apple juice or water. You can buy *char siu* sauce at Chinese specialty stores, and it makes a fine glaze, but it doesn't make ribs that taste like Chinese restaurant ribs. That's because you need to marinate the meat in a thin sauce first.

Here's what Craig shared with us about this recipe: "I love the barbeque pork and ribs in Chinatown. They have a distinct pork flavor, a glossy sheen that implies the sweet glaze beneath, and a glowing red-pink color that penetrates the surface. Unlike traditional southern American smoke-roasted low-and-slow barbeque, there is no smoke flavor, even though there is a pink ring beneath the surface of the meat. How do they do it?

"Well, it turns out that *char siu*, even though it sounds like charcoal, is not grilled or smoked. It is roasted in a special oven. And it gets its ruddy tone from red food coloring. Sigh. But it still tastes great."

ANYTHING BUTT

149

TONY STONE, PHB

Paul says this recipe is a perfect example of one of the good old boys of barbequing stealing his grandmother's recipe and claiming it's his own creation! Tony and his wife, the lovely Dean, are renowned for hosting a Thursday night reception before the Cookeville Cookoff, as well as for their New Year's Day open house. The country ham should be trimmed of most of its fat before you dice it. You can adjust the amount of ham as needed to fit a different size of baking dish.

COUNTRY HAM PIE

Serves 4

4 cups country ham in ½-inch dice

8 tablespoons (1 stick) butter

1 (11-ounce) box Betty Crocker pie crust mix, prepared according to package directions

4 to 6 hard-boiled eggs, peeled and thinly sliced

Place the ham in a saucepan, cover it with water, and bring it to a boil over high heat. Boil for about 2 minutes. Pour off the water and rinse the ham with hot water to rid it of excess salt. The process may be repeated one or two more times if the ham is very salty.

Leave the ham in the saucepan and cover it with about 2 inches of water. Bring the ham to a boil over high heat, reduce the heat so the liquid simmers, add the butter, and simmer for 1 hour, or until tender. Drain the meat and reserve the broth.

Preheat the oven to 375°F. Grease a 9-inch pie plate and line it with half of the prepared pie crust. Alternate layers of ham and egg slices until the dish is full. Add the broth from cooking the ham until it is the same level as the meat and eggs (or higher). This is important, as the pie has a tendency to dry out otherwise. Cover with the remaining pastry, making slits in the top so the steam from cooking can escape.

Bake for 1 hour, or until the crust is browned and the pie is bubbly.

When it comes to cooking sausage, there are basically three ways to do it: Split and grill them, boil and grill them, and straight grill them. The main problem is getting good sausages grilled through without drying out the casing (or worse, having the casings burst open). We're talking about kielbasa, bratwurst, and similar large sausages. Try these methods for grilling sausages:

SPLIT AND GRILL: With this method, cut the sausage lengthwise about 80 percent of the way through, so you can fold it out and lay it flat. This way you cook the insides quickly because you can lay it skin side up; at least the skin won't dry out. But you have a 90 percent chance of losing the juices that drip out. While this might be a healthier way of cooking, it tends to dry out the sausages and leave them a bit lacking in flavor.

BOIL AND GRILL: Another good way to grill sausages is to parboil them before you put them on the grill. This partially cooks them before you grill. Fill a pot with half water and half beer. You can add spices or seasonings to enhance the flavor. Drop the sausages into the boiling liquid and cook for long enough to tighten the skin. When you pull the sausages out, the fat inside should be just starting to liquefy. Next, place the sausages on your grill over a medium-low fire and finish cooking. This method gives you juicy sausages and is a popular way of grilling them.

STRAIGHT GRILLING: For this method, you place the sausages right on the grill and cook them the old-fashioned direct way. The biggest problem is that people use a high heat and burn the surface before the middle gets cooked. The other problem is that when a sausage cooks it leaks juices that can cause flare-ups and add to the burning problem. To eliminate burning and the flare-ups, you need to keep the fire low. This increases the cooking time but lets the sausages cook gently and hold in their flavor. Some people will tell you to puncture the skin, but this will just let the juices out to start more flare-ups. Keep the sausage casing intact and the heat low.

GRILLING
SAUSAGE

AL LAWSON

Besides being a good sauce maker, Al was known for making this sausage, and you could always count on getting a free sample when you stopped by his booth. You can still order it from his son, Ed. We recommend Al's People's Choice sauce with it, which Ed still makes.

AL LAWSON'S ITALIAN SAUSAGE

Makes 10 pounds

¼ cup salt

1 tablespoon paprika

2 tablespoons monosodium glutamate (MSG) (optional)

1 tablespoon black pepper

1 tablespoon ground anise

1 tablespoon ground oregano

1 tablespoon fennel seeds

1 tablespoon garlic powder

1 tablespoon cayenne pepper

1 handful parsley flakes

10 pounds boneless pork butt, cubed and chilled

¾ pound provolone cheese, cut into chunks and chilled

2 cups water

In a small bowl, combine all the seasonings and mix well. Pour the mixture over the meat and stir before you grind the meat and cheese. Grind the meat and cheese together using the $\frac{5}{16}$-inch or $\frac{3}{8}$-inch plate. Add the water, mix well, and stuff the mixture into 35-millimeter casings.

PA'S SAUSAGE WITH MA'S CHEESY BUNS

Serves 6

CHEESY SPREAD

8 tablespoons (1 stick) butter, softened

½ teaspoon dried basil leaves

½ teaspoon dried oregano leaves

½ teaspoon lemon pepper

2 cloves garlic, minced, or ¼ teaspoon garlic powder

6 Italian sub rolls

6 slices Monterey Jack cheese

Your favorite pasta sauce, for serving (optional)

6 Italian sausages, hot, mild, or sweet,
grilled the way you like them

Hot peppers, for serving (optional)

Sweet peppers, for serving (optional)

Set up your grill to cook indirectly.

To make the cheesy spread, combine the butter, basil, oregano, lemon pepper, and garlic and mix well. Spread the mixture on the rolls. Cut 1 slice of the Monterey Jack cheese in half to fit a sub roll lengthwise and place in the roll. Repeat with the remaining Monterey Jack and rolls. Wrap each roll in aluminum foil and grill over indirect heat for 15 to 20 minutes, until the cheese melts.

Meanwhile, warm the pasta sauce in a heatproof saucepan on the grill. Remove the rolls from the grill and place a grilled sausage in each. Spread pasta sauce on top, then top with the hot and sweet peppers or with the condiments of your choice. Enjoy with your favorite moonshine.

LINDA AND PETE GRASZER

Ma (Linda) and Pa (Pete) have been involved in competition barbeque since 2007. In addition to being competition cooks, both are KCBS Certified Judges. Linda, they say, is "the rub and sauce expert," and Pete "is the process guy." They add, "We are codependent and proud of it!"

ANYTHING BUTT

153

JOHN RAVEN, PHB

John Raven, PhB, is the Commissioner of Barbecue. He has been actively involved in the world of chili and barbeque competitions since day one. In his younger days they called him Daredevil Bad McFad, human cannonball. Today we call him Bad, and he's good. John introduces his original blast-off recipe as follows: "Anyone can come up with a barbeque recipe. Man does not live by barbeque alone. Quihi is the camp of the Quihi Rangers down in the Texas brush country west of San Antonio. I guarantee a plate of these breakfast migas will keep you running until late in the evening when it's grilling time again. Here it comes. Duck!"

BAD'S QUIHI MIGAS

Serves 6 to 8

1 pound hot-style breakfast sausage, preferably Owens

1 large yellow onion, diced

2 cloves garlic, minced

1 jalapeño chile, seeded and minced, or more to taste

½ red bell pepper, minced

1 teaspoon freshly ground black pepper

2 teaspoons chili powder

8 corn tortillas, 4 cut into ½-inch strips and 4 cut into ¼-inch strips

8 eggs, beaten until well combined

1 large ripe tomato, chopped

¾ cup shredded cheddar cheese

Salt, if needed

Canola oil, for frying

Picante sauce, for serving (optional)

In a large, heavy, lightly greased skillet, brown the sausage over medium heat, breaking it up as it cooks.

When the sausage is done, add the onion, garlic, jalapeño, and bell pepper.

Stir and cook until the onion is transparent, 5 to 6 minutes longer; the peppers will be a little crunchy. Add the black pepper and chili powder, stirring to combine well. Add the ½-inch tortilla strips and cook until they are limp, just a minute or so. Pour in the eggs and cook, stirring, until they are cooked through, 5 to 6 minutes. Add the tomato and cheese and stir until the cheese melts and combines with the rest of the ingredients, another minute or two. Check the taste and add salt if necessary. Remove the pan from the stove and set it aside.

In a deep pan, in about 2 inches of canola oil, fry the ¼-inch tortilla strips until golden brown and crisp. Drain on paper towels.

Serve the hot sausage mixture topped with the fried tortilla strips and picante sauce.

Note: *For variety, you can substitute cooked chopped ham for the sausage or use half ham and half sausage.*

THAT'S BLASPHEMY!

BEANS WITH MIGAS? YES AND NO!

We have enjoyed migas for breakfast many times in central Texas restaurants and homes. Invariably the plates served to us thus far have included refried beans or seasoned pinto beans on the side. Sometimes the beans are layered with the eggs, tortilla, and cheese. Add salsa or hot sauce and migas make a memorable feast to start your day.

When we asked a few Texans if they serve beans with their migas, they replied, "That's blasphemy!" John Raven is among the most vocal on the blasphemy side of the question. When we asked him why his migas recipe omits beans, he replied, "Beans are good and nice. Eggs are good and nice. Beans and eggs mixed are an abomination in the eyes of the Lord."

The jury is still out on the question of beans with migas. We've found recipes with and recipes without. You'll have to decide for yourself. If you add beans to John's migas recipe, just don't tell him!

LEW MILLER

Almost everyone has cut their teeth in basic grilling with brats on the grill. Grill 'em too hot and they burst. Grill 'em too low and your face turns red when the inside of your guests' brats are pink. In this recipe, Lew introduces a tried-and-true method of giving your brats a refreshing bath in beer for added flavor during the grilling process. Be sure to save a cold beer for the cook!

BEER BRATS AND KRAUT

Serves 6 to 8

2 pounds bratwurst

½ (12-ounce) bottle beer

1 (14-ounce) can sauerkraut, drained

½ cup packed brown sugar

1 Granny Smith apple, cored and minced, skin on

1 tablespoon caraway seeds

Preheat your smoker to 230° to 250°F. Smoke the brats for 1 hour. Remove them from the smoker, place them in a large, shallow dish, pour the beer over them, cover the dish, and refrigerate for 30 minutes while you make the sauerkraut mixture.

In a large saucepan, combine the sauerkraut, brown sugar, apple, and caraway seeds. Bring to a boil over medium-high heat, reduce the heat, and simmer for 20 minutes.

Remove the brats from the beer bath, slice them, and add them to the sauerkraut mixture. Cook until heated through and serve warm.

SKILLET-GRILLED POTATOES AND ITALIAN SAUSAGE

Serves 8

2 pounds russet potatoes, peeled and sliced ¼ inch thick

2 tablespoons extra virgin olive oil

1 green bell pepper, minced

1 red bell pepper, minced

1 medium sweet onion, minced

1 pound mild Italian sausage, bulk or links

Salt and black pepper

Preheat your gas or charcoal grill to medium-high heat. Put a large cast-iron skillet over the direct fire, add the potatoes and olive oil, and cook, stirring and turning the potatoes, for 10 minutes. Add the peppers and onion, stirring and turning for another 5 minutes. Add the sausage, stirring and turning all of the ingredients until done, about 30 minutes. Remove from the fire and serve immediately.

JAY JOHNSTON

When the late Jay Johnston fired up his grill and brought out the cast-iron skillets, neighbors soon followed the aroma to Jay's driveway and gathered for a feast. This version is built from memories of Jay's wife, Nancy, and neighbors, George Reising and Tom Hyde. It goes great with Italian garlic bread and cold beer.

RICK BROWNE, PH8

Rick told us he borrowed this technique from a barbeque contest cook years ago at the Blue Springs Barbeque Blazeoff. When Rick asked what it was, the cook replied, "Why, it's beer-butt chicken." That cook could have been the late Hank Lumpkin, who coined the "beer-butt chicken" expression. Here's Rick's version.

RICK BROWNE'S BEER-BUTT CHICKEN

Serves 4 to 6

1 teaspoon packed brown sugar

1 teaspoon garlic powder

1 teaspoon onion powder

1 teaspoon dried summer savory

¼ teaspoon cayenne

1 teaspoon chili powder

1 teaspoon paprika

1 teaspoon dry mustard

1 tablespoon finely ground sea salt or kosher salt

1 (4- to 5-pound) chicken

1 (12-ounce) can warm beer

1 cup apple cider

2 tablespoons olive oil

2 tablespoons balsamic vinegar

In a small bowl, combine the brown sugar, garlic powder, onion powder, savory, cayenne, chili powder, paprika, mustard, and salt and stir until well incorporated. Apply the rub all over the chicken, even in the cavity. Work the mixture gently into the skin and under the skin wherever possible. Cover the chicken and set aside at room temperature for 30 minutes.

Pour half of the can of beer into a spray bottle; add the cider, olive oil, and vinegar; and set aside.

Preheat a charcoal or gas barbeque for indirect heat over a water pan at 375°F.

Hold the beer can (with the remaining beer inside) in one hand and slide the chicken, tail side down, over the can. Place the chicken on the can over direct heat on the barbeque and cook, using the spray bottle to baste once or twice, for 20 minutes, or until it's just beginning to brown all over. Move the chicken to the cool side of the grill over the water pan. Lower the lid and cook, spraying with the basting spray several times, for 1 to 1½ hours, until the internal temperature at the thigh reaches 180°F and the chicken is very brown, almost a mahogany color.

Using a barbeque glove, remove the chicken from the barbeque and present it on the can to your guests. After they have reacted appropriately, remove the chicken from the beer can with tongs. Be careful, as the can and the liquid inside are very hot.

Spray the chicken again with the basting spray. Carve and serve. Or, wearing barbeque gloves, pull the chicken apart with your hands and serve.

AL LAWSON'S GRILLED CHICKEN HALVES

Serves 12 to 16

12 chicken halves

¾ cup Al Lawson's Dry Poultry Seasoning (page 224)

1 cup canola oil

8 tablespoons (1 stick) butter, melted and cooled

1 tablespoon fresh lemon juice

1 (12-ounce) can beer (optional)

Set up your grill to cook indirectly (230° to 250°F). Rinse the chicken in cold water and wipe it dry with paper towels. Rub 1 tablespoon of poultry seasoning on each chicken half. Refrigerate, covered, for at least 5 hours or overnight.

Combine the oil, butter, lemon juice, and beer. Grill or smoke the chicken, covered, for about 4 hours, or until done, mopping frequently with the oil and lemon juice mixture.

AL LAWSON

Al and Bob Lawson were two of the pioneers of competition barbeque and they won many ribbons with this recipe. Al was a great cook and a true gentleman.

DON PRZYBYLA

Don is a barbeque nomad who follows barbeque like a religion, gathering all of the information he can in order to get it just right. Don't turn your nose up at white barbeque sauce until you have tried it on your chicken. You will be pleasantly surprised. It's a north Alabama tradition. Don suggests serving this over noodles or rice.

WHITE SAUCE CHICKEN

Serves 2

2 boneless, skinless chicken breasts

2 teaspoons dried basil

2 tablespoons butter, or as needed

1 medium yellow onion, chopped

1 (4.5-ounce) can or jar mushrooms

½ to 1 cup dry sherry

2 cups (1 pint) whipping cream

1 large tomato, chopped

Sprinkle the chicken with the basil. Melt the butter in a large skillet over medium heat. Add the chicken and onion and brown the chicken on both sides, about 5 minutes per side. Add the mushrooms and sherry, cover, and simmer for 20 to 30 minutes.

Transfer the chicken along with some of its juices to a shallow ovenproof pan, cover the pan, and place it in a warm oven while you make the sauce. Add the whipping cream and chopped tomato to the juices, mushrooms, and onion remaining in the skillet. Simmer over medium-low heat until well blended and reduced to a sauce consistency. Remove the chicken from the oven, pour the sauce over it, and serve.

Turkey That Tastes Like *"PONCAKES"*

AS TOLD BY DON PRZYBYLA

When I first started to experiment with smoking woods, I was using a gas grill, wrapping soaked wood chips, and putting one packet on each side of the drip pan. The Wednesday before Thanksgiving, my wife asked if I could do the turkey on the grill the next day because my brother-in-law and sister-in-law, along with their sons, were coming over. The oven wasn't large enough to cook everything. Sure, I could do the turkey on the grill. But I had to find some wood chips. The local hardware chains had none in November, but American Sales—which sells pools, spas, and outdoor furniture—had maple chips. So Thanksgiving morning out to the grill I went with about an 18-pound bird and the chips. Both burners were as low as they could go. About halfway through I used just one burner. After the bird was done, I brought it into the house, let it rest, and carved it up. My nephews didn't like turkey. But when they ate this bird, they said it tasted like PONCAKES. According to my sister-in-law, they ate more turkey than they ever had before. There was no leftover bird that day.

ANYTHING BUTT

18th ANNU

THE WORLD'S LARGEST BARBECUE

AMERICAN ROY BARBECUE

FRIDAY, OCTOBER 3,
SATURDAY, OCTOBER 4

Donation
Children 12 & Under

KELL PHELPS

Kell is carrying on his parents' (Joe and Carlene's) dream for the *National Barbecue News.* You cook this chicken on a beer can half filled with liquid to help balance the can. You can use a variety of liquids, from beer to apple juice, water, stock, or root beer—use your imagination.

JUICED-UP CHICKEN

Serves 2 to 4

1 (3½- to 4-pound) whole chicken

½ (12-ounce) can frozen apple juice concentrate, thawed

1 tablespoon minced garlic

1 tablespoon barbeque rub

Olive oil, for rubbing and brushing

1 (12-ounce) beer can, half full of liquid (see sidebar)

Preheat the grill to 300°F. Rinse the chicken inside and out and pat it dry with paper towels.

Place the apple juice concentrate in a bowl and whisk in the garlic and barbeque rub to form a paste. Coat the chicken lightly with oil, rub on an even coating of the paste, and put the cavity of the chicken down over the top of the beer can. Press down firmly and put the chicken on the grill, balancing it evenly. Cook for 2 hours, or until the internal temperature of the chicken registers at least 180°F with the thermometer inserted in the breast or thigh. When that temperature is reached, remove the chicken from the grill, cover it with foil, and let it sit for 15 minutes before carving and serving.

BIG BILLY'S SOUTHERN-STYLE FRIED CHICKEN

Serves 4 to 6

COATING

1 tablespoon white pepper

2 teaspoons black pepper

½ teaspoon dry mustard

½ teaspoon garlic powder

½ teaspoon rubbed sage

½ teaspoon ground coriander

½ teaspoon celery seeds

⅔ teaspoon ground cardamom

½ teaspoon ground mace

½ teaspoon ground cloves

½ teaspoon ground cinnamon

2 tablespoons plus ½ teaspoon salt

1 teaspoon monosodium glutamate (MSG) (optional)

3 cups all-purpose flour

CHICKEN

1 (3½- to 4½-pound) chicken, cut up

Vegetable oil or lard, for frying

Whisk together all the coating ingredients. Divide the mixture into two bowls. Add enough water to one bowl to form the consistency of a thin pancake batter, usually 1 to 1½ cups. Dip your chicken pieces in the batter first, then dredge them in the dry mixture.

Heat vegetable oil or lard (about ½ inch deep) in a 10- to 12-inch cast-iron skillet until it registers 360°F on a deep-frying thermometer. Place the chicken pieces skin side down in the hot oil and fry until golden brown, 5 to 7 minutes per side. The internal temperature of the meat should reach 165° to 170°F on a meat thermometer. Drain the chicken on a rack and serve hot.

BILLY RODGERS

I discovered this technique while watching a well-known chef in New Orleans prepare her chicken. This is definitely a keeper!

PAUL KIRK, FOR BRIAN HEINECKE

When Brian Heinecke retired from marketing Procter & Gamble products out of the company head-quarters in Cincinnati, he launched a new full-time volunteer career in competition barbeque. With clip-board in hand and wearing a KCBS polo shirt, Brian was a fixture and go-to guy at every major contest in the country, plus many smaller contests. He was loyal, reliable, a stickler for details, always polite and friendly, and always looked for ways to improve a contest the next year. This recipe, created by Paul Kirk, is one we think Brian would love. For more on why, read the ac-companying story.

You'll need to soak the chicken livers and the onion rings in milk. To time everything right, do that in advance so that everything is as fresh and hot as possible when you serve it. It's well worth it!

REDNECK MOTHER CHICKEN LIVERS WITH BACON, SPICY CHEESE GRITS, AND CRISPY ONION RINGS

Serves 2

SPICY CHEESE GRITS

3 cups water

1 teaspoon salt

¾ cup quick-cooking grits

1 cup frozen whole kernel corn, thawed

1 (6.5-ounce) container pepper-Jack-and-jalapeño spreadable cheese

½ teaspoon freshly ground black pepper

ONION RINGS

1 large yellow onion, sliced into very thin rings

1½ cups whole milk

2 cups all-purpose flour

2 teaspoons salt

1 teaspoon freshly ground black pepper

Oil, for frying

FRIED CHICKEN LIVERS

1 pound chicken livers, trimmed

1 cup whole milk

6 slices bacon

2 cups self-rising flour

½ cup cornmeal

1 tablespoon salt

1 teaspoon freshly ground black pepper

1 teaspoon poultry seasoning

Oil, for frying

Texas Pete Hot Sauce or your favorite, for serving

To make the grits, bring 3 cups water and the salt to a boil in a large saucepan over medium-high heat; gradually stir in the grits. Reduce the heat to medium-low and cook, stirring often, for about 5 minutes, or until thickened. Stir in the corn, cheese, and pepper and cook, stirring constantly, for about 1 minute, or until the cheese is melted. Keep warm while you fry the chicken livers and onion rings.

Put the onion rings in a large bowl, pour the milk over them, and toss to coat. Cover and refrigerate for at least 1 hour. About 45 minutes before you want to serve the dish, soak the chicken livers in the milk, covered, in the refrigerator, for 30 minutes.

Combine the flour, salt, and pepper for the onions in a large bowl and blend well.

Heat about 2 inches of oil in a deep pot or deep-fryer until it registers 350°F on a deep-frying thermometer. Remove the onions from the refrigerator. Shake off any excess milk, place in the flour mixture, and toss to coat all over. Shake off any excess flour. Deep-fry for 2 to 3 minutes, or until golden and crisp. Drain on paper towels.

Fry the bacon in a skillet over medium heat until crisp. Drain on paper towels, crumble, and set aside. Reserve the bacon grease.

Combine the flour, cornmeal, salt, pepper, and poultry seasoning for the chicken livers in a small baking dish. Drain the livers and discard the milk. Dredge each liver in the flour mixture, shaking off any excess. Transfer them to a plate.

Heat the frying oil and the reserved bacon grease in a skillet to 365° to 375 °F, until it sizzles. Fry the livers in batches until golden brown, 3 to 4 minutes, turning once, covering the pan with a splatter screen. Transfer the livers to a paper towel–lined plate to drain.

To serve: Place several big spoonfuls (about 2 cups) of grits on a plate and top with livers, crumbled bacon, and onion strings. Top with hot sauce.

In addition to many other fine qualities, Brian Heinecke had empathy, a great sense of humor, and a deep appreciation for classic American country music. There has never been a greater fan of Jerry Jeff Walker than Brian. This recipe is reminiscent of the year that Jerry Jeff Walker was the featured entertainer at the North Carolina Blue Ridge Barbecue Festival in Tryon, North Carolina. On a dare, Brian tracked down Jerry Jeff before the concert for a photo op and gave him a plate of Texas spareribs. Later, in the concert, Jerry Jeff dedicated the song "Up Against the Wall Redneck Mothers" to his "barbeque buddies, Brian and Remus." Two grown men have never been prouder than at that moment.

Earlier that evening, Tana Shupe, Gary and Carolyn Wells, Paul Kirk, Jim and Kathleen Tabb, John Ross, Tammy Williams, Ardie Davis, Brian, and other barbequers had dined at a favorite restaurant, the Caro-Mi Dining Room. Brian and several of the rest ate Caro-Mi's delicious fried chicken livers. The recipe here is not the Caro-Mi recipe. Instead, Paul Kirk gourmeted up chicken livers to a level we know Brian would love. Rest in peace, Brian.

INN AT FOX HALL'S WARM CHICKEN SALAD

Serves 6 to 8

3 cups cubed cooked chicken

1 cup seedless green grapes, halved

1 cup sliced celery (optional)

1 cup mayonnaise

½ cup toasted slivered almonds

2 tablespoons fresh lemon juice

2 tablespoons minced onion

½ teaspoon salt

½ cup freshly grated Parmesan cheese

½ cup bread crumbs, fresh or dried

Preheat the oven to 325°F and lightly grease a 2-quart baking dish.

In a large bowl, mix together all the ingredients except the Parmesan and bread crumbs. Spoon the mixture into the baking dish. Mix the Parmesan and bread crumbs together and sprinkle them over the chicken mixture. Bake until the mixture is warm and the cheese is melted, about 20 minutes.

JENNIFER B. STANLEY

This dish was enjoyed by supper club members in Jennifer's barbeque mystery novel *Stiffs and Swine*. Serve the salad on croissants or toasted buns.

TANA FRENSLEY-SHUPE, PHB

In the process of coordinating the Jack Daniel's World Championship Invitational Barbecue, Tana became part of the barbeque family. Tana says the sauce is savory and wonderful over rice or mashed potatoes, and she suggests doubling the recipe, since it is just as good the second day.

CHICKEN CASSEROLE
Serves 4 to 6

1 (2.25-ounce) jar Armour Star Sliced Dried Beef

4 to 6 boneless, skinless chicken breasts or 1 (12- to 16-ounce) package chicken tenders

1 (10¾-ounce) can condensed cream of mushroom soup

1 (8-ounce) container sour cream

Preheat the oven to 325°F. Arrange the dried beef rounds across the bottom and up the sides of an 8-inch casserole dish. Top with the chicken. Pack the chicken in; it will shrink as it cooks. Bake for 45 minutes.

Mix together the soup and sour cream and spread the mixture over the top of the meats, to the edges of the casserole dish. Bake for another 45 minutes, until bubbling.

SMASHED CHICKEN

Serves 4 to 6

1 (3½- to 4½-pound) chicken

1 cup margarita mix

Remove the giblets from the bird, along with any fat. Rinse the chicken inside and out with cold water. Pat the chicken inside and out with paper towels to dry it. Marinate the chicken in the margarita mix in a covered bowl in the refrigerator overnight.

Prepare the grill for indirect cooking (230° to 250°F). Put the chicken on a cutting board, breast side down, with the tail pointing away from you. Pull the chicken to an upright position on its neck end. With a sharp knife, cut down the right or left side of the backbone, through the thigh joint, which is just gristle, then go down the backbone, cutting through the rib bones. Be careful to keep to the backbone, not the breast bone. Repeat the process on the other side of the backbone.

Open the chicken, breast or skin side down, with the breast end pointing toward you. In the middle of the breast you'll see the keel bone. Some people call it the breast bone, but it's the keel bone. At the top of the keel bone, in the center, there is a white piece of gristle about the size of a quarter; with your knife, cut straight down the center of the gristle.

Place your thumbs on either side of the cut, and with your fingers under the keel bone or your fingers on the skin side of the breast, push down with your thumbs and up with your fingers and the keel bone will pop up; you can then pull out the keel bone and attached gristle. Turn the chicken over and press on the breast, flattening the chicken out.

Place the chicken on a hot grill and put a foil-covered brick on top to weigh it down and flatten it so it cooks evenly. Cook for 20 minutes; then turn and cook for 20 minutes more, or until the internal temperature registers 185°F on a meat thermometer.

Use two forks to shred the chicken before serving.

LEW MILLER

This juicy "drunk" chicken would be great with tortilla chips and Lew's Mango Salsa (page 17).

ANYTHING BUTT

169

CHRIS MALANGA

No, the name of this recipe isn't spelled incorrectly. It's a play on words. Chris came up with this recipe the morning after Chris's mother's funeral when there was a ton of leftovers from all the people bringing food over to the house. It was a nice change from all of the stuffed shells and ziti, plus the chicken didn't go to waste. This is excellent by itself or in a wrap. You can add shredded cheese as a topping if desired. Variations can include chopped celery, bell peppers, tomatoes . . . you name it. The spice and mayonnaise amounts can also be adjusted to suit individual tastes.

MOURNING AFTER CHICKEN SALAD

Serves 4 to 6

½ pound bacon

1½ cups mayonnaise

1 teaspoon freshly ground black pepper

1 teaspoon ground cumin

1 teaspoon dry mustard

1 teaspoon garlic powder or granulated garlic

1 teaspoon onion powder

1 teaspoon ground oregano

Pinch of cayenne, if desired, for heat

4 cups torn or diced leftover smoked of fired chicken

In a large skillet over medium heat, cook the bacon until crispy. Set the bacon aside on paper towel–lined plate until cool enough to crumble.

In a medium bowl, combine all of the ingredients except the crumbled bacon and cooked chicken. Mix until completely blended, then add the chicken and bacon and toss until well distributed and coated.

HERBED CHICKEN

Serves 4 to 6

1 handful fresh mint

1 handful fresh basil

1 handful fresh parsley

1 tablespoon minced fresh thyme leaves

2 tablespoons fresh lemon juice

1 to 2 cloves garlic, minced

½ cup olive oil

1 teaspoon kosher salt

½ teaspoon white pepper

1 (3½- to 4½-pound) whole chicken

Set up your grill to smoke at 230° to 250°F. Place all the ingredients except the chicken in a blender and blend until smooth. Rinse the chicken inside and out and pat it dry with paper towels. Paint the paste onto the chicken with a pastry brush. Smoke for about 3 hours, basting every 30 minutes with the herb mixture. Cook until the internal temperature registers at least 165°F.

Note: *To make juicing citrus fruits easier, warm them in a microwave oven for 10 to 15 seconds before squeezing.*

BUDDY FOSTER

This recipe is Buddy's own creation, and he says it came about over 40 years of cooking. The herb mixture gives the chicken a very zesty, fresh flavor, and this is an especially tasty roasted chicken recipe for the spring and summer months, when fresh herbs are plentiful. You can use a whole chicken or pieces. Remember that pieces will cook faster than a whole, so adjust your times accordingly. Buddy's friend Alan augmented this recipe by throwing one jalapeño into the blender while he was making the sauce, and he cooked the chicken "beer can" style. Buddy suggests cooking extra; the leftovers are great!

MASON STEINBERG

The culinary forefathers of the Chinese developed a unique dry rub that was believed to include five flavors found in food: sour, bitter, sweet, pungent, and salty. Mason Steinberg, founder of Oldmill BBQ in Omaha, Nebraska, says this is his favorite smoked duck recipe.

SMOKED YUM-YUM DUCK

Serves 2 to 4

RUB

3 tablespoons anise seeds

1½ teaspoons fennel seeds

1¼ teaspoons Szechuan peppercorns

⅔ teaspoon ground cloves

½ teaspoon ground cinnamon

½ teaspoon salt

¼ teaspoon white pepper

DUCK

1 (4- to 5-pound) whole duck, thawed if frozen

¼ cup dark sesame oil

YUM-YUM SAUCE

¼ cup hoisin sauce

¼ cup apricot jam, puréed until smooth

1 tablespoon clover honey

Combine the rub ingredients in a spice or coffee grinder or a blender and finely grind them. You can store the ground spice mixture in an airtight jar in a cool, dry, dark area for up to 2 months before using it.

Use a 40 to 60 percent combination of oak and applewood for smoking and prepare your smoker to cook at 225° to 250°F.

BARBEQUE IS THE PURSUIT OF HAPPINESS.

Remove anything that's in the cavity of the duck, rinse the duck in cold water, and pat dry. Use a pronged fork to pierce the skin of the duck all over to allow the fat to render out of the bird, trying not to go too deep into the meat.

Lightly paint the duck inside and out with the sesame oil. Season the duck inside and out with the rub. It is helpful to tie the legs and wings together with butcher's twine so they do not flop around.

Place the duck on the rack in the smoker, breast side up. Cook for about 2 hours and 45 minutes and then begin checking the temperature of the duck with a meat thermometer every 20 minutes until the thermometer reads 165°F in the thickest part of the thigh. Normal cooking time is 3 to 3½ hours, depending on the weight of the bird.

While the duck is cooking, place all of the Yum-Yum Sauce ingredients in a saucepan over medium heat and bring to a simmer. Simmer for 5 minutes, stirring often; then cool before serving.

When the duck reaches the necessary temperature, remove it from the smoker and allow it to rest for 15 minutes. Using a cleaver, cut the duck in half. Then cleave the duck into serving pieces roughly 2 inches square. Serve with your favorite fruity barbeque sauce or Yum-Yum Sauce on the side for dipping.

JIM "TRIM" TABB, PHB

Jim "Trim" Tabb has been around barbeque for a long time and has traveled the world in its pursuit. He's famous for his award-winning Pig Powder, but in this recipe he shows his expertise with lamb. Rumor has it that he stole this recipe from Bob Carruthers (pictured above right) while visiting him in Australia.

TABB'S GRILLED MARINATED LAMB

Serves 8 to 10

MARINADE

1 cup white wine

3 tablespoons olive oil

2 tablespoons soy sauce

Juice of 1 lemon

6 cloves garlic, crushed

1 teaspoon salt

1 teaspoon ground black pepper

½ teaspoon ground ginger

1 bay leaf, crumbled

½ teaspoon dried thyme

½ teaspoon rubbed sage

½ teaspoon dried marjoram

½ teaspoon dried cumin

½ teaspoon dried savory

LAMB

1 (6-pound) butterflied leg of lamb, trimmed of fat

Mint jelly, for garnish

Fresh mint leaves, for garnish

In a medium bowl, whisk together all the marinade ingredients. Marinate the lamb, covered, in the refrigerator, for at least 2 hours or overnight. Remove the lamb from the marinade and reserve the marinade.

Set up a hot grill and cook the lamb for about 20 minutes on each side, or until the internal temperature registers 140°F if you like it rare or 160°F for medium.

While the lamb is cooking, place the marinade in a medium saucepan and bring it to a boil over medium-high heat. Boil for 3 to 5 minutes, then turn down the heat and keep it warm while you finish cooking the lamb.

When the lamb is done, slice it at an angle about ¼ to ½ inch thick and pour warm marinade on it. Serve garnished with mint jelly and mint leaves.

LACHLAN VALLEY BBQ LAMB

Serves 12 to 14

MARINADE

6 tablespoons tomato relish or salsa

1 tablespoon curry powder

3 tablespoons brown sugar

2 tablespoons soy sauce

1 tablespoon brown cider vinegar

1 teaspoon ground ginger

½ teaspoon allspice

Grated lemon zest

Salt and black pepper

LAMB

1 (4- to 6-pound) leg of lamb, boned and butterflied

Whisk together all the marinade ingredients. Marinate the lamb in the mixture, covered, in the refrigerator, for at least 4 hours or overnight.

Set up your grill to cook on low to medium heat. Place the lamb on the grill, fat side down, and cook for 40 minutes. Turn and cook for an additional 20 to 50 minutes, until it reaches your desired doneness.

CHRIS ROYLANCE

Here's a lamb recipe from an Aussie. This delicious lamb is a little out of the ordinary, with hints of Indian cuisine.

ANYTHING BUTT

JOHN RAVEN, PHB

John Raven, the Commissioner of Barbeque, is never at a loss for good recipes. This one is great mixed with a little of your favorite sauce and served on a bun with pickles and onion, and, of course, with a couple of Shiners (as in Shiner Bock) or Lone Star beers.

CABRITO, TEXAS STYLE

Serves 8 to 10

1 (10- to 12-pound) cabrito (baby goat), backbone removed, quartered

¼ cup Texas-style rub with chili powder

1 quart mop sauce of your choice

Give the meat a good rub with the spices, seal it in a plastic bag, and keep in the refrigerator overnight.

Remove the bag from the refrigerator and keep it sealed at room temperature for about 2 hours before cooking. Grill or smoke as you would any cut of this size, about 6 to 8 hours at 230° to 250°F, basting every hour or so with mop sauce. The internal temperature needs to register 160°F on a meat thermometer. To ensure tenderness, when the meat has reached the 160°F internal temperature, you could wrap it tightly in heavy-duty foil and keep it on medium heat for another hour. Cut into serving portions or shred the cabrito à la pulled pork.

COOKING CABRITO

Due to its low fat content, cabrito will lose moisture and can toughen quickly if it is exposed to high, dry cooking temperatures. Therefore, there are two basic rules for cooking it: Cook it slowly (low temperature). Cooking any meat at low temperatures results in a more tender and flavorful product with more juice. You should also cook it with moisture (use a mop to baste it).

The tenderness of a meat cut determines the method of cooking. Tender cuts of meat are usually best when cooked by a dry-heat method such as smoke-roasting, broiling, or frying. The tender cuts of goat meat are the legs, ribs, portions of the shoulder, the loin roast, and the breast.

TABB'S BAKED EGGS

Serves 1

Butter for greasing the casserole, plus 1 tablespoon

3 slices bacon

2 eggs

⅓ cup heavy cream

2 to 3 teaspoons dried onion flakes

1 teaspoon dried chives

Dash of dried or minced fresh parsley

Dash of onion powder

Dash of salt

Dash of black pepper

2 tablespoons freshly grated Parmesan cheese

Dash of paprika

Preheat the oven to 400°F. Rub the bottom and sides of a small oval ovenproof dish or ramekin with butter and set it aside.

In a small skillet, cook the bacon until it's about half done and still limp. Line the sides of the prepared dish with the bacon. Break the eggs into the center of the dish, then pour the cream over the eggs. Sprinkle with the dried onion flakes, chives, and parsley. Add the onion powder, salt, and black pepper. Cover with the Parmesan cheese. Place 1 tablespoon butter on top. Finish with a dash of paprika. Bake for 15 minutes and serve warm.

Note: *Sometimes Jim adds thinly sliced fresh mushrooms before serving.*

JIM "TRIM" TABB, PHB

On the Sunday following the Blue Ridge Barbecue Festival in Tryon, North Carolina, Jim always served his friends and family these baked eggs. They are fabulous!

TONY STONE, PHB

Tony is past president of the KCBS. He loves to experiment with new recipes, and he made Jasper the Pig, a metal pig that is filled with everyone's regrets for the year and then burned annually at The Jack by the master distiller. Traditional scotch eggs are boiled eggs wrapped in sausage and then deep-fried. You can also cook the eggs in a smoker. Omit the breading, don't deep-fry them, and instead place the eggs on a perforated flat grill pan and cook indirectly at 230° to 250°F for about an hour to cook the sausage.

SCOTCH EGGS

Serves 8

1 pound sausage, preferably Tennessee Pride mild sausage, at room temperature

2 raw eggs

1 (10-ounce) container seasoned bread crumbs, preferably Old London

8 small or medium hard-boiled eggs, at room temperature, peeled

Canola oil, for frying

Mix the sausage with one of the raw eggs and ¼ cup of the bread crumbs. Cover and place in the freezer until the mixture is firm enough to handle (no more than 15 minutes). Take about one-eighth of the sausage mixture, form a patty, and then mold the sausage evenly around 1 hard-boiled egg. Repeat with the remaining 7 hard-boiled eggs.

Mix the remaining raw egg with about 2 tablespoons of water to form an egg wash. Place the remaining bread crumbs on a plate. Roll each sausage and egg ball in the egg wash; then roll in the bread crumbs until well coated. Place the coated eggs in the refrigerator for about 15 minutes to firm up. Meanwhile, heat 2 inches of oil in a deep-fryer to 350°F.

Drop the eggs into the hot oil and cook for about 7 minutes, or until golden brown. Drain on paper towels and serve.

JASPER FEELS YOUR PAIN

Many customs and rituals take place at barbeque contests. One of our favorites happens annually on Friday night at a party on Barbecue Hill in Lynchburg, Tennessee. Hundreds of barbeque cooks, judges, friends, and relatives dine on country fare of fried chicken, fried catfish, beans, greens, and other delights, with fiddle, guitar, and banjo music from the Jack Daniel's Distillery Band setting a party mood befitting the annual Jack Daniel's World Championship Invitational Barbecue Contest—the one contest that every team would do just about anything to be invited to. Just to be there, win or lose, is one of the greatest accomplishments a team can achieve. Not being there is a thing to regret.

Besides not getting invited to The Jack, barbequers, like everyone else, have many regrets. The annual burning of Jasper the Pig is a symbolic means of putting our regrets behind us and moving on to the next year of competition with a clean slate. Jasper is not as large as Santa Fe's Zozobra, the Old Man of Gloom, but his burning is as meaningful to barbequers as the burning of Zozobra is to the thousands who gather in Santa Fe each year.

Here's how it works. Readers of the *KC Bullsheet* and the *National Barbecue News* are reminded to write down their regrets and mail them to the office of The Jack or to take their regrets with them if they are going to be in Lynchburg for The Jack. All correspondence to Jasper is confidential and not opened or read by anyone. What goes in Jasper stays in Jasper and burns in Jasper. Regrets could be poor scores at a contest or the loss of love or a loved one—any personal losses or behaviors that a person regrets and wants to be rid of through a symbolic cleansing.

At the appointed hour, the partygoers on Barbecue Hill are asked to remain silent for a few minutes. They are given a last-minute chance to bring forward any regrets, and then Jasper's belly is filled with all of the papers containing regrets. The Master Distiller pours some Jack on the papers to enhance their flammability and add some magic to the mix, then takes a sip out of the bottle, and then pours more Jack on the papers. Jasper is lifted into the fire in the big fireplace, and the papers go up in flame and smoke as the partygoers cheer!

Why is the pig named Jasper? That was Jack Daniel's first name. We don't know if the fact that he preferred to be called Jack means he regretted being named Jasper, but it's possible.

By the way: Jasper is made of heavy metal, designed and welded by former KCBS president Tony Stone and staff at his welding shop in Cookeville, Tennessee. And we'll let you in on one and only one secret about a piece of paper that goes in Jasper every year. Ardie writes, on behalf of Jack Daniel, "I wish I hadn't kicked that safe!"

VAN McLEMORE

This recipe was modified from an online BBQ Forum posting by Louie on April 9, 2003, in response to the question "What's your favorite 'anything butt' recipe?" Van uses this recipe at competitions for a morning breakfast. It's simple to make up before they go and when they get the smoker going in the morning for competition, they just put the pockets in the smoker with everything else. Serve it with a little salsa if you like. You can also warm the pockets in a low oven if you don't have a grill or smoker.

POCKET BREAKFAST

Serves 8 to 10

10 eggs

1 cup diced summer sausage

1 cup diced ham

¾ cup shredded pepper Jack cheese

¾ cup shredded cheddar cheese

½ cup diced onion

¼ cup crumbled crisp-cooked bacon

¼ cup diced green bell pepper

¼ cup diced red bell pepper

1 tablespoon diced pickled jalapeños

Salt and black pepper

8 round pocket breads

Set up your smoker to cook at 225°F.

In a greased large skillet over medium heat, scramble the eggs, place them in a bowl, and put them in the refrigerator to cool. Mix everything else except the pocket breads in a large bowl. After the eggs are cooled, chop them and add them to the rest of the filling mixture.

Cut each pocket bread to make two half-moon pockets. Fill each pocket with the egg mixture and place the filled pockets upright in an aluminum pan. Cover the pan with foil and place the pan in the smoker for 45 minutes to 1 hour, until heated throughout.

BREAKFAST CASSEROLE

Serves 6

8 eggs, lightly beaten

2 cups shredded potatoes (Mary uses thawed frozen plain hash browns)

½ cup grated cheddar cheese

½ pound bulk sausage, browned and crumbled

¾ cup chicken broth

½ teaspoon garlic salt

Prepare the smoker to cook indirectly (230° to 250°F). Mix together all the ingredients in a large bowl.

Smoker directions: Coat a foil half-pan with butter-flavored cooking spray. Pour the ingredients into the pan and cover it loosely with aluminum foil. Place the pan in the smoker and smoke until the eggs are set, which could take 1½ to 2 hours, depending on the temperature of your smoker.

Oven directions: Preheat the oven to 350°F. Coat a 9 by 13-inch pan with butter-flavored cooking spray. Pour the ingredients into the pan. Bake for 30 to 40 minutes, or until the eggs are set.

MARY IRONS

Mary told us this is the breakfast she and the JR Smokers fix when they are at a barbeque contest. She also said that as a variation you could use ½ cup sour cream instead of chicken broth.

ANYTHING BUT

PAUL KIRK, PHB

When Paul was teaching his pitmaster class in Portland, Oregon, his host served brisket and gravy for breakfast, and it was outstanding, so Paul decided to create his own recipe. Anyone in barbeque who likes biscuits and gravy will enjoy this version.

BRISKET AND GRAVY

Serves 4

½ pound bulk mild sausage

¼ cup all-purpose flour

½ pound barbequed brisket point, diced

2 to 3 cups milk

Salt and black pepper

Crumble the sausage into a skillet and cook over medium heat until browned. Sprinkle the flour over the browned sausage, stirring constantly. Blend in the brisket. When the mixture is thoroughly combined, slowly add the milk a little at a time until you reach your desired thickness. Stir constantly until creamy and bubbly, about 3 minutes. Season to taste with salt and pepper. Serve hot over homemade biscuits, such as the following recipe.

FLAKY BISCUITS

Makes 10 to 12 biscuits

1½ cups all-purpose flour

½ cup bread flour

1 tablespoon baking powder

½ teaspoon sea salt

5 tablespoons unsalted butter, chilled

3 tablespoons lard or solid white vegetable shortening, chilled

¾ cup cold milk

2 tablespoons butter, melted

Preheat the oven to 425°F and make sure the rack is in the center of the oven.

In a large bowl, combine the flours, baking powder, and salt and mix well. With your fingertips, two knives, or a pastry blender, cut in the chilled butter and lard until the mixture resembles cornmeal. Stir in the cold milk and mix just until the dry ingredients are moistened. Gather the dough into a ball and place it on a lightly floured work surface.

Roll the dough into a rectangle about ½ inch thick. Using a 2-inch round biscuit cutter, flouring the cutter in between cuts, cut out the biscuits, gather up the scraps, and form the dough into another ½-inch-thick piece of dough, being careful not to work it too much.

Place the biscuits 1½ inches apart on an ungreased baking sheet and brush the tops with melted butter. Bake for 10 to 14 minutes, until golden brown. Serve immediately.

PAUL KIRK, PHB

To Paul's taste, a biscuit should be crusty and golden brown on the top—and even lightly browned on the bottom—with an interior that is soft, light, and tender but not too fluffy. Top these with Brisket and Gravy (preceding recipe) or sausage gravy or serve with sweet butter and homemade strawberry preserves.

IF NUTS COULD TALK!

For almost two decades, no team has won grand champion at the Jack Daniel's World Championship Invitational Barbecue, aka The Jack, without a magic hickory nut. If a team doesn't have the magic nut, it won't win. "How do I know this is it?" head cooks ask when invited to pick a nut the first time they compete at The Jack. "You'll know when they call your team name at the awards ceremony on Saturday night" is the reply. Every grand champion at The Jack has had the magic hickory nut since the tradition began.

It happens only at The Jack. Each team takes a shagbark hickory nut out of a bag made from a Jack Daniel's bandana. "That nut was marinated in Jack Daniel's Whiskey and a combo of secret barbeque seasonings for a solid week," they are told. "Then it was rinsed with Kansas City water and dried in Kansas City sunshine. That's powerful magic in itself, but the rest is up to you. Take good care of your nut and your nut will take good care of you. Kiss it. Rub it. Say nice things to it and give it some Jack. It hasn't had a drink of Jack for a week. It's thirsty!"

Teams don't tell us everything they do with their nut to enhance its magic, but we've heard stories. One team, for example, didn't take grand champion their first year at The Jack. They kept their magic nut, however, and pampered it for a full year. One of the members of that team told us she wore that nut in her bra all year. Sure enough, they were grand champions the next year!

The widow of one of our dearly departed barbeque friends told us she buried her husband with his magic nuts from their two years of competing at The Jack in his hands. Magic hickory nuts are all over the world. If only they could talk!

PIZZA DOUGH

Makes enough for 1 large pizza

1 cup warm water

1 teaspoon sugar

1 (¼-ounce) package active dry yeast

2½ cups all-purpose flour, plus more for kneading

1 cup semolina flour or cornmeal

1 teaspoon salt

1 tablespoon dried Italian seasoning

¼ cup olive oil

Combine the water and sugar. Stir in the yeast to dissolve and then let the mixture stand for 10 minutes, until foamy.

In a large bowl, combine the all-purpose flour, semolina flour, salt, and Italian seasoning. Add the yeast mixture and olive oil. Knead to a soft dough, adding enough flour to make a soft dough. Alternatively, you can mix the dough in a food processor or stand mixer following the manufacturer's instructions.

Cover the bowl and let the dough rise in a warm place until doubled. Punch it down, turn it out onto a lightly floured surface, and roll it to the desired thickness.

STEVE PARMAN

Steve is a woodworker and a gourmet cook. Each month he plays guest chef at the Old Store, a sandwich and quilting shop in Johnson City, Kansas. He shared several pizza recipes with us, and this all-purpose crust is great for all of them. For a really good sourdoughlike crust, make the dough up to 48 hours in advance and refrigerate it until you're ready to use it. Bring it to room temperature before using it.

GRILLED PIZZA

Some people grill pizza dough directly on the grill, but Steve Parman likes using a heavy pizza stone. His goes from the oven to the grill every summer. A hot grill and a good pizza stone with a little practice will make for a really fine pie.

Heat a pizza stone on a grill at medium-high heat for 15 to 20 minutes. Remove the hot stone from the grill to place the dough on it. Since this recipe makes a large pizza, it's tricky to transfer the dough to the stone without good peel skills. If you're good with a pizza peel, by all means use it. Steve finds it easier to fold the dough in quarters and unfold it on the stone and then add the ingredients. Return the hot stone to the grill.

The pizza should be ready in 12 minutes or so, but check it at 8 minutes until you've had enough experience with your grill to know how long it takes.

STEVE PARMAN

Steve and his brother David started building furniture in 1976, but in 1984 they changed their focus and began making wooden kaleidoscopes. Their kaleidoscopes are all individually hand-crafted from a variety of woods—red gum, black walnut, maple, beech, eucalyptus, and oak. This recipe from Steve, who is also a great cook, is a creative use of sweet potatoes.

SWEET POTATO PIZZA

Makes 1 large pizza

1 recipe Pizza Dough (page 185)

CILANTRO PESTO

1 bunch of fresh cilantro

1 to 2 chipotle chiles, fresh or packed in adobo

2 tablespoons pine nuts

1 clove garlic

Pinch of salt

2 to 3 tablespoons olive oil

TOPPINGS

1 (8-ounce) package Mexican-blend shredded cheese

1 sweet potato, peeled and thinly sliced

1 medium yellow onion, thinly sliced

Preheat the oven to 450°F or follow the grilling instructions on page 185.

To make the cilantro pesto, combine all the pesto ingredients in a food processor and purée them.

Place the rolled-out dough on a baking sheet. Spread the pesto on the dough, top with the cheese, and then with the sweet potatoes and onions. Bake or grill, covered, for about 12 minutes, or until the crust is golden brown and the cheese is melted.

CARAMELIZED ONION PIZZA

Makes 1 large pizza

1 recipe Pizza Dough (page 185)

3 medium yellow onions, thinly sliced

2 tablespoons olive oil

2 tablespoons sugar

1 (8-ounce) package Italian-blend shredded cheese

1 Granny Smith apple, cored and thinly sliced

½ cup coarsely chopped walnuts

2 to 3 ounces feta cheese, crumbled

Preheat the oven to 425°F or follow the grilling instructions on page 185.

To caramelize the onions, place them in a large skillet with the olive oil and sauté over medium-high heat for 5 to 7 minutes. Add the sugar and sauté for 7 to 8 minutes, stirring constantly, until the onions are caramelized.

Place the rolled-out pizza dough on a baking sheet and top it with the Italian cheese, followed by the sliced apples, caramelized onions, walnuts, and feta cheese. Bake or grill, covered, for 12 to 14 minutes, until the crust is golden brown and the cheese is melted.

STEVE PARMAN

Steve's wife, Ann Davis, teaches English at the local high school and is a world traveler. Steve and Ann are part of an art board that brings artists from all points to Johnson City, Kansas, and they end up entertaining a lot of artists. Their hospitality is world class. This pizza is simple and delicious and an elegant dish for entertaining.

ANYTHING BUTT

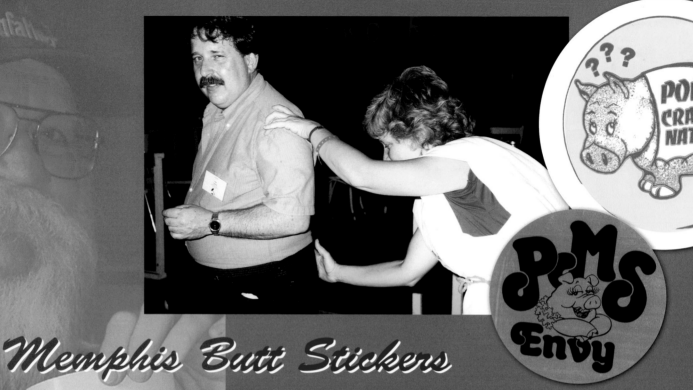

Memphis Butt Stickers

There was a period of several years at the Memphis in May World Championship Barbecue Cooking Contest when men and women of all ages and sizes walked the miles of team booths in Tom Lee Park wearing stickers on their bodies— especially on their buttocks or breasts. The stickers bore names of cooking teams and/or slogans. As a rule, the more endowed the body, the more bountiful the stickers.

Apparently someone in authority decided to ban the tradition. Maybe there were complaints, or maybe someone feared complaints. Imagine, for example, what could have happened if Tom Roberts's Bite My Butt barbeque team had decided to compete in Tom Lee Park. Though we don't know the reason for the ban, we do know it was a lot of fun, and we miss it!

MASHED POTATO PIZZA

Makes 1 large pizza

1 recipe Pizza Dough (page 185), rolled for a thick-crust pizza

3 to 4 slices bacon

About 2 cups prepared mashed potatoes (about 4 medium potatoes), skins reserved

1 (8-ounce) package Mexican-blend shredded cheese

Preheat the oven to 425°F or follow the grilling instructions on page 185.

In a skillet over medium-high heat, fry the bacon until it's crispy. Remove the bacon from the skillet and set it aside to cool. Add the potato skins to the skillet and fry them until crisp. Remove them from the skillet and set them aside cool. Crumble the cooled bacon and chop the cooled potato skins.

Place the rolled-out thick-crust dough on a baking sheet or pat the dough into a deep-dish pizza pan. Spread the mashed potatoes about ½ inch thick over the dough, then top with the cheese, crumbled bacon, and chopped potato skins. Bake or grill, covered, for 20 to 25 minutes, until the crust is golden brown.

STEVE PARMAN

Don't throw away your leftover mashed potatoes! Here is a great way to use them. Steve likes to prepare his potatoes with lots of butter, milk, and chopped fresh rosemary.

BILLY RODGERS

This is a great basic pizza dough recipe you can top with your own favorite toppings—or use one of Billy's recipes, which follow. Billy makes it for pizza night at his house. It reminds him of the New York–style pizza that he and his wife used to eat when they were high school sweethearts. Enjoy!

NEW YORK–STYLE PIZZA DOUGH

Makes enough dough for 1 (14-inch) pizza

⅓ cup plus 1½ teaspoons water

½ teaspoon kosher salt

½ teaspoon sugar

1¼ cups bread flour

½ teaspoon active dry yeast

½ teaspoon canola oil

Put the water into the bowl of a stand mixer fitted with a dough hook. Add the salt and sugar, then add the flour and the yeast. Mix at low speed for about 2 minutes, then mix at medium speed until all of the flour is incorporated into the dough. Add the oil and mix for 2 minutes at low speed; then mix the dough at medium speed until it develops a smooth, satiny appearance, 8 to 10 minutes. Place the dough in a lightly oiled bowl, cover the bowl, and place it in the refrigerator.

The dough will be ready to use after about 24 hours of refrigeration. To use the dough, remove it from the refrigerator and allow it to warm at room temperature for 2 to 3 hours. The dough will then be ready to be stretched and dressed with your favorite toppings.

TERIYAKI CHICKEN PIZZA

Makes 1 (14-inch) pizza

1 recipe New York–Style Pizza Dough (page 190)

2 tablespoons thinly sliced scallion

¼ cup thinly sliced green, red, and yellow bell pepper

½ cup fresh pineapple chunks

1 teaspoon dark sesame oil

¾ cup grated mozzarella cheese

¼ cup teriyaki sauce

2 grilled chicken breasts, boned and cubed

Place a pizza stone on your grill and preheat the grill to 500°F.

Combine the scallion, peppers, and pineapple with the sesame oil. Stretch the pizza dough out on a lightly floured surface. Sprinkle ¼ cup of the mozzarella cheese on top of the dough. Spread the pineapple mixture evenly across the top. Drizzle on the teriyaki sauce. Top with the remaining ½ cup of mozzarella cheese and then the cubed chicken breast. Carefully slide the pizza onto a pizza peel dusted lightly with flour or cornmeal, transfer the pizza to the pizza stone, and grill, covered, for 5 to 6 minutes, until the crust is browned and the cheese is melted.

BILLY RODGERS

If you are looking for a unique pizza to wow your friends, this is it!

BILLY RODGERS

The marinara sauce is really what helps the Buffalo sauce to shine in this recipe.

BUFFALO CHICKEN PIZZA

Makes 1 (14-inch) pizza

1 recipe New York–Style Pizza Dough (page 190)

¾ cup marinara or pizza sauce

¼ cup Wing-Time Garlic Buffalo Wing Sauce

¾ cup grated mozzarella cheese

2 grilled chicken breasts, boned and cubed

Place a pizza stone on your grill and preheat the grill to 500°F.

Combine the pizza or marinara sauce with the wing sauce and blend well. Stretch the pizza dough out on a lightly floured surface. Spread ½ cup of the sauce on the dough. Add ¼ cup of the mozzarella cheese, followed by the cubed chicken breast. Top with the remaining ½ cup mozzarella cheese. Carefully slide the pizza onto a pizza peel lightly dusted with flour or cornmeal, transfer the pizza to the pizza stone, and grill, covered, for 5 to 6 minutes, until the crust is browned and the cheese is melted.

HAWAIIAN PIZZA

Makes 1 (14-inch) pizza

1 recipe New York–Style Pizza Dough (page 190)

¾ cup marinara sauce

¼ cup Fischer & Wieser Charred Pineapple Bourbon Sauce

¾ cup grated mozzarella cheese

1 cup diced or sliced Canadian bacon

1 cup fresh pineapple chunks

Place a pizza stone on your grill and preheat the grill to 500°F.

Combine the marinara sauce with the charred pineapple bourbon sauce and blend well. Stretch the pizza dough out on a lightly floured surface. Spread ½ cup of the sauce on the dough. Top with the mozzarella cheese, then add the Canadian bacon and pineapple chunks. Carefully slide the pizza onto a pizza peel dusted lightly with flour or cornmeal, transfer the pizza to the pizza stone, and grill, covered, for 5 to 6 minutes, until the crust is browned and the cheese is melted.

BILLY RODGERS

This pizza brings the flavor of the Big Island to your kitchen table!

ANYTHING BUTT

193

BRAD BARRETT

This is an easy pizza recipe you can assemble when you're in a hurry.

EASY BBQ PIZZA

Makes 1 (14-inch) pizza

Olive oil, for brushing

Mama Mary's Thin & Crispy Pizza Crust or other partially baked crust from the deli section

½ cup barbeque sauce

½ cup pulled barbequed pork

1 cup shredded mozzarella cheese

Preheat your grill to 400°F.

Lightly brush olive oil on the bottom side of the pizza crust. Spread the sauce over the top side of the crust, followed by the pork and then the cheese.

Carefully slide the pizza onto the grill and close the lid. After 3 minutes, lift up the edge of the crust to peek at the sear marks on the bottom and give the pizza a quarter turn. If the sear marks are black, your grill is too hot, so reduce the heat. Check again in 3 minutes, give it another quarter turn, and see how well the cheese is melting. The pizza should take 8 to 10 minutes total and is ready when the crust is browned around the edges and the cheese is melted.

HERBED LOBSTER PIZZA WITH A FRENCH ACCENT

Makes 1 (14-inch) pizza

1 recipe New York–Style Pizza Dough (page 190)

½ cup tomato sauce
1 cup caramelized onions

2 lobsters, steamed in dry white wine and herbs (parsley, chervil, tarragon), then gently smoked with apple chips, meat removed and chopped

1½ cups shredded gruyere cheese
Unsweetened whipped cream, for serving

Place a pizza stone on your grill and preheat the grill to 500°F. Stretch the pizza dough out on a lightly floured surface. Spread the tomato sauce over the dough, leaving about 1 inch of crust around the edges. Distribute the caramelized onions over the sauce, then follow with the lobster meat. Spread the cheese evenly over the top.

Carefully slide the pizza onto a pizza peel lightly dusted with flour or cornmeal, transfer the pizza to the pizza stone and grill for 5 to 6 minutes, until the crust is browned and the cheese is melted.

Top each slice with a dollop of whipped cream before serving.

PAUL KIRK, PHB, FOR JULIA CHILD

She touched the lives of millions with her winning personality, enthusiasm for life, and childlike joy at discovering a new gadget or culinary technique. Everyone loved Julia, present company included. We asked Paul to take liberties with Julia's recipe for "lobster steamed in wine with herb sauce" and make a pizza with it. We think she would love the result.

GUIDO AND CATHY MEINDLE ON JULIA CHILD

We loved that lady. Drop the chicken on the floor, pick it up, and put it back in the pan—that's our kind of cookin' and no BS! About six months before she died, she signed autographs in one of our Gourmet Cookin' Kitchen Supply Stores in Pasaloony. Before we went, we put together a little package of Guido's Serious Sauces and Seasoning. When we gave it to her, she was so excited she ripped the package open, looked at all the goodies, stood up, thanked us, and gave us both a big hug. What a lady she was! We will never forget her.

RICH AND BUNNY TUTTLE, K CASS BBQ

Rich and Bunny told us, "We have experimented with grilling all kinds of different pizzas, and this one is exceptionally delightful and healthy."

GRILLED SEAFOOD FOCACCIA

Serves 2 to 4

½ cup seafood cocktail sauce

1 (9-inch) focaccia

Fresh spinach leaves to cover the bread

1 pound crabmeat or crab blend

½ pound feta cheese, crumbled

¼ cup freshly grated Parmesan cheese

Prepare your coals and let them die down to a low heat.

Spread the cocktail sauce over the bread as you would a pizza. Arrange the fresh spinach leaves over the sauce so they are close enough that they are touching each other. Spread the crabmeat evenly over the spinach. Follow with the feta cheese and sprinkle the Parmesan cheese on top.

Place the focaccia on the grill and close the lid. Check on the pizza about every 5 minutes to make sure the bottom is not burning. It should take approximately 20 minutes and is ready when it's hot and the cheese is completely melted.

PORTOBELLO FAJITAS

Serves 4

2 teaspoons oil

4 large portobello mushroom caps

2 medium bell peppers, sliced

1 medium yellow onion, sliced

1 (1-ounce) package fajita seasoning

⅓ cup water

8 (8-inch) flour tortillas, warmed

8 lettuce leaves

Sour cream, for serving

Lime wedges, for serving

Fresh cilantro sprigs, for serving

Heat 1 teaspoon of the oil in each of two skillets. Add the mushrooms to one skillet, and the peppers and onion to the other. Cook each for about 6 minutes, turning the mushrooms and stirring the pepper mixture until firm-tender. Transfer the mushrooms to a cutting board. Stir the fajita seasoning and water into the pepper mixture. Cook for about 1 minute, or until saucy. Slice the mushrooms. Place the tortillas on a work surface and top each with a leaf of lettuce. Divide the mushrooms among the fajitas, then top each with the pepper and onion mixture. Serve with sour cream, lime wedges, and cilantro sprigs.

PAUL KIRK, PHB

This is a fast, easy, and delicious meat-alternative fajita recipe.

CHERISH GRABAU

Cherish admits, "I don't like venison, but if it's prepared like this, I just can't stop eating it!" You'll need some skewers to make this, and if you're using wooden skewers, soak them in water for at least 30 minutes first.

GRILLED VENISON TENDERLOIN

Serves 4

2 pounds venison back strap (tenderloin), cut into 2-inch chunks

1 quart apple cider (not apple juice), or as needed

2 (12-ounce) bottles original Demon Pig BBQ Sauce

1½ pounds thick-sliced bacon

Olive oil, for brushing

Place the chunks of venison in a shallow baking dish. Pour in enough apple cider to cover them. Cover and refrigerate for 2 hours.

Remove the meat from the refrigerator and discard the apple cider. Pat the venison dry and return it to the dish. Pour the barbeque sauce over the chunks. Cover and refrigerate for 2 to 3 more hours.

Remove the venison from the refrigerator and let it stand for 30 minutes, or until it reaches room temperature. Preheat an outdoor grill for high heat. Charcoal is best, but if you must, use gas.

Wrap each chunk of venison in a slice of bacon and thread them onto skewers, leaving some space between the chunks. Brush the grill grate with olive oil when hot and place the skewers on the grill so they are not touching. The bacon will kick up some flames, so be ready with a spray bottle filled with water. Grill, turning occasionally, until the bacon becomes very slightly burned, 15 to 20 minutes. The slower, the better. Dig in and prepare to want more!

BBQ BEAVER'S BODACIOUS GRILLED BACK STRAP

Serves 4

4 back strap steaks, butterfly style or disks, cut ¾ inch thick

¼ cup best-quality balsamic vinegar

2 tablespoons extra virgin olive oil

1 tablespoon granulated garlic

2 tablespoons Johnny's Pork, Chicken & Turkey Seasoning (see Note)

1 tablespoon coarsely ground black pepper

Place the steaks in a shallow pan or dish and sprinkle with the vinegar. Turn often for 20 minutes.

Prepare a hot fire of coals, lump or briquettes, with some cherrywood to be added 5 minutes before the steaks go on.

Take the steaks out of the vinegar and pat them dry. Liberally paint one side of the steaks with the olive oil. Then apply liberal amounts of garlic granules, followed by Johnny's seasoning, and finally the pepper. Make sure all other side dishes are ready and the table is set. These game steaks should be served hot and fresh with no standing time.

Place the steaks, seasoned side down, over the hot fire. Apply more olive oil to the top side, followed by liberal amounts of each of the other ingredients, in the same order as before. (What barbeque cook needs forearm hair anyway?) The steaks should be served rare to medium-rare. If you see juice coming to the surface on the top side, they need to be turned with tongs.

Note: *Johnny's Pork, Chicken & Turkey Seasoning is manufactured by Johnny's Fine Foods (johnnysfinefoods.com) of Tacoma, Washington. If you need a substitute for the Johnny's, use a seasoning salt that does not contain sugar. You will be grilling at a high enough temp that sugar will burn, leaving an off taste.*

JIM ERICKSON

Jim is with the Beaver Castors team. This is great for back strap loin steaks from (in descending order of quality) a Columbian black-tailed deer (best), a Roosevelt elk (next best), Rocky Mountain elk, a high-country mule deer, or a flat-land or desert mule deer, a farm-raised elk, or, if you have to, a white-tailed deer.

ANYTHING BUTT

BOB LYON, PHB

Bob told us he entered this meat loaf in a contest. It didn't win, but Bob notes, "Steve Holbrook likes it." We know Steve Holbrook, and we like his taste—so if Steve likes it, we like it! It is Bob's adaptation of a Paul Prudhomme fiery-flavored "strangler." Bob's version is milder. Bob also shared that "somehow the venison left over from hunting season doesn't get used up. It sits in the freezer and eventually gets thrown out. Farmer John's lean ground pork has just the answer for using it up. Thaw, trim, and grind a package of venison from the freezer or carefully trim and grind pieces and then keep in 1-pound packages in the freezer for this super meat loaf."

VENISON MEAT LOAF

Serves 6 to 8

SEASONING MIX

2 bay leaves

2 teaspoons salt

¼ teaspoon cayenne

1 teaspoon chili powder

1 teaspoon black pepper

½ teaspoon white pepper

½ teaspoon ground cumin

½ teaspoon ground nutmeg

MEAT LOAF

3 tablespoons butter

3 good-size garlic cloves, put through a press

⅔ medium yellow onion, minced

2 scallions, minced

2 medium celery stalks, minced

½ green bell pepper, minced

¼ teaspoon Scorned Woman hot sauce or 2 teaspoons Cajun Power Garlic Sauce or 6 sprinkles of Tabasco sauce

2 teaspoons Worcestershire sauce

⅓ cup canned condensed milk

⅓ cup ketchup

1 pound ground venison, all fat and silver skin removed, or 1 pound lean ground beef

½ pound Farmer John California Natural Extra Lean Ground Pork, or your favorite brand

2 eggs, lightly beaten

⅔ cup dried bread crumbs

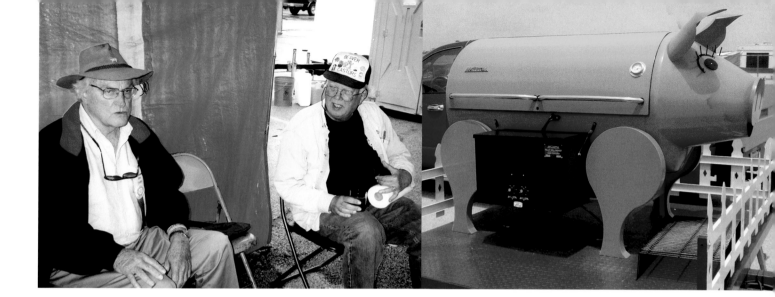

Preheat the oven to 350°F. Combine the seasoning mix ingredients in a small bowl and set aside.

Melt the butter in a medium nonstick skillet over medium heat. Toss in the garlic, onion, scallions, celery, green pepper, hot sauce, Worcestershire sauce, and seasoning mix. Sauté for about 6 minutes, stirring every so often and scraping the bottom of the pan well. Then stir in the milk and ketchup and cook for 2 more minutes, stirring and scraping as before. Remove the pan from the heat and allow it to cool. Remove and discard the bay leaves.

Put the venison and pork in a large bowl. Add the eggs, bread crumbs, and cooked vegetable mixture. Mix thoroughly. Put the results in your favorite ovenproof glass dish or baking pan. Bake, uncovered, until the meat loaf registers an internal temperature of 165°F, about 45 minutes. Cut and serve immediately after you remove it from the oven.

KENNA JO LAMBERTSEN

Kenna Jo created this recipe for the specialty meat category at the Iowa Farm Bureau 2008 cookout contest. It won grand champion at Tama County and first place in the specialty meat category at the Iowa State Fair. She wanted to showcase the ease of cooking elk. It's great made into cheesesteaks, too. Just slice the elk and top with grilled onions, green peppers, and Cheez Whiz on toasted ciabatta rolls.

ELK FOR DUMMIES

2 to 3 pounds elk tenderloin

2 cups packed brown sugar

1 cup chili powder

1 (12-ounce) jar beef gravy

1 (6-ounce) can whole cranberry sauce

2 teaspoons balsamic vinegar

Prepare your grill or smoker to cook at 230° to 250°F over indirect heat.

Place the elk on a sheet of heavy-duty aluminum foil. Combine the brown sugar and chili powder and rub the mixture on the elk. Combine the gravy, cranberry sauce, and vinegar and brush the mixture on the elk. Pour the remaining sauce over the elk. Seal the foil and cook until the internal temperature registers 135°F (or your desired degree of doneness) on a meat thermometer, 2 to 3 hours. Allow the meat to rest for 10 minutes before serving with the sauce from the foil.

BUFFALOST

Serves 4

6 ounces fresh spinach

1 tablespoon butter

6 ounces fresh mushrooms, stemmed and rinsed

1 (10-ounce) beef flatiron steak, pounded to ¼ inch thick

1 (8-ounce) buffalo sirloin steak, pounded to ¼ inch thick

1 (6-ounce) ostrich sirloin steak, pounded to ¼ inch thick

Salt and black pepper

2 shallots, chopped and sautéed

Steam the spinach over medium-high heat until soft. Drain it, lightly pressing on it to get most of the moisture out, then chop it. Set aside.

Melt the butter in a skillet over medium heat. Sauté the mushrooms until soft, 5 to 7 minutes, then chop them and set them aside.

Set up a medium-hot grill to cook the steaks over indirect heat.

Season all of the steaks with salt and pepper. Lay the beef steak on your work surface and spread the spinach over the top of it; top with the buffalo steak. Spread the mushrooms over the buffalo steak; top with the ostrich steak. Spread the shallots over the ostrich steak. Roll tightly and tie with culinary twine.

Cook for 1½ hours, or until the internal temperature registers 130°F (or your desired degree of doneness) on a meat thermometer. Allow the meat to rest for 15 minutes before slicing and serving.

KENNA JO LAMBERTSEN

Kenna Jo created this recipe for the specialty meat category at the Iowa Farm Bureau 2007 cookout contest because, as she told us, "I wanted to create a recipe that used Iowa domestically raised meats in a new way." It won first place in Tama County.

DAVE CONTI

Connecticut barbequer and KCBS member Dave Conti likes his food spicy, on or off the grill. He shared his jambalaya recipe with Hartford's WSFB-TV and with his friends at KCBS for this book. Chef Paul has tweaked it a bit and suggested other products in case you can't find the ones in the recipe in your area. If you can't get Luzianne Cajun Spice, you could mix 1 teaspoon salt, ½ teaspoon cayenne, ½ teaspoon black pepper, and 1½ teaspoons fresh thyme (or ½ teaspoon dried).

RED PLANET JUMPIN' JAMBALAYA

Serves 10 to 12

¼ cup olive oil

6 chicken thighs

1 to 3 tablespoons Luzianne Cajun Spice (see sidebar), or more to taste

2 cups chopped celery

2 cups chopped onion

2 cups chopped green bell pepper

1 whole head of garlic, peeled and chopped

2 cups chicken or vegetable broth

1 lemon, cut in half

1 (12-ounce) bottle Saranac Pale Ale or ale of your choice

1 bag shrimp boil (optional)

2 cups chopped chorizo sausage

2 cups chopped ham

2 (28-ounce) cans whole Sclafani tomatoes, with juice

2 pounds shrimp, any size, peeled and deveined

2 (8-ounce) boxes Goya Yellow Rice, prepared according to package directions

Heat the olive oil in a skillet over medium-high heat, add the chicken, and season with the Luzianne seasoning. Sauté the chicken until brown, 7 to 8 minutes. Set the chicken aside to cool and add the celery, onion, green pepper, and garlic to the pan. Sauté until the vegetables are tender, 6 to 8 minutes. At this point you could add more Luzianne seasoning (about 2 tablespoons), depending on your taste. Remove from the heat.

In a 2-quart saucepan, heat the broth over medium-high heat, then add the sautéed vegetable mixture, the lemon, half of the ale, and the shrimp-boil. Tear the chicken skin and meat off the chicken thighs and discard the bones. Chop the meat and skin into bite-sized pieces and add them to the pan. Add the sausage, ham, tomatoes, and the rest of the ale. Cook until the mixture is bubbling, then reduce the heat and simmer for 30 to 45 minutes. During the last 7 to 8 minutes, add the shrimp (so the shrimp don't overcook).

Add the freshly cooked rice and mix well to combine. Enjoy!

SNAIL'S SMOKY CHILI CON CARNE

Serves 10

2 pounds mild or hot Jimmy Dean breakfast sausage, or your favorite brand

4 celery stalks, chopped

2 large yellow onions, chopped

2 (15-ounce) cans corn

3 (15-ounce) cans diced tomatoes

2 (15-ounce) cans light red kidney beans

2 (15-ounce) cans dark red kidney beans

1 (6-ounce) can tomato paste

½ cup white distilled vinegar

6 tablespoons cornstarch

3 tablespoons chili powder

2 tablespoons salt

2 tablespoons garlic powder

1 tablespoon dried cumin

1 tablespoon baking soda

1 tablespoon black pepper

1 teaspoon cayenne

1 teaspoon dried Italian seasoning

1 drop liquid smoke (optional)

In a large skillet over medium heat, brown the sausage, celery, and onions. Add the corn, tomatoes, beans, tomato paste, vinegar, cornstarch, chili powder, salt, garlic powder, cumin, baking soda, black pepper, cayenne, Italian seasoning, and liquid smoke, mixing well, and simmer for 1 hour before serving.

JAY "THE SNAIL" VANTUYL

Snail tells us this is a nice dish that even children can eat because it's not too spicy. The drop of liquid smoke in the ingredient list is actually a little inside joke. Snail threw it in there so this recipe would have something to do with barbeque. "If you want to live dangerously," he says, "go ahead and put it in."

How to Market Roadkill

O ur friend the late Billy "Shug" Powell of Columbus, Georgia, was never at a loss for mischief and practical jokes. One of his favorites was to relabel 3-ounce cans of potted meat with his Nature Cured Georgia Possum label. It is definitely a "product" you'll want to completely understand before you spread it on a cracker and pair it with sweet potatoes, RC Cola, and a Moon Pie!

America's No. 1 Choice
Nature Cured
GEORGIA POSSUM

CONTENTS: PURE POSSUM TENDERIZED BY A LOADED DUMP TRUCK ON HIGHWAY 27, ABOUT 2 MILES FROM THE BRIAR PATCH IN COLUMBUS, GEORGIA.

GUARANTEED SUN CURED FOR ONE DAY.

BRUNSWICK STEW

Makes 5 quarts, 12 to 14 servings

1 whole fryer chicken

1 pound barbequed pork shoulder, chopped

4 slices thick hickory-smoked bacon

4 cups diced peeled potatoes

2 (10-ounce) packages frozen baby lima beans

1 (28-ounce) can crushed tomatoes

2 medium Vidalia onions, chopped

4 teaspoons kosher salt

½ teaspoon black pepper

1 cup Georgia barbeque sauce, such as Johnny Harris Original or Hickory Bar-B-Cue Sauce

1 tablespoon Worcestershire sauce

2 (10-ounce) packages frozen whole kernel corn

Rinse the chicken and cut into 4 to 6 pieces. Put the chicken pieces in a large stainless-steel kettle and cover with water. Bring the water to a boil, reduce the heat, and simmer until tender, about 1 hour. Remove the chicken from the broth; remove and discard the skin and bones when the meat is cool. Cut the meat into small pieces. Add enough water to the broth to make 8 cups.

Add the chicken, pork, bacon, potatoes, lima beans, tomatoes, onions, salt, pepper, barbeque sauce, and Worcestershire to the broth. Simmer, uncovered, over low heat for 1 hour, stirring occasionally. Add the corn and simmer for another 30 minutes.

ARDIE A. DAVIS, PHB, FOR BILLY "SHUG" POWELL

This popular southern dish has been prepared many ways with a variety of meats. Few people these days put traditional squirrel meat in their stew. I adapted this recipe from notes I found in my file of correspondence with the late Billy "Shug" Powell.

ANYTHING BUTT

207

SUSAN AND BRAD SPARR

This recipe is from the Sue-B-Q BBQ Team from McKinney, Texas. If you like your chili with beans, this is a quick and easy recipe. If you like your chili spicy, you can chop some jalapeño peppers and add them to the chili. If you like your chili really spicy, you can also add white pepper in small increments until you achieve the level of heat you like. Be careful with the white pepper, as it will add quite a kick.

EASY TURKEY CHILI

Serves 8 to 10

3 (15-ounce) cans tomato sauce

1 (1-ounce) package Williams Chili Seasoning

1 (8-ounce) can mushroom stems and pieces

2 (15-ounce) cans ranch-style beans

2 pounds ground turkey

1 large yellow onion, chopped

Salt

Place the tomato sauce, chili seasoning, mushrooms, and beans in a slow cooker and blend together. While the mixture is warming, brown the turkey and onion together in a large skillet over medium heat. Then add the contents of the skillet to the slow cooker and heat everything together for at least 30 minutes before serving. Add salt to taste.

CROSS-DRESSING AT BBQ AND CHILI EVENTS

Q Why do grown and otherwise manly men dress up like rowdy women at barbeque and chili contests?

A Our short answer is: For fun! We'll leave other explanations to armchair psychologists or professionals of a Freudian or Jungian bent. From the Texas Hula Men of the Green County Pod to the Miss Piggy Memphis in May contestants, the air is alive with smoke, mirrors, music, dancing, and faux flirting when the "girls" make the scene. Embrace your cognitive dissonance and enjoy the fun!

JIM "TRIM" TABB, PHB

Jim Tabb was one of the pioneers of competition barbeque. He held competitions in his backyard in Jacksonville while stationed there as a fighter pilot more than 40 years ago. According to Jim, the smell of barbeque was a chick magnet that "baited" the JAX girls. Time sure flies. Jim allows that he was never very fond of Thanksgiving turkey, but always looked forward to making tacos with the leftovers.

TURKEY TACO GOOP

Serves 6

3 tablespoons olive oil

1½ cups chopped yellow onion

3 green chiles such as jalapeños, seeded and chopped

1 cup diced green bell pepper

3 cloves garlic, diced

3 cups cooked turkey in thin strips

1 (8-ounce) can tomato sauce

½ cup hot Mexican salsa

1 (6-ounce) can tomato paste

3 tablespoons ketchup

1 tablespoon monosodium glutamate (MSG) (optional)

1½ teaspoons sugar

½ teaspoon ground coriander

2 teaspoons chili powder or taco seasoning powder

¼ teaspoon salt

Taco shells, for serving

Sour cream, for serving

Sliced black olives, for serving

Heat the olive oil in a large, heavy skillet over medium heat and sauté the onion, chiles, green bell pepper, and garlic until tender, 5 to 10 minutes. Add the turkey, tomato sauce, salsa, tomato paste, ketchup, MSG, sugar, coriander, chili powder, and salt. Simmer for 5 to 10 minutes. Serve in taco shells topped with sour cream and olives.

OLE RAY'S SOUTHERN BBQ STEW

Serves 10 to 12

1½ to 2 pounds ground or chopped pork

1 medium yellow onion, chopped

1 (14.5-ounce) can green peas, with juice

1 (14.5-ounce) can green lima beans, with juice

1 (14.5-ounce) can diced or sliced potatoes, with juice

1 (14.5-ounce) can diced tomatoes, with juice

1 (14.5-ounce) can corn, with juice

1 (14.5-ounce) can cream-style corn, with juice

1 cup Ole Ray's Kentucky Red Bourbon Barbeque Sauce
or your favorite

2 tablespoons Ole Ray's Rubb-It or your favorite

1 teaspoon onion powder

1 teaspoon garlic powder

1 teaspoon vinegar

Salt and black pepper

In a large pot over medium heat, brown the pork and drain off the grease. Add the rest of the ingredients to the pot and bring the mixture to a boil over medium-high heat. Reduce the heat to low and cook, covered, for 1 hour, adding water or broth if needed to maintain a stew consistency.

RAY GREENE

This isn't your everyday stew, and it's great with corn bread.

SEASONINGS: MARINADES, BRINES, RUBS, BASTES, PASTES, AND SAUCES

Paul would argue that the most important chapter in any cookbook—especially a barbeque cookbook—is the one that deals with seasonings. The most important part of any recipe is the seasonings, and the more you can learn and know about seasoning, the better cook you will be.

When using any seasoning, a good rule of thumb is that a little goes a long way, so don't smother food with spices, herbs, or other flavorings. Mark Twain's famous observation about how using the right word makes a difference as dramatic as light from a firefly versus lightning can also be applied to seasoning. Done in moderation, seasoning can be fantastic. Done to excess, it can overpower other flavors in a dish. Seasonings have the potential to deliver culinary lightning. When you don't use them, your dish may be as unremarkable as a firefly's twinkle in a lighted room. Use just enough and your dish will be as remarkable as lightning in a lighted room.

The seasoning recipes in this chapter run the gamut of the taste spectrum, from Citrus Marinade for Chicken to Crawlin' Cajun BBQ Rub to the sweetness of Big Billy's Very Cherry Dr Pepper Barbecue Sauce. These recipes also show the creativity of barbequers as they search for the perfect flavoring for their meat, whether it's mustard seed, paprika, wasabi, coffee, molasses, soda pop, or any of the many seasonings that go great with barbeque.

JEREMY RAVENSHAW FOWLER

The barbeque team Jeremy captains won grand champion at the 2009 British BBQ Championships.We're grateful for this recipe he sent us. This marinade, when cold, will enhance the flavors of most proteins and vegetables, yet it is best with chicken, beef, and pork. It's best to marinate the meat overnight, depending on the size of the cut, but it will have a marked flavor after 2 hours.

JAPANESE MARINADE

Makes about 1 quart

⅔ cup sugar

¾ cup malt vinegar

¼ cup dark corn syrup

1 teaspoon garlic purée

1 tablespoon molasses

2 tablespoons Kikkoman soy sauce

½ cup pineapple juice concentrate

½ cup orange juice concentrate

2 tablespoons fresh lemon juice

1 large yellow onion, minced (about 1 cup)

1½ cups water

2 teaspoons ginger purée

1 tablespoon wasabi purée

½ teaspoon hot red pepper flakes

½ teaspoon black pepper

¼ teaspoon cayenne

½ teaspoon dried basil

1 bay leaf

¼ teaspoon dried marjoram

¼ teaspoon dried oregano

¼ teaspoon minced fresh savory

¼ teaspoon dried cumin

½ teaspoon mustard seed

2 tablespoons cornstarch dissolved in 3 tablespoons water

⅔ cup sake (Jeremy uses Kasumi Tsuru Kimoto), or mirin

1 cup soybean oil

for real barbecue

Seriously BBQ

Combine the sugar and vinegar in a saucepan and slowly bring them to a boil, cooking until caramelized. Be careful to not boil too long as this can easily burn.

Take the pan off the heat and set it on a heatproof surface before adding the rest of the ingredients, as hot caramel can give bad burns if things are added to it too quickly. Add the corn syrup, garlic purée, molasses, soy sauce, pineapple juice concentrate, orange juice concentrate, lemon juice, onion, and water.

Put the ginger purée, wasabi, red pepper flakes, black pepper, cayenne, basil, bay leaf, marjoram, oregano, savory, cumin, and mustard seed into a mortar and grind it down with a pestle to release the flavors and scents. You can also use a food processor or blender. Stir this mixture into the liquid mixture and simmer for 20 minutes. Then bring to a rolling boil, whisk in the cornstarch mixture to thicken the liquid slightly, and cook until the marinade becomes clear, about 2 minutes. Reduce the heat to a simmer. You want to avoid boiling at this point, for that would kill the strength of the sake you are about to add. Add the sake and soybean oil and stir. Remove from the heat and cool before using the marinade.

DON PRZYBYLA

This marinade is great for ribs. A slab of ribs takes 2 cups of marinade, so you'll need to multiply this recipe accordingly. Or you could add your favorite soda or beer to the marinade. Do not use diet soda or light beer. It is less flavorful. Just add your meat to the bag, squeeze out any excess air, and keep it in the refrigerator for 6 to 8 hours or overnight.

MODIFIED PAUL KIRK MARINADE

Makes about 1½ cups

3 tablespoons dried Italian seasoning

2 tablespoons sea salt or kosher salt

2 tablespoons sugar

2 tablespoons granulated garlic

2 tablespoons dry mustard

1 tablespoon black pepper

¼ cup balsamic vinegar

2 tablespoons lemon juice concentrate, thawed

2 tablespoons lime juice concentrate, thawed

¼ cup olive oil

¼ cup ketchup

½ teaspoon Worcestershire sauce (optional)

½ teaspoon liquid smoke (optional)

Mix the Italian seasoning, salt, sugar, garlic, dry mustard, and pepper together in a glass, stainless-steel, or plastic bowl. Add the vinegar, lemon juice concentrate, and lime juice concentrate. Mix well and let stand for about 30 minutes to an hour. Beat or whisk in the oil and ketchup. Add the Worcestershire and liquid smoke, if using. Pour the marinade into a resealable 1-gallon freezer bag.

MARINADE FOR FLANK STEAK

Makes about 1½ cups

1 cup Burgundy wine

⅓ cup soy sauce

¼ cup vegetable oil

1 tablespoon chopped garlic

¼ teaspoon ground oregano

In a small bowl, whisk together the wine, soy sauce, oil, garlic, and oregano. Place the steaks in a 1-gallon resealable plastic bag. Pour in the marinade, seal the bag tightly, and turn the steaks to coat. Marinate overnight in the refrigerator.

STEAK OR CHICKEN MARINADE

Makes about 12 cups

1¾ cups plus 2 tablespoons soy sauce

1 cup apple cider vinegar

2½ cups sherry

6 cups pineapple juice

1½ cups sugar

Garlic salt

Combine all the ingredients and mix well. Marinate the meat overnight.

LEW MILLER

Lew says this is a great way to tenderize flank steak.

STEVE OWNBY

Steve Ownby is a member of the KCBS board of directors, as well as a judge and promoter. He helps put on a barbeque contest in Sevierville, Tennessee, home of Dolly Parton, and he always tells anyone who will listen that Sevierville is known for two things—and Dolly has both of them. Steve is often mistaken for the late Conway Twitty.

DON PRZYBYLA

This makes enough to marinate a 10- to 12-pound brisket.

DON'S BEER MARINADE

Makes about 2½ cups

¼ cup packed dark brown sugar

¼ cup raw sugar, such as turbinado

1 teaspoon sea salt

1 teaspoon hickory powder

½ teaspoon black pepper

1 (12-ounce) can premium beer

½ cup fresh lemon juice

1 tablespoon liquid smoke, or to taste

½ cup salad oil

3 bay leaves

In a small bowl, mix together the brown sugar, raw sugar, salt, hickory powder, and pepper and set aside. In a large bowl, mix together the beer, lemon juice, and liquid smoke. Add the brown sugar mixture to the beer mixture and mix well. Slowly pour in the oil, beating rapidly and continuously to emulsify the mixture. Add the bay leaves.

Place your meat in the marinade in a sealed container and let it rest in the refrigerator for 6 to 8 hours or overnight, turning occasionally.

CITRUS MARINADE FOR CHICKEN

Makes a little more than 1 cup, plenty for 1 (3½- to 4½-pound chicken)

⅓ cup fresh lime juice

⅓ cup fresh orange juice

½ cup canola oil

1 teaspoon chicken bouillon granules

1 teaspoon garlic powder

2 teaspoons hot chili sauce, or more to taste

Combine all the ingredients in a jar. Shake. Pour the mixture over the chicken and marinate, covered or sealed in a plastic bag, for at least 2 hours in the refrigerator.

TENNESSEE BBQ CHICKEN BASTE

Makes about 3 cups

2 cups apple cider vinegar

¼ cup salt

⅔ cup canola or vegetable oil

2 tablespoons plus 2 teaspoons Tabasco or other hot sauce

2 tablespoons Worcestershire sauce

½ teaspoon garlic powder

Combine all the ingredients and mix well. Use the mixture to baste chicken as it cooks.

MARILYN CLEMENT

This is a great marinade for chicken. Grilled Asparagus (page 82) is a great accompaniment to citrus marinated chicken.

STEVE OWNBY

Steve sold his insurance agency to his brothers, retired, and has since taken up catering and promoting barbeque in east Tennessee. This baste goes especially well with Tennessee chickens.

SARAH KRAUSE

When the Krause family fires up the grill on their Fairway, Kansas, backyard deck, Alan could be set to grill eggplant, soy burgers, meat burgers, brats, hot dogs, kebabs, pineapple slices, peach halves, or chicken. Sarah's marinade works great with many different foods, even tofu, but is especially good with chicken or turkey thighs. This recipe makes enough for about 12 chicken thighs or 6 turkey thighs.

MARINADE FOR CHICKEN AND TURKEY

Makes 3¼ cups marinade

¼ cup Worcestershire sauce

¼ cup fresh lemon juice

¼ cup good-quality soy sauce

¼ cup canola oil

¼ cup cider vinegar

2 cups nondiet Mountain Dew, Coca-Cola, Pepsi, or Dr Pepper

Mix the Worcestershire, lemon juice, soy sauce, oil, vinegar, and Mountain Dew. Marinate the meat overnight in a resealable plastic bag before cooking.

GARY WELLS
BY REMUS POWERS, PHB

Gary Wells, cofounder of KCBS, earned a few nicknames over his two decades of KCBS leadership. For example, in the late 1980s and early 1990s, it seemed that every time Gary showed up for a contest it rained! We nicknamed him "Raindance."

Given his exemplary skills at resolving conflicts and growing a small group of organized barbeque enthusiasts into the world's largest barbeque organization, he could have also aptly been called "Esteemed Cat Herder." He led us with a steady hand, not losing sight of the mission.

Through it all, Gary also exemplified humility. Given his position as a founder and longtime president of the KCBS, he had unquestionable

DIVA Q CITRUS CHICKEN BRINE

Makes about 8½ cups, enough for about 36 chicken thighs

1½ cups freshly squeezed blood orange juice

6 cups water

¾ cup kosher salt

1 tablespoon black pepper

1 tablespoon ground ginger

1 cup pure Canadian maple syrup

1 teaspoon hot red pepper flakes

Combine all the ingredients in a large saucepan and bring the mixture to a boil over medium-high heat. Remove the pan from the heat and let it cool completely. Place your chicken in the brine, cover the pan, and let it marinate overnight in the refrigerator. Rinse the chicken before cooking it.

DANIELLE DIMOVSKI

This brine adds a nice citrus accent to the meat and makes it tender and juicy. This makes a large amount of brine. You can halve the ingredient quantities and marinate a smaller batch of chicken thighs, or you can make a full recipe and reserve half for basting the chicken. If you can't find blood oranges, use 1¼ cups orange juice and ¼ cup lime juice.

bragging rights. Yet he was not one to brag. Any who mistook his humility for weakness, however, quickly learned otherwise. He suffered no fools, nor was he intimidated by big egos, macho anger, greedy ambition, or narcissistic whining. He was fair. He was decisive. Like all of us, he could get frustrated and irritated, but he seldom lost his cool, and never in public.

FLAVORED BUTTERS

Butter is one of the best flavor enhancers there is.

Here are a few good recipes from Chef Paul's collection.

Just remember that the possibilities are endless and you can

experiment with a variety of seasonings and other additions

to make your own flavored butters.

ANCHO BUTTER

Makes about ¼ cup

4 tablespoons (½ stick)
unsalted butter, chilled

1 tablespoon steak sauce,
such as A.1. or Heinz 57

1 tablespoon ground ancho chile

½ teaspoon onion powder

½ teaspoon garlic powder

½ teaspoon sea salt

⅛ teaspoon cayenne

Put the butter, steak sauce, ground ancho chile, onion and garlic powders, salt, and cayenne into a food processor. Pulse the processor and scrape down the sides three or four times to ensure that all the ingredients are mixed in and well blended. Do not mix too long or the butter will melt. Remove the blended butter mixture from the processor and form a small loaf of the butter on a sheet of wax paper. Roll up the paper to form a neat roll of butter. Place in the refrigerator to firm up and blend the flavors, about 30 minutes to an hour.

SEASONED BUTTER BASTE

Makes about ¼ cup

4 tablespoons (½ stick) unsalted butter, softened

½ teaspoon paprika

¼ teaspoon onion salt

1 large clove garlic, pressed

In a grill-safe custard cup, blend all the ingredients. Place on the edge of the cooking grid or upper cooking rack. When the butter has melted, remove the dish from the grill and brush the butter on meats, seafood, fish, or vegetables during grilling.

ROSEMARY LEMON BUTTER FOR POULTRY OR LAMB

Makes about ¼ cup

1 teaspoon dried rosemary leaves, crushed

½ teaspoon grated lemon zest

4 tablespoons (½ stick) unsalted butter, softened

¼ teaspoon onion salt

1 large clove garlic, pressed

In a grill-safe custard cup, blend all the ingredients. Place on the edge of the cooking grid or upper cooking rack. When the butter has melted, remove the dish from the grill and brush the butter on poultry or lamb during grilling.

DILL LEMON BUTTER FOR SEAFOOD

Makes about ¼ cup

½ teaspoon dried dill weed

½ teaspoon grated lemon zest

4 tablespoons (½ stick) unsalted butter, softened

¼ teaspoon onion salt

1 large clove garlic, pressed

In a grill-safe custard cup, blend all the ingredients. Place on the edge of the cooking grid or upper cooking rack. When the butter has melted, remove the dish from the grill and brush the butter on fish or seafood during grilling.

Note: *This is also great on steaks, baked potatoes, and vegetables, not to mention on a fluffy biscuit hot out of the oven.*

AL LAWSON

Al Lawson was one of the KCBS pioneers. He was a very good amateur cook, but he had to cook in the professional division because he built barbeque pits and it was perceived that he made his living selling barbeque pits. KCBS doesn't make that distinction now.

AL LAWSON

When it comes to barbeque recipes, Al was not one to keep secrets. He set a standard for sharing recipes and this is a keeper.

AL LAWSON'S DRY RIB SEASONING

Makes 1 cup

6 tablespoons salt

6 tablespoons sugar

1 tablespoon dry lemonade powder (such as Country Time), not sugar-free

2 tablespoons monosodium glutamate (MSG) (optional)

2½ tablespoons black pepper

1 tablespoon paprika

Combine all the ingredients in an airtight container and mix well. The mixture will keep, stored away from heat and light, for up to 6 months.

AL LAWSON'S DRY POULTRY SEASONING

Makes 1 cup

6 tablespoons salt

3 tablespoons black pepper

2 tablespoons monosodium glutamate (MSG) (optional)

2 tablespoons garlic powder

2 tablespoons ground bay leaves

1 tablespoon paprika

2 tablespoons dry mustard

Combine all the ingredients in an airtight container and mix well. The mixture will keep, stored away from heat, light, and moisture, for up to 6 months.

GINGER'S SWEET GLAZE RIB RUB

Makes about ½ cup, enough for 1 (3- to 4-pound) slab of ribs

¼ cup packed dark brown sugar

2 teaspoons Hungarian paprika

1 teaspoon garlic powder

1 teaspoon chili powder

1 teaspoon ground cumin

½ teaspoon cayenne

Pinch of ground cinnamon

Pinch of ground nutmeg

Pinch of ground allspice

Combine all the ingredients in an airtight container and mix well. The mixture will keep, stored away from heat, light, and moisture, for up to 6 months.

DON PRZYBYLA

Ginger is a barbeque friend of Don Przybyla. The large amount of brown sugar imparts a nice glaze to the ribs, as long as it is done low and slow.

MASON STEINBERG

Mason got this recipe in the 1950s, when he was crawling around Louisiana at the cost of his employer, the original "Good Old U.S. Government." That's right, "In the Army now." Mason says, "I like to use it on ribs and shoulder/butt when I want a Cajun-type flavor. The cayenne can be more according to one's taste. This recipe will do one slab, or one medium butt. For shoulder I would double it."

CRAWLIN' CAJUN BBQ RUB

Makes about ¼ cup

2 tablespoons onion powder

1½ tablespoons garlic powder

2 teaspoons white pepper

2 teaspoons black pepper

2 teaspoons salt

½ teaspoon cayenne, or to taste

1 teaspoon dry mustard

½ teaspoon dried oregano

½ teaspoon ground bay leaves

½ teaspoon dried thyme

Combine all the ingredients in an airtight container and mix well. The mixture can be stored, away from heat, light, and moisture, for up to 6 months.

Order of the Magic Mop

In barbeque jargon mops are a liquid baste applied during the cooking process or the basting tool itself. For purists the only acceptable mop has a wooden handle with a clump of cotton strings attached. We want the cotton mop to be attached with stainless-steel wire and a single nail, no glue. The handheld mop was invented for washing dishes. Today they are used for barbeque more than for dish washing.

The Magic Mop concept was born in a Memphis Piggly Wiggly. In 1987, Phil and Cheryl Litman and Ardie Davis were in town for the Memphis in May Barbecue and had stopped at the Piggly Wiggly on Winchester Avenue to browse for local barbeque products. They noticed an abundance of mops on display near the barbeque sauces and rubs and again near the charcoal briquettes and wood chips for smoking. Those mop treasures were selling for less than a dollar. There must have been twenty of them, and they bought them all. Buying up those mops became an annual tradition. In 1989 Phil and Ardie had the good fortune to meet the mops' creator, Mr. Gattuso, a true gentleman who was very enthusiastic about his product. "These handles are made of solid olive wood," he explained, "and this cotton is high-quality Egyptian cotton." He went on to note that he used no glue to attach the mop to the handle. "I use stainless-steel wire and a stainless-steel nail, no glue," he said. Right then and there Mr. Gattuso's mops inspired the creation of the Order of the Magic Mop.

Membership in the Order of the Magic Mop is by invitation only. You never know when it could happen to you. The only requirement for induction into the order is that a member of the order catches you doing something of merit for the benefit of better barbeque and humankind. No dues and no membership roster. Members live all over the USA, Canada, Australia, and Ireland. Some are celebrities. Most are salt-of-the-earth everyday people who are great at what they do and often pay it forward with a random act of kindness.

There's a simple induction ceremony. The inductee assumes a posture of reverence, with bowed head. Then, with a personalized Magic Mop, signed by two members of the order, the cotton end of the mop is placed on the inductee's right shoulder, left shoulder, and, finally, his or her head, as this litany is pronounced: "In the name of the steer, the hog, and the holy smoke, you are hereby inducted into the Order of the Magic Mop."

Sadly, we've lost track of Mr. Gattuso and can no longer find his mops. The Piggly Wiggly that sold his mops now sells mops made in China. When our supply of the Gattuso mops is gone, members of the order will have to find a worthy replacement or close the door to future prospective members.

JAY "THE SNAIL" VANTUYL

Jay, aka "the Hogfather," is a builder of specialty barbeque barrels. To make this sauce your own, you could substitute Worcestershire sauce for the soy sauce. Or instead of using tomato paste, you could substitute tomato sauce, ketchup, mustard, or mayonnaise. Snail tells us that mayo is the sleeper here. Try it and see for yourself.

SNAIL'S SIMPLE SAUCE

Makes about 8 cups

4 cups sugar

⅔ cup soy sauce

1⅔ cups white vinegar

½ cup water

2 (6-ounce) cans tomato paste

2 tablespoons coarsely ground black pepper

¼ cup garlic salt

2 teaspoons hot red pepper flakes

2 teaspoons celery seeds

1 teaspoon canning salt

Combine all the ingredients in a large stockpot over medium-high heat, stirring constantly to dissolve the seasonings. Simmer for about 30 minutes, stirring every 10 minutes or so to prevent scorching. (Or you could do like Snail and make this in a double boiler.) Discard the bay leaves after cooking.

BIG BATCH SNAIL'S SIMPLE SAUCE

Makes about 12 cups

5 pounds sugar

1⅓ cups soy sauce

3⅓ cups white vinegar

1 cup water

4 (6-ounce) cans tomato paste

1 (15-ounce) can tomato sauce

¼ cup coarsely ground black pepper

6 tablespoons garlic salt

1 tablespoon plus 1 teaspoon hot red pepper flakes

1 tablespoon celery seeds

3 tablespoons canning salt

Combine everything and cook it just as you would for the small batch (preceding recipe).

SNAIL'S GREAT GLAZE

Makes 1½ cups

1 cup sugar

¼ cup Kikkoman soy sauce

¼ cup Sprite soda

In the top of a double boiler over boiling water, combine all the ingredients and mix until the sugar dissolves and the mixture becomes fully liquefied.

JAY "THE SNAIL" VANTUYL

If you want to make a big batch of Snail's sauce, the ingredient list is a little different from that of the small batch. We think you'll like the small-batch version so much you'll want to make a big batch next time, so here's the recipe.

JAY "THE SNAIL" VANTUYL

This is one of the Hogfather's very special sauces and it's great with ribs and chicken. He wasn't going to give us the recipe, but we made him a deal he couldn't refuse.

MONTY SPRADLING

When you're looking for a party, stop by Monty's Voodoo Barbecue booth. Fun, beer, and barbeque get together with as much spirit as Mardi Gras. The team motto is "Eat the cook!" but we recommend Voodoo Ribs instead. Brush your spares or baby backs with Voodoo Glaze during the last 15 to 30 minutes of cooking and you'll be more than ready when neighbors shout, "Show me your ribs!"

VOODOO GLAZE

Makes about 2 cups

1 cup sugar

¾ cup Texas Pete Hot Sauce

¼ cup apple cider vinegar

¼ cup tomato paste

¼ cup Gulden's mustard or your favorite

1½ teaspoons minced garlic

1½ teaspoons kosher salt

1½ teaspoons black pepper

1½ teaspoons mustard seeds

1 teaspoon celery salt

2 bay leaves

Combine all the ingredients in a pot over low heat. Bring to a simmer and cook, stirring occasionally, until the sugar is dissolved. The glaze should be the consistency of thick syrup. Discard the bay leaves after cooking.

AMBERBOCK BEER SAUCE FOR WINGS

Makes about 3 cups

1 (12-ounce) bottle Michelob AmberBock beer or your own favorite

1 teaspoon onion powder

1 tablespoon chopped garlic

1 teaspoon Worcestershire sauce

1 tablespoon hot red pepper flakes

½ cup hot sauce

½ cup packed brown sugar

2 tablespoons white vinegar

1 tablespoon Dijon mustard

½ cup molasses

Combine all the sauce ingredients in a medium saucepan over medium heat and simmer for 20 minutes.

LEW MILLER

Either smoke or fry some wings until crisp, toss them in this sauce before serving, and enjoy with a cold one.

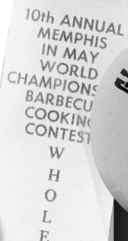

BILLY RODGERS

This is the recipe that Billy used in a barbeque contest that was held at Smoke 'N' Fire in Overland Park, Kansas, and sponsored by Steven Raichlen. Billy placed sixth using this sauce. Use it as a dipping sauce or glaze for any meat.

BIG BILLY'S VERY CHERRY DR PEPPER BARBEQUE SAUCE

Makes about 6½ cups

3 cups Heinz Chili Sauce

1 cup cherry Dr Pepper, allowed to go flat

1 (12- to 13-ounce) jar cherry preserves or jam

½ cup sugar

¼ cup honey

2 tablespoons molasses

¼ cup port vinegar

1 tablespoon salt

1 tablespoon granulated onion

1½ teaspoons granulated garlic

1 teaspoon ground coriander

½ teaspoon black pepper

¼ teaspoon cayenne

Mix all the ingredients except the cayenne together in a 2-quart stockpot. Bring to a low boil over medium-high heat. Reduce the heat to medium-low and simmer, uncovered, stirring often with a rubber spatula to prevent scorching, about 50 minutes. Stir in the cayenne. Transfer the sauce to a bowl and cool it completely.

KATHY'S PIG POWDER SAUCE

Makes about 5 cups

¼ cup peach pie filling (mashed to the consistency of Jell-O)

½ cup molasses

1 cup ketchup

1 cup cider vinegar

1 cup apple juice

1 cup packed dark brown sugar

1 cup Pig Powder or your favorite rub

Combine all the ingredients in a medium saucepan and warm them over medium heat until the brown sugar and Pig Powder are dissolved. Serve warm.

STRAWBERRY BBQ SAUCE

Makes about 5 cups

4 cups strawberries, chopped

½ cup chili sauce

¼ cup apple cider vinegar

3 cloves garlic, minced

In a large saucepan over medium heat, combine half of the strawberries, the chili sauce, vinegar, and garlic. Bring the mixture to a boil and simmer for 20 minutes to thicken. Add the remaining strawberries and cook just until heated through.

KATHLEEN TABB

This is a great sauce for dippin' your pig pickin'.

KENNA JO LAMBERTSEN

Kenna Jo created this recipe "to use a surplus of strawberries." She said it "brings a fresh and sweet take on traditional barbeque sauce." It's fantastic over pork or chicken, and it also makes a great sauce to serve with corn bread. Kenna Jo calls that "Strawberry BBQ Shortcake."

KEN MISHOE

Ken told us he eats a lot of barbeque sauce, so he thought he should try to make it healthier. He uses this at home when cooking for family and guests. You can freeze any extra in freezer bags and thaw it as needed.

3 X BBQ SAUCE

Makes about 4 quarts

2 cups raisins

2 cups water

4 cups apple cider vinegar

3 cups malt vinegar

8 (12-ounce) cans tomato paste

2 cups honey (optional; Add more Sugar Twin Brown sugar if honey is omitted.)

5 tablespoons frozen apple juice concentrate

¼ cup prepared yellow mustard

¼ cup liquid smoke

¼ cup Worcestershire sauce

¼ cup prepared instant coffee

2 tablespoons olive oil or canola oil

2 tablespoons fresh lemon juice

2 tablespoons molasses

1 tablespoon fresh lime juice

1 tablespoon bourbon

1 tablespoon rum

3 dashes Tabasco or your favorite hot sauce

3 cups Sugar Twin Granulated Brown Sugar

6 tablespoons sodium-free salt (potassium chloride)

3 tablespoons onion powder

1 tablespoon ground turmeric

Combine the raisins and water in a blender and purée into a paste.

Combine the raisin purée and the rest of the ingredients in the order given in a large saucepan. Bring the mixture to a boil, then lower the heat and simmer for 20 minutes. Cover the pan, remove it from the heat, and let the sauce cool. Refrigerate any leftovers.

ADAM'S RIBBERS' SPICY BARBEQUE SAUCE

Makes about 3 cups

1½ tablespoons olive oil

1 large yellow onion, chopped

1 tablespoon minced garlic

1¼ cups jarred chili sauce

⅓ cup tomato paste

¼ cup Worcestershire sauce

¼ cup red wine vinegar

¼ cup honey

1 tablespoon fresh lemon juice

1½ teaspoons hot sauce, preferably Tabasco

1 tablespoon dried oregano

½ teaspoon hot red pepper flakes

Heat the olive oil in a medium sauté pan and sauté the onion and garlic until tender, about 5 minutes. Stir in the remaining ingredients and bring to a boil over medium-high heat. Reduce the heat to low and simmer for 30 minutes. Remove from the heat and brush the sauce on your food while grilling.

JENNIFER B. STANLEY

In Jennifer's barbeque mystery novel *Stiffs and Swine*, one of the competition teams has good luck with this sauce. For an even spicier sauce, add more hot red pepper.

SEASONINGS: MARINADES, BRINES, RUBS, BASTES, PASTES, AND SAUCES

235

DESSERTS

Some think that if the barbeque is fantastic, who needs dessert? But many KCBS members—especially the judges—are always at the ready to tickle their sweet tooth. After judging a minimum of twenty-four portions of sanctioned meats, plus side dishes, sauces, and Anything Butt entries, you'd think the judges had reached capacity.

Yet they're ready to "bring on the dessert!"

There's more than enough here to make your sweet tooth tweet with delight. Mary Beth Lasseter's groundbreaking Valomilk Cookies and Pies, Mary Anne's Warm Chocolate Mud Pudding from Matthew Shropshall, and Dawn Endrijaitis's Ooey-Gooey Cake will please any fussy palate—as will the many other outstanding sweet treats we selected for this chapter. Some have won the dessert category in a contest or two. All are, in our judgment, winners!

DREW VOLPE

Drew told us, "My recipe has been refined over the years, and I really enjoy it. It's a great finisher to an afternoon barbeque." We wholeheartedly agree! You can substitute a premade crust in a pinch.

BOURBON SWEET POTATO PIE

Makes 1 (9-inch) pie

1 pound 3 ounces (about 4 medium) sweet potatoes

CRUST

5 ounces vanilla wafers (about ½ box)

2 tablespoons sugar

5 tablespoons unsalted butter

½ shot bourbon

FILLING

8 tablespoons (1 stick) butter

1 cup sugar

¼ teaspoon ground cinnamon

1 teaspoon ground nutmeg

½ cup whole milk

1 shot bourbon (Maker's Mark, Elijah Craig, Jim Beam, or your favorite)

Peel and cook the potatoes. Drew usually cuts them into 1-inch cubes and steams them until tender. The potatoes are done when a fork stuck into them goes in easily; they should not fall apart.

Put the potatoes into a large mixing bowl and mash them with a potato masher until smooth. You do not want to whip them or make them too smooth (as you would with a pumpkin pie). This can be done a day ahead of time; store, covered with plastic wrap, in the refrigerator.

Then start on the crust. Preheat the oven to 325°F. Crush the wafers into crumbs by placing them in a large plastic bag and crushing them with a rolling pin. This can also be done with 30 seconds in a food processor (though that's less fun). Place the crumbs in a large bowl and whisk in the sugar until thoroughly combined. Melt the 5 tablespoons of butter in the microwave and then add the bourbon to it. Slowly drizzle the butter and bourbon mixture over the crumbs as you whisk them to evenly distribute the butter. Once you have a consistent mixture, press the crumbs into the pie plate using your thumb or the back of a spoon so there's an even layer over the whole surface and up to just shy of the top of the plate.

Bake the crust until it begins to brown (about 15 minutes), then remove it from the oven and allow it to cool. Increase the oven temperature to 375°F.

To make the filling, melt the stick of butter and pour it and the other ingredients into the bowl with the potatoes. Stir until well mixed and then pour the mixture into the cooled crust. Bake until a toothpick inserted into the center comes out dry, 30 to 45 minutes. It's best served warm.

RICK BROWNE, PHB

Here's Rick's version of a very popular and unique spin on traditional apple pie. It's cooked in a 9-inch metal pie pan on the grill in a brown paper bag. Although in this recipe Rick calls for removing the pie from the bag before serving, he is also on record as liking to "bring the bag right to the table on a serving tray, tear open the bag, and enjoy the reaction." Regardless of your presentation, this pie is a guaranteed hit.

RICK BROWNE'S BROWN BAG APPLE PIE

Serves 6 to 8

3 cups plus 2 tablespoons all-purpose flour

½ teaspoon salt

½ cup solid white vegetable shortening

5 tablespoons ice water

¼ cup granulated sugar

½ teaspoon ground nutmeg

1 teaspoon ground cinnamon

⅛ teaspoon ground cloves

2 tablespoons fresh lemon juice

8 cups peeled, cored, and sliced apples

½ cup firmly packed brown sugar

5⅓ tablespoons unsalted butter

Vanilla ice cream, for serving (optional)

Extra-sharp cheddar cheese, thickly sliced, for serving (optional)

Preheat a charcoal or gas grill to 400°F.

In a mixing bowl, combine 2½ cups of the flour, the salt, and the shortening. Use 2 forks or a pastry blender to cut in the shortening until the mixture resembles coarse crumbs. Stir in the water a little at a time, until the dough forms a ball.

On a lightly floured surface, roll out the dough to an 11- or 12-inch round and fit it into a 9-inch pie pan, fluting the edges.

In a large bowl, combine the sugar, 2 tablespoons of the remaining flour, the nutmeg, cinnamon, cloves, and lemon juice. Add the apples, stirring to coat. Transfer the apple mixture to the pie pan, smoothing out the filling; set aside.

To prepare the topping, in a medium bowl, combine the brown sugar and the remaining ½ cup of flour. Using two knives or a pastry blender, cut in the butter until the mixture resembles coarse crumbs. Sprinkle the topping evenly over the apple filling.

Place the pie in a brown paper bag and transfer the bag to a baking sheet; loosely fold the top of the bag under the pie. If you don't have a cookie or baking sheet, cut 3 large pieces of heavy-duty aluminum foil and cover the grill with this triple layer of foil. Transfer to the grill rack over direct heat. Close the grill lid and cook the pie until the apples are tender, 50 minutes to an hour.

Carefully remove the pie from the bag, avoiding the hot steam when you open the bag. Serve with generous scoops of ice cream and slices of cheddar cheese.

Reprinted with permission from the author from *The Best Barbecue on Earth* (Ten Speed Press, 2008).

DESSERTS

WILLIAM WRIGHT

Big Will and his Will Deal Catering and BBQ Company out of Topeka, Kansas, have garnered honors in all categories at KCBS-sanctioned contests, including the American Royal and the Great American Barbecue. When Will offered to share this recipe for his award-winning cheesecake, we were thrilled. Will's generosity goes beyond the barbeque pit and the kitchen. He shares recipes and mentors aspiring cooks. He donates his time and expertise in community service. Big. Bold. Generous. That's Big Will. That's this cheesecake.

BIG WILL'S TRIPLE-CHOCOLATE CHEESECAKE

Makes 1 (9-inch) cheesecake

CRUST

3 cups Oreo cookie crumbs

¼ cup sugar

8 tablespoons (1 stick) butter, melted

FILLING

3 (8-ounce) packages Philadelphia cream cheese (don't skimp), softened

1 (8-ounce) package mascarpone cheese, softened

2 (14-ounce) cans Eagle brand sweetened condensed milk

1 cup Hershey's chocolate syrup

1 cup Hershey's cocoa powder

½ cup Ovaltine mix

1 cup sugar

2 tablespoons real vanilla extract

3 large eggs

Preheat the oven to 350°F. To make the crust, combine the cookie crumbs, sugar, and melted butter in a large bowl and mix with your hands until the cookie crumbs start to get sticky; then press the mixture into a 9-inch springform pan or silicone cake pan. Bake for 10 minutes; remove from the oven and cool on a wire rack.

Reduce the oven temperature to 300°F. To make the filling, place the cream cheese and mascarpone cheese in a stand mixer fitted with a paddle attachment and mix until smooth. Add the sweetened condensed milk, chocolate syrup, cocoa powder, Ovaltine, sugar, and vanilla; mix until incorporated. Add the eggs one at a time, allowing each one to incorporate well before adding another. Mix for 10 minutes at low speed, scraping the bowl often. Pour the filling into the pan and bake for 1 hour and 20 minutes.

Turn off the oven, but leave the pan in the oven for 1 hour to cool. After the cheesecake cools, place it in the freezer to chill for at least 4 hours or overnight. Remove the cheesecake from the pan while frozen, allow it to sit for 20 minutes, slice, and enjoy.

POUND CAKE SAUCE

Makes about 3½ cups

8 tablespoons (1 stick) butter

1½ cups Malibu rum or dark rum

1 cup packed brown sugar

½ cup chopped pecans

1 cup sliced fruit, such as bananas, strawberries, or pineapple

Combine the butter, rum, and brown sugar in a medium saucepan over medium heat and cook, stirring often, until the sugar dissolves. Stir in the pecans and fruit.

LEW MILLER

This is a great sauce to serve over toasted pound cake slices topped with ice cream, whipped cream, or whipped topping.

NO-BAKE COOKIES

Makes 3 to 4 dozen

2 cups sugar

¼ cup unsweetened cocoa

½ cup milk

8 tablespoons (1 stick) margarine

1 teaspoon vanilla extract

½ cup peanut butter

4 cups quick rolled oats

Combine the sugar, cocoa, milk, and margarine in a large saucepan. Cook over medium heat until the mixture begins to boil. Bring to a hard boil for 1 minute; then remove from the heat. Cool for 1 minute; then add the vanilla, peanut butter, and oats, stirring well. Drop by teaspoons onto wax paper and cool.

KELLY CAIN

This is one of Kelly's favorite recipes and is a big hit with family and friends. She has tweaked it over time, and the result is these fantastic, easy-to-make cookies.

PHIL AND ROSEMARY MORROW, AM AND PM SMOKERS

Phil and Rosemary told us that for all the effort this takes to put together, if you follow the directions, the reward will be like a first-place ribbon.

BLUEBERRY AND WHITE CHOCOLATE CHEESECAKE

Makes 1 (9-inch) cheesecake

CRUST

1½ cups crumbs from Oreo cookies (filling removed)

5⅓ tablespoons butter, melted

FILLING

½ cup blueberry preserves

4 (8-ounce) packages cream cheese, softened

1¼ cups sugar

½ cup sour cream

2 teaspoons vanilla extract

5 eggs

4 ounces white chocolate, chopped into chunks, plus 2 ounces white chocolate, shaved, for garnish (optional)

2 cups blueberry syrup, reduced (by about half) until thickened, for garnish

Preheat the oven to 475°F. Line the bottom and sides of a 9-inch springform pan with parchment paper. Create a water bath by placing a large pan filled with about ½ inch of water into the oven while it preheats.

Put the chocolate cookie crumbs into a medium bowl. Mix in the melted butter and stir until the crumbs are moistened evenly. Press the crumbs into the prepared pan. Use the bottom of a drinking glass to press the crumb mixture flat into the bottom of the pan and about two-thirds of the way up the sides.

Wrap a large piece of heavy-duty aluminum foil around the bottom of the pan to keep the cheesecake dry in the water bath. Put the crust in your freezer until the filling is done.

Put the blueberry preserves into a small bowl and stir to loosen, leaving the blueberry pieces intact. In a large mixing bowl, use an electric mixer to combine the cream cheese with the sugar, sour cream, and vanilla. Mix for a couple minutes, or until the ingredients are smooth and creamy. Be sure to scrape down the sides of the bowl. Whisk the eggs in a medium bowl and then add them to the cream cheese mixture. Blend the mixture just enough to incorporate the eggs.

Remove the crust from the freezer and sprinkle the 4 ounces of white chocolate chunks onto the bottom of the crust. Pour half of the cream cheese filling into the crust. Drizzle the blueberry preserves over the entire surface of the filling. Use a butter knife to swirl the blueberry preserves into the cream cheese. Pour the other half of the filling into the crust and spread it evenly.

Carefully place the cheesecake in the water bath in the oven. Bake for 12 minutes; then turn the oven down to 350°F and bake for 50 minutes to 1 hour, or until the top of the cheesecake turns a light brown or tan color. Remove the cheesecake from the oven to cool.

When the cheesecake is cool, remove it from the water bath, cover it with foil, and chill it in the refrigerator for at least 4 hours. Before serving, sprinkle the entire top surface of the cheesecake with the 2 ounces of shaved white chocolate. Slice the cheesecake and place each piece on individual serving plates, then garnish with a drizzle of reduced blueberry syrup.

Fred tells us this recipe is well over a century old. Note that there are no spices and not even any vanilla. Fred's wife, Jill Sauceman, learned the recipe from her grandmother, Nevada Parker Derting, who lived at the foot of Clinch Mountain in the southwestern corner of Virginia. Jill is the only grandchild who makes the cake. Its ingredients are simple—right off the farm and the shelf. Its adornments— scalloped edges, fork pricks, and sprinkled sugar—are elegant in their simplicity. This is the dessert perhaps most closely identified with the mountains of southern Appalachia, but because of the work involved, it's rarely found on restaurant menus. Its thin layers and their consistency are reminiscent of the tortes of

continued on page 247

DRIED APPLE STACK CAKE

Makes 1 (8- or 9-inch) cake

1 pound dried tart apples

½ cup sorghum syrup

½ cup sugar, plus sugar for sprinkling

½ cup buttermilk

1 egg

1 teaspoon baking soda

1 teaspoon baking powder

½ teaspoon salt

⅓ cup solid white vegetable shortening

About 4½ cups White Lily flour or cake flour, plus enough for flouring the board

In a saucepan, cover the dried apples with water and cook over medium-low heat until most of the water is absorbed and the apples break up when stirred. If the apples are not soft enough to break up, add more water and keep cooking. If desired, add a tablespoon or so of sugar or to taste. Cool the mixture and run the apples through a sieve or food mill to produce a smooth sauce. Set the filling aside.

Preheat the oven to 400°F. Grease enough baking sheets to hold the number of 8- or 9-inch layers you want to bake. Combine the sugar, buttermilk, egg, baking soda, baking powder, salt, shortening, and flour in a large bowl and mix well. The dough should be the consistency of stiff cookie dough. Separate the dough into 5 to 7 balls, depending on how many layers you want. Roll each ball of dough to a ⅛- or ¼-inch thickness. Cut into 8- or 9-inch rounds. Nevada Derting used a pie pan with a scalloped edge to cut out the

Germany, and central Europe may have been the cake's origin. In the mountains of the American South, it was often served as a wedding cake, with neighbors taking individual layers to the home of the bride. Dried Apple Stack Cake is a good barbeque-ending dessert, since it's not overly sweet or heavy. It must be made ahead of time, though, since it has to "cure" for about 3 days. This recipe first appeared in volume one of Fred's book series *The Place Setting: Timeless Tastes of the Mountain South, from Bright Hope to Frog Level.*

rounds. Prick each layer with a fork, making a nice design. Sprinkle individual layers with sugar and bake on greased baking sheets until golden brown, 5 to 8 minutes, depending on the thickness. Mrs. Derting sometimes baked her layers in iron skillets.

Cool the layers on baking racks. Save the prettiest layer for the top. Place the first layer on a cake plate. Divide the apple filling into enough equal portions to spread between the layers (but not on top). Spread a coating of cooked apples over the first layer to within ½ inch of the edge. Stack the other layers, alternating cake and apples and ending with a cake layer on top. Store, covered, in a cool place for several days before serving.

DAWN ENDRIJAITIS

This cake recipe has been in Dawn's family for years. She can remember her grandmother making this cake for brunch when Dawn was younger. She added the frosting a few years back, and it complements the cake nicely. With or without the frosting, it is wonderful.

EASY PINEAPPLE CAKE WITH CREAM CHEESE FROSTING

Makes 1 (9 by 13-inch) cake

CAKE

2 cups sugar

2 cups all-purpose flour

2 teaspoons baking soda

2 eggs

1 (20-ounce) can crushed pineapple, undrained

FROSTING

1 (8-ounce) package cream cheese, softened

4 tablespoons (½ stick) butter

1¾ cups confectioners' sugar, sifted

1 teaspoon vanilla extract

Preheat the oven to 335°F. Grease a 9 by 13-inch pan.

To make the cake, mix all the cake ingredients together, stir until the dry ingredients are moistened and incorporated, and pour the batter into the prepared pan. Bake for 40 minutes, or until a toothpick inserted in the center of the cake comes out clean.

To make the frosting, with an electric mixer on medium speed, beat the cream cheese and butter together in a large bowl until smooth. Gradually mix in the confectioners' sugar, beating until smooth, and stir in the vanilla. Spread on the cake while still warm.

CHOP SUEY CAKE

Makes 1 (9 by 13-inch) cake

CAKE

2 cups all-purpose flour

2 teaspoons baking soda

2 cups sugar

2 eggs

¾ cup chopped pecans

1 (20-ounce) can crushed pineapple, undrained

FROSTING

1 (8-ounce) package cream cheese, softened

8 tablespoons (1 stick) margarine or butter, softened

1¾ cups confectioners' sugar, sifted

½ teaspoon vanilla extract

Preheat the oven to 350°F. Grease a 9 by 13-inch pan.

In a large bowl, combine all the cake ingredients and mix well. Pour the batter into the prepared pan and bake for 35 minutes, or until a toothpick inserted in the center comes out clean.

To make the frosting, beat the cream cheese and margarine together in a large bowl until smooth. Gradually mix in the confectioners' sugar, beating until smooth, and stir in the vanilla. Spread on the cake while still warm.

CONTRIBUTOR UNKNOWN

A lot of KCBS members sent us their favorite recipes for this book. Unfortunately, the name of the contributor for this one eludes us, but it sounds good, so here it is. Thanks to the unsung person who sent it!

DAWN ENDRIJAITIS

This delicious dessert is the epitome of "too much of a good thing." Dawn often serves this dessert for family gatherings because it is so rich a little goes a long way. It's best served warm with a large glass of milk!

OOEY-GOOEY CAKE

Makes 1 (9 by 13-inch) cake

1 (18.25-ounce) box yellow cake mix

⅓ cup canola or vegetable oil

2 eggs

2 cups semisweet chocolate chips

1 cup white chocolate chips

1 cup toffee bits

1 (14-ounce) package caramels

1 (14-ounce) can sweetened condensed milk

Preheat the oven to 350°F. Grease a 9 by 13-inch pan.

In a large bowl, blend together the cake mix, oil, and eggs. The consistency will be very thick. Stir in the semisweet chips, white chocolate chips, and toffee bits. Pour half of the batter into the prepared pan and bake for 10 minutes. Meanwhile, melt the caramels with the sweetened condensed milk in a medium saucepan over medium-low heat until smooth, stirring often. Remove the cake mixture from the oven and pour the caramel mixture over it. Drop spoonfuls of the remaining half of the cake mixture over the melted caramel and bake for 20 to 25 minutes. Serve warm or cool it and cut it into squares.

GRILLED MIXED FRUIT

Serves 4

4 tablespoons (½ stick) salted butter

⅓ cup extra virgin olive oil

2 medium peaches

2 large apricots

4 medium plums

2 tablespoons cinnamon sugar

Vanilla ice cream

Prepare the grill for medium-high cooking over direct heat. In a saucepan, melt the butter and add the olive oil. Stir to combine. Slice the fruits in half and remove the pits (Gordon uses an old spoon that he's sharpened the tip of). Brush the fruit with the butter and oil mixture and place it flat side down on the grill. Usually, 3 or 4 minutes will produce nice grill marks and fruit that is softened about halfway through. Watch carefully as you cook, as the natural sugar in the fruit will burn easily if you aren't careful. Turn and cook on the round side for a couple of minutes to complete the process.

Place a few pieces of the grilled fruit in shallow bowls, sprinkle lightly with the cinnamon sugar, and top with vanilla ice cream.

GORDON HUBBELL

One night before a contest, Gordon watched a guy, on a dare from a friend, try to grill a banana. "He chose a nice soft one," Gordon told us, "peeled it, slathered a little cooking oil on it, then plopped it on the grid over super-hot coals. Instead of grilling into a tender flavorful morsel, the banana slipped halfway through the grate, where it couldn't be retrieved. Some of the fruit dropped onto the coals and was incinerated. The rest of the banana was inedible goo." Gordon recommends grilling fruits that are "just ripe," meaning "fruit that is tender and just ripe, not stuff ready for the compost pile." Gordon also suggests using really good ice cream. He says the cheap stuff turns into white, sweet water.

DESSERTS

251

MATTHEW SHROPSHALL

Matthew is a member of the Best British BBQ Cookery Team, Company and Trade. The team has competed in international cooking competitions worldwide ten times, with more than thirty barbeque awards, including 2007 Best International Team and a bronze medal in Culinary Olympics 2009. Matthew is a Certified KCBS Judge and a British barbeque celebrity chef. Here's his story about how this recipe got its name:

"On a Continental Airlines flight from the United Kingdom to the USA, an airline staffer showed great interest in our group of Brits traveling over the pond to compete in the country known for 'Kings of BBQ.' Mary Anne was her name, and she was from Nashville. I told her that the recipe

continued on page 253

MARY ANNE'S WARM CHOCOLATE MUD PUDDING

Serves 8

2 tablespoons butter

4 eggs

¼ cup superfine sugar, plus ¼ cup for the meringue

2 cups whole or skim milk

1 whole vanilla bean

1 cup sponge cake crumbs

6 ounces semisweet chocolate, melted

Toffee bits, for garnish

Chocolate shavings, for garnish

Your favorite cookies, for serving

Preheat the oven to 350°F. Coat a 9-inch pie pan with the butter and set it aside.

Separate 3 of the eggs, placing the yolks in a medium bowl and the whites in a large mixing bowl. Set the whites aside. Add the fourth egg to the 3 yolks and briefly whisk this egg mixture with the ¼ cup of the superfine sugar. Set aside while you heat the milk.

Place the milk and vanilla bean in a medium saucepan and bring to a boil over medium heat. Remove the pan from the heat, remove the vanilla bean, and pour the milk into the egg and sugar mixture. Whisk well.

Place the cake crumbs in the bottom of the prepared pan. Strain the pudding mixture onto the crumbs. You will need to bake the pudding in a water bath. To do that, place the pie pan in a 9 by 13-inch baking dish and add enough boiling water to come halfway up the sides of the pie pan. Bake for about 30 minutes, or until set. Allow to cool in the water bath.

When the pudding is cool, preheat the broiler. Beat the egg whites with a mixer on medium-low speed until they look frothy. Increase the speed to medium and slowly add the ¼ cup sugar a little at a time. Beat until soft peaks form. Touch the top of the meringue lightly with a spoon or spatula; it should form peaks that don't quite stay up straight.

Spread the melted chocolate over the cooled pudding. Using a large star tube, pipe the meringue over the top to cover the chocolate. Brown the meringue under the broiler. Garnish with toffee bits, chocolate shavings, and serve each portion with a cookie.

we were cooking for the contest was a chocolate mud pudding—a dessert she loved. After some 7 hours on the plane, and a free bottle of champagne, Mary Anne explained what Americans like to eat. 'Sweet, sweet, and more sweet,' she said. At that point I decided to name the dessert at the Jack after her. The British Barbecue Team thanks Mary Anne very much for her input."

When you cook your dessert in the pit, try to avoid too much smoke!

—BBQ tip by Matthew Shropshall, Master Chef from the British BBQ Team

DESSERTS

STEVE HOLBROOK

Steve found this recipe while rummaging in memorabilia related to his fellow Masonic Lodge member in Independence, Missouri, the late Harry S. Truman. In 2008 Steve spearheaded the lodge-sponsored "Old Timers BBQ Contest" in Independence in memory of Harry and good times past. The recipe Steve found was clipped from a magazine, no name or date, and attributed to Mrs. Harry S. Truman. If it is indeed her recipe, we think Bess would have approved of how Steve tweaked it. It is delicious served warm or chilled, with whipped cream or vanilla ice cream.

OZARK PUDDING

Serves 8

1 egg

¾ cup sugar

2 tablespoons all-purpose flour

1¼ teaspoons baking powder

⅓ teaspoon salt

¼ teaspoon baking soda

½ cup chopped pecans

½ cup peeled and diced Granny Smith apple

Preheat the oven to 350°F. Butter a 9-inch pie pan.

Beat the egg with the sugar until light. Sift the flour with the baking powder, salt, and baking soda. Add the egg mixture to the flour mixture and beat well. Stir in the pecans and apples.

Pour the mixture into the prepared pan and bake for 20 to 25 minutes. The pudding will rise very high, then fall when almost done.

INSTANT STICKY TOFFEE PUDDING

Serves 6

1 (8-ounce) container Cool Whip

1 tablespoons instant vanilla pudding powder

3 ounces Heath English Toffee Bits

Butterscotch or caramel sundae syrup, for serving

Whisk together the Cool Whip and pudding. Fold in the toffee bits. Pour the mixture into 6 (3-ounce) dessert cups. Drizzle the syrup over the top of each. Chill 4 to 6 hours or overnight before serving.

MIKE LAKE, PHB, AND THERESA LAKE

Mike is the president of the board of the KCBS. He's a Contest Rep, a Master Certified Judge, and a Judge Instructor. He's also in the livestock hauling business and sponsors a barbeque contest in Illinois. Theresa fixes this to sweeten him up. You can find Heath English Toffee Bits in the baking aisle with the chocolate chips.

KELL PHELPS

According to Kell, there is no need to use precise measurements for this, as practice will make these perfect! He admitted these can be done in the oven on medium heat, but frankly, he doesn't think they are quite as good as when they're grilled.

GRILLED BANANA SPLIT

Serves 6

6 underripe bananas

2 (1.55-ounce) Hershey's chocolate bars, broken into small pieces

1 quart vanilla ice cream or your favorite flavor

¼ cup chopped peanuts or pecans (optional)

Prepare a grill to cook at medium heat.

Using a sharp knife and leaving the peels intact, slit the bananas from end to end so the flat part is on the bottom. Go deep into the banana, but do not cut the bottom peeling, as this will be your bowl for the finished product. Force the slits wide open by pressing on the ends of the slit banana and stuff it with the chocolate pieces. The amount you put into each banana is usually determined by the size of the banana.

Wrap the bananas in foil. Place them on the grill for about 10 minutes, or until the chocolate is melted. Open the foil and use this as a catchall to keep from making too big a mess. Add the vanilla ice cream and top it off with chopped nuts if desired.

BANANA NUT BREAD

Makes 1 loaf

8 tablespoons (1 stick) butter

1 cup sugar

2 eggs, lightly beaten

2 cups all-purpose flour

1 teaspoon baking soda

Pinch of salt

1 tablespoon sour milk or buttermilk

3 bananas, mashed (1 cup)

1 cup chopped nuts

Preheat the oven to 350°F. Lightly grease a standard loaf pan.

In a large bowl, cream the butter and sugar. Add the beaten eggs and mix well. In a medium bowl, sift together the flour, baking soda, and salt. Stir the flour mixture into the butter mixture. Add the sour milk and mix well. Fold in the bananas and nuts. Transfer the batter to the prepared pan and bake for 1½ hours, or until a knife inserted in the center comes out clean.

DON PRZYBYLA

This is a good way to use your overripe bananas.

MARY BETH LASSETER

This recipe started with one Mary Beth found online, and she has tweaked it and made it her own. Mary Beth told us, "There's a lot of debate about the name for this dessert in my house. Some of us think that Valomilk will want to be the featured candy, and thus referring to a 'Moon Pie' will detract from the featured ingredient, even though the chocolate, marshmallow, and graham cracker elements clearly hark back to the age-old Moon Pie favorite. Others think we Valomilk lovers are being too sensitive. You decide." Mary Beth highly recommends doubling the Marshmallow Ice Cream quantities and making more than you need for the pie. It's delicious on its own, especially sprinkled with chopped Valomilks.

VALOMILK MOON PIE (OR VALOMILK ICE CREAM PIE)

Makes 1 (8- or 9-inch) pie

MARSHMALLOW ICE CREAM

5 ounces mini-marshmallows

1 cup half-and-half

1 tablespoon vanilla extract

1 cup whipping cream

PIE

1 (8- or 9-inch) graham cracker pie crust

8 Valomilk candies

Magic Shell chocolate, for garnish

Whipped topping or whipped cream, for garnish

Heat the marshmallows and half-and-half in a large saucepan over low heat until all the marshmallows are melted. Stir constantly to prevent scorching. After the mixture is smooth and combined, cool in the refrigerator for 20 to 30 minutes (or put the pot in an ice bath for 15 minutes to bring the mixture to slightly below room temperature). When cool, stir in the vanilla.

In a large mixing bowl with a mixer, beat the cream at medium speed until soft peaks form. Fold the whipped cream into the cooled marshmallow mixture. Add this ice cream mixture (it's not really a custard, since there are no eggs) to your ice cream maker and follow the manufacturer's instructions to chill the mixture to the soft-serve ice cream stage.

Spread half of the soft-serve marshmallow ice cream in the bottom of the pie crust. Layer the Valomilks on top of the ice cream. Cover the Valomilks (and fill to the top of the pie crust) with another layer of ice cream. Stash in the freezer until thoroughly frozen, about 2 hours. Drizzle the top of each pie slice with Magic Shell chocolate and top with a dollop of whipped topping.

Note: *Slicing the pie can be difficult, because the marshmallow hardens a bit when frozen, but letting it sit out for a minute or two (and using a good knife) will overcome the difficulty. Or Mary Beth's preferred method—again messy–is to put a layer of crumbled Valomilks, rather than whole Valomilks, between the ice cream layers. It's important to sprinkle the crushed Valomilks on top of the ice cream but not mix them in. When they're mixed with the ice cream, the marshmallows get cold, the Valomilks tend to clump together, and you don't get even distribution in the ice cream. If you use chopped Valomilks, chop them by hand. If you use a food processor to do the job, you'll be scrubbing the marshmallow goodness off the blades for days! If you'd prefer to stay away from a Moon Pie theme, the filling is also good in an Oreo crust, but a baked flaky pie crust just doesn't seem sweet enough for an ice cream dessert.*

THE PINK SATIN JACKET AS TOLD BY WILLIAM E. "BILLY BONES" WALL

Aside from the Red Laces (page 92), there is an item awarded to team members who have "served time" for five years on the road. A pink satin jacket, embroidered with a red-and-pink logo, is awarded with proper ceremony at the end of the barbeque season. Some of the male members of the team have pointed out that pink didn't seem like appropriate attire for a "real man," but when another color was offered as an alternative, the "pink number" was gratefully accepted and given with appropriate tongue-in-cheek remarks to celebrate the occasion properly. I suspect many pink jackets are kept in closets out of reverence. These pink jackets inspire their proud owners. I'm sure that while showing the pink jacket to friends, comments like, "The audacity of that Billy Bones . . . To think I would keep such a thing and wear it, too!" are often heard. However, I know their true feelings.

DESSERTS

Reprinted with permission from the *National Barbecue News*, April 2005.

BRAD BARRETT

Flour tortillas make a wonderful platform for grilled desserts. Two tortillas form a sandwich that can be filled with sliced fruits and cheeses or in this case with a sweet ricotta cheese filling and chocolate morsels. This one hits all the sweet spots for a great grilled dessert, and it's an easy dessert that can be made several hours ahead. It's great served with a dollop of ice cream.

GRILLED CHOCOLATE RASPBERRY QUESADILLAS

Serves 2

1 (16-ounce) container whole-milk ricotta cheese

¾ cup confectioners' sugar, sifted

1 teaspoon vanilla extract

4 large flour tortillas

½ cup semisweet chocolate morsels

½ cup fresh raspberries

Prepare a grill to cook at medium heat (400°F).

Place the ricotta, confectioners' sugar, and vanilla in a food processor and process until smooth. Place a tortilla on a cutting board or rimless baking sheet. Spread a third of the filling on the tortilla. Sprinkle half of the semisweet morsels over the filling, then place another tortilla on top of the morsels. Spread a thin layer of filling on top. Cut the raspberries in half and arrange half of the raspberry halves on top of the filling. Add a few more chocolate morsels for color. Repeat with the remaining ingredients.

Use a grilling spray or wipe the raised rails with oil. Slide the quesadillas off the cutting boards or baking sheets onto the grill and close the lid. Cook for 3 to 4 minutes, then lift an edge to check the sear marks. If the sear marks are dark (almost black), give the quesadillas a quarter turn. If not, cook for 2 to 3 minutes more before giving them a quarter turn. Grill until the quesadillas feel firm and the tortillas are crispy. Let the quesadillas cool for 2 minutes, then cut and serve.

ROSEMARY'S FRUIT SALAD

Serves 10 to 12

1 (21-ounce) can peach pie filling

1 (8-ounce) can pineapple chunks, drained

1 (11-ounce) can mandarin oranges, drained

1 (1-pound) package frozen strawberries or
fresh strawberries (about 1 cup sliced)

2 medium bananas

In a large serving bowl, combine the peach pie filling, pineapple chunks, mandarin oranges, and strawberries; mix well and refrigerate overnight. Right before serving, slice the bananas, add them to the mix, and stir.

ROSEMARY MORROW, AM AND PM SMOKERS

Rosemary and her husband, Phil, love the barbeque circuit because they get to see our friends and share the pride that comes with being a proud member of the Kansas City Barbeque Society. They not only compete but also are KCBS Contest Representatives. Yes, they are the couple that wears the pig hats, pink pig suspenders, and don't forget those awesome pig shorts! Rosemary's fruit salad recipe is excellent served for breakfast or even as a light dessert. You could even serve it in waffle cone bowls with a little whipped cream as a topping. It is delicious.

DESSERTS

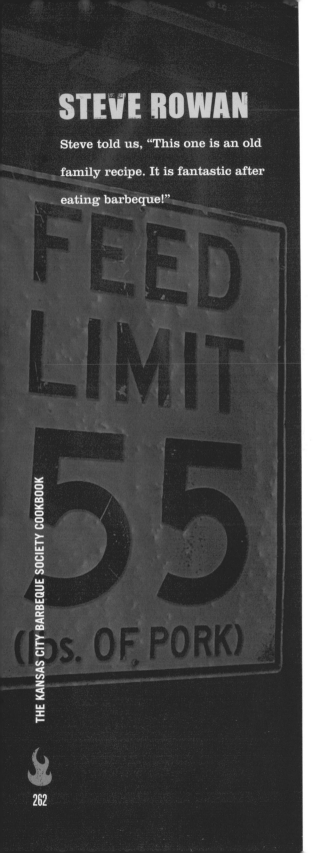

STEVE ROWAN

Steve told us, "This one is an old family recipe. It is fantastic after eating barbeque!"

BLUEBERRY DELIGHT

Serves 6 to 8

1 (15-ounce) can crushed pineapple

½ cup sugar

1 (3.5-ounce) package raspberry-flavored gelatin

1 (15-ounce) can blueberry pie filling

TOPPING

1 (8-ounce) package cream cheese, at room temperature

1 cup confectioners' sugar, sifted

2 cups whipped cream

Place the crushed pineapple in a medium saucepan and bring to a boil. Add the sugar and boil for 5 to 7 minutes. Remove from the heat and add the gelatin, stirring well to mix. Let it cool to room temperature and stir in the blueberry pie filling. Place in a 9 by 13-inch glass dish and refrigerate overnight.

Put the cream cheese into a bowl and beat in the confectioners' sugar with an electric mixer on medium speed. Use a spatula to fold in the whipped cream. Spread the topping mixture over the gelatin mixture and chill for at least 1 hour before serving.

SMOKIN' WALLY'S ABC (APPLE-BACON-CRANBERRY) PIE

Makes 1 (9-inch) pie

TOPPING

¼ cup all-purpose flour

¼ cup maple sugar

1½ tablespoons butter

6 cups peeled and sliced apples, preferably the tart-sweet Fuji

¾ cup sugar

2 tablespoons all-purpose flour

1 teaspoon apple pie spice

⅓ cup dried cranberries

1 (9-inch) pie crust

¾ pound thin-sliced bacon

Preheat your smoker (or your oven to 300°F).

To make the crumb topping, combine the ¼ cup of flour and the maple sugar and use a pastry blender or fork to cut in the butter until a crumblike texture forms. Set aside.

Then mix together the apples, sugar, 2 tablespoons flour, apple pie spice, and cranberries. Turn well to coat all sides of the apple slices. Place in the unbaked pastry shell. Sprinkle the crumb topping over the pie.

Use the bacon as your top crust. Weave the bacon strips over the top in a lattice pattern and seal the edges of the crust over the loose ends of the bacon.

If using your smoker, place the pie in a covered cast-iron Dutch oven and bake for 50 minutes, or until the juices are bubbly. Carefully remove the pie from the Dutch oven, place it directly in your smoker, and finish with your choice of smoking wood (Walt and Jo like hickory) for about 15 minutes. It is done when the bacon is crisp and done to your liking.

WALT VANSTONE AND JO LEVERETT

Walt and Jo made this pie in the Smokin' Red Dirt Cookoff in Enid, Oklahoma, in 2009. They told us, "We didn't realize that it did not have to be cooked on-site, so we had racked our brains (and looked through all of Grandma's recipes) for what we could cook on the smoker. And to say the least, we were very pleasantly surprised with the outcome. All our neighbors came over with spoons for the taste test on Friday night and raved about it; then the judges honored it with a prize on Saturday. It might even be better served à la mode."

VALOMILK COOKIES AND PIES

MARY BETH LASSETER

After completing the assignment we gave Mary Beth to develop some Valomilk recipes, here's her report: "So many pounds later, here I am, with no single recipe to offer you. Instead, I have two recipes, and one includes variations. Our family favorite still seems to be Valomilks straight out of the pack. It's just so hard to improve upon something that starts out so good in the first place!"

She submitted her Valomilk recipes to us with disclaimers and notes included in the recipe text and invited us to feature the one we liked best—or the one that best went with the other sweet treats in this chapter. Did we already have too many pies, in which case cookies would be the best bet? Or, can you never have too many pies—especially when the pie in this chapter is so tasty! In the end, we decided to include both.

One confession from Mary Beth: "I tried a number of baked pie variations, only to find that either the Valomilk milk chocolate got lost in the mix and the marshmallow hardened (if it was the center of the pie when baked) or the Valomilks scorched on top (since the pies had to cook so long to be done in the center). We had about 12 Valomilk casualties, with attempts at Valomilk brownie pie and Valomilk peanut butter pie, but—in the end—the majority of Valomilks made tasty treats for our tests."

VALOMILK PEANUT BUTTER COOKIES

Makes 12 large cookies

1 cup creamy peanut butter (Mary Beth uses Jif)

1 egg

1 cup sugar

4 Valomilks, chilled and then chopped into
one delicious gooey mess

MARY BETH LASSETER

This is a delicious twist on the classic peanut butter cookie, with melted chocolate and marshmallow goodness on top— or in the middle (see the note below).

Preheat the oven to 375°F.

Combine the peanut butter, egg, and sugar in a medium bowl and mix into a soft dough. Shape the dough into cookie balls about 2 inches in diameter and place them on a baking sheet. Gently and evenly flatten each dough ball with the tip of your finger. After flattening, make sure the cookies are at least 1 inch apart. Top each cookie with a spot of Valomilk crumbles, being very careful to keep the Valomilk in the center of the dough. (This is important because the milk chocolate will scorch if it melts off the cookie and onto the baking sheet.)

Bake for 10 to 12 minutes. Cool on a wire rack.

Note: *Rather than top each cookie with the Valomilk crumbles, Mary Beth prefers to secrete a bit of gooey Valomilk in the middle of each peanut butter dough ball before lightly flattening it. The cookies will look like plain peanut butter cookies on the outside, but when you bite inside, you will get chocolate and marshmallow goodness. This method is a little messier than the first, as the Valomilk gets all over your fingers, but Mary Beth notes "the cleanup [aka licking your fingers] at the end is a treat!" To make the prep work a little less messy, you could form the dough into 1-inch balls and gently flatten half of the dough balls on the baking sheet. Then top each with a little bit of crumbled Valomilks and place a second slightly flattened dough disk on top, pressing the edges gently to seal them.*

JAMES L. BOGLE

Serve this with vanilla ice cream for a sweet summer treat. You can substitute other in-season fruits for the peaches.

PEACH CRUMBLE

Serves 6

1 cup packed brown sugar

1 cup all-purpose flour

½ cup steel-cut oats

8 tablespoons (1 stick) butter, cut into cubes and softened

1 teaspoon ground cinnamon

1 teaspoon ground nutmeg

1 pound peaches, fresh or individual quick frozen

Preheat the oven to 350°F. Place a 9-inch square baking dish in the oven to warm while you prepare the rest of the ingredients.

In a large bowl, use a pastry blender or fork to combine the brown sugar, flour, oats, butter, cinnamon, and nutmeg.

Slice the peaches in half, remove the pits, and slice each peach into 6 to 8 wedges.

Remove the baking dish from the oven and layer the peaches across the bottom of the dish. Top with the crumble mixture and bake for 15 to 20 minutes, until the crumble is golden brown.

SKILLET PEACH COBBLER WITH BLACKBERRIES

Serves 6 to 8

1 (29-ounce) can sliced peaches, juice reserved

1 teaspoon cornstarch

8 tablespoons (1 stick) unsalted butter

1 cup self-rising flour

½ cup sugar

1 cup milk

1 teaspoon baking powder

¼ teaspoon ground nutmeg

½ cup fresh blackberries

Preheat the oven to 350°F.

Use a wire whisk to whip about ¼ cup of the peach syrup with the cornstarch until well blended. Set aside.

Place the butter in an 8- or 10-inch cast-iron skillet and melt over medium heat. In a large mixing bowl, combine the flour and sugar. Slowly pour in the milk, whisking constantly. Add the baking powder and continue to whip until well blended. The batter will appear to be slightly lumpy.

Once the butter is melted, remove the pan from the heat and allow the butter to cool slightly. Pour the batter directly into the skillet over the melted butter. Blend the dissolved cornstarch with the remaining syrup, peaches, and nutmeg. Gently fold in the blackberries. Pour the fruit mixture over the batter. Bake on the bottom shelf of the oven for 50 minutes to an hour, until the cobbler is golden brown. Cool slightly before serving.

STUART CARPENTER

Stu promises us, "These are darned good!" And Stu wouldn't lie.

DESSERTS

267

STUART CARPENTER

This is a fresh, delicious, and light summer dessert.

STU'S GRILLED PEACHES

Serves 6

6 canned peach halves

2 tablespoons sugar

2 tablespoons plus ¼ cup peach brandy, or more if desired

1 tablespoon fresh lemon juice

⅓ cup mascarpone cheese, at room temperature

¼ teaspoon vanilla extract

1 teaspoon ground cinnamon, or to taste, plus cinnamon for dusting

Dash of ground nutmeg

6 maraschino cherries or 6 tablespoons raspberry jam

Whipped cream, for topping (optional)

Prepare the grill to cook at medium-high heat.

Lightly brush the grill rack with olive oil. Place the peaches, cut side down, on the grill and do not move them while grilling. If you do, you will not have those great grill marks. Grill the peaches until the grill marks are formed and the peaches are slightly softened and heated through, 2 to 3 minutes.

Meanwhile, stir together the sugar, 2 tablespoons of the brandy, and the lemon juice in a medium bowl and set aside.

As the peaches are ready, remove them from the grill and place them in a metal pan. Top them with the brandy mixture and toss to coat. Set aside to marinate for 15 minutes, tossing occasionally.

Meanwhile, stir the mascarpone, vanilla, cinnamon, and nutmeg together in a small bowl to blend. Roll the cheese blend into 6 balls and lightly flatten them. Stuff each ball into the hollow of each peach half. Top the cheese mixture with either a maraschino cherry or raspberry jam.

Place the peaches back in the metal pan and place the pan on the grill. Spoon the ¼ cup of brandy over the peaches until it ignites. The peaches are done when the cheese is soft and the peaches are warm.

To serve, place the peaches on a plate and spoon the leftover pan juices over them. Dust with cinnamon and top with whipped cream if desired.

FORGOTTEN COOKIES

Makes about 24 cookies

2 egg whites

1 teaspoon vanilla extract

Dash of salt

⅔ cup sugar

1 cup chocolate chips

½ cup pecans, chopped

Preheat the oven to 350°F.

In a medium mixing bowl with an electric mixer on medium speed, beat the egg whites, vanilla, and salt, adding the sugar a little at a time while beating until stiff. Use a spatula to fold in the chocolate chips and nuts. Drop by teaspoonfuls onto a greased baking sheet. Place in the pan in the oven, turn off the heat, and leave the cookies in the oven overnight to bake and firm up.

TANA FRENSLEY-SHUPE, PH&

Sweets for the sweet—that's Tana. These meringue cookies are quick and easy. So easy, in fact, you can forget all about them (at least overnight). They're great to keep on hand for when a sugar craving hits.

MIKE DAVIS

Grilling cake isn't that common, but it is relatively easy. Just be careful not to burn it! This is a simple and unique dessert to serve your guests.

GRILLED ANGEL FOOD CAKE WITH FRUIT AND HOMEMADE CARAMEL SAUCE

Serves 10 to 12

1 store-bought or homemade angel food cake

Melted butter, for brushing

Fresh ripe fruit, such as pears, peaches, apples, or peeled bananas

Caramel sauce (homemade, recipe follows, or store-bought), for topping

Cool Whip, for topping

Set up your grill to cook at medium-high heat.

Cut the cake into slices. Brush each side of each slice with melted butter, put them on the grill, and toast on each side. Place the fruit on the grill and cook for 2 to 3 minutes, until it has grill marks.

Place the cake on individual serving plates, top with fruit, drizzle with caramel sauce, and finish with a dollop of Cool Whip. Enjoy.

HOMEMADE CARAMEL SAUCE

Makes about 1 cup

1 cup sugar

6 tablespoons butter

½ cup heavy whipping cream

Heat the sugar in a heavy 2- or 3-quart saucepan over moderately high heat. As the sugar begins to melt, stir vigorously with a whisk or wooden spoon. As soon as the sugar comes to a boil, stop stirring.

As soon as all the sugar crystals have melted (the liquid sugar should be dark amber in color), immediately add the butter to the pan. Whisk until the butter has melted.

Once the butter has melted, take the pan off the heat. Count to three, then slowly add the cream to the pan and continue to whisk to incorporate. When you add the butter and the cream, the mixture will foam up considerably. This is why you must use a pan that has at least a 2-quart (preferably 3-quart) capacity.

Whisk until the caramel sauce is smooth. Let it cool in the pan for a couple minutes and then pour it into a glass Mason jar and let sit to cool to room temperature.

PAUL KIRK, PHB

Make sure you have all of the ingredients ready to go before you start this. Making caramel is a fast process that cannot wait while you hunt around for ingredients. You can store the sauce in the refrigerator for up to 2 weeks and warm it just before serving.

AWARD WINNING

IT'S OVER!

One of our favorite ceramics artists has set aside a portion of her rural central Texas property for her "boneyard." Any piece of pottery that comes out of her kiln with the slightest imperfection goes to the boneyard instead of the marketplace. Friends and family who come to visit are welcome to take whatever they want.

We like to think of that ceramics boneyard as a metaphor for the boneyard in this section. To some cooks, items such as Koolicles, Sugar-Free Margaritas, and such don't fit into any category other than miscellaneous and may appear to be novelties instead of serious foods and beverages, but to us they are too good to be discarded. You be the judge.

THE
BONEYARD

BILLY RODGERS

Billy grew up in the Washington, D.C., area, where it was not uncommon to see kids coming from the corner store dipping their kosher dill or sour pickles into a cup of Kool-Aid. This recipe is a variation of that unique treat!

KOOLICLES

Makes 1 (46-ounce) jar

1 (46-ounce) jar whole dill pickles

2 cups water

1 pound sugar

2 (.13-ounce) packages unsweetened red Kool-Aid

Drain and discard half of the brine from the pickle jar. Mix the water with the sugar and Kool-Aid and stir until the sugar has completely dissolved. Pour enough into the jar so that the pickles are covered. If necessary, add more water. Cover the jar and refrigerate for at least 3 days before serving.

PICKLED JALAPEÑOS

Makes 1 (1-quart) jar

Enough jalapeños to pack the jar (at least 2 cups)

¼ cup olive oil

1 teaspoon salt

1 teaspoon pickling spice

1 cup white vinegar

Rinse the jalapeños with warm water; pat dry with paper towels. Pack the peppers tightly in pint or quart jars. Loosely packed peppers will float to the top and leave empty space in the bottom of the jar.

In a medium saucepan, combine ¼ cup water, the olive oil, salt, pickling spice, and vinegar. Heat to boiling. Pour into the jar of packed peppers until all are covered; seal the jar and simmer in a hot water bath for 10 minutes.

JOHN ROSS, PH8

These are a delicious garnish for a plate of barbeque. This recipe makes a quart jar full, but you can multiply it according to the number of peppers you have. For best results, keep the sealed jars in a cool place for 2 weeks before opening, and refrigerate after opening.

MICHAEL AND DIANE PHILLIPS

This is one of Michael's favorite accompaniments to grilled sausages or hot dogs. It's also good on hamburgers.

ZEE SMOKED FOODS COMPANY RELISH

Makes about 7 pints

2 cups diced red pepper

1 cup diced poblano pepper

1 cup diced tomatillo

1 cup diced Vidalia onion

¼ cup olive oil

Salt and black pepper

8 cups chopped dill pickles

¼ cup prepared horseradish

¼ cup maple syrup

¼ cup prepared yellow mustard

2 tablespoons pickle juice

2 tablespoons apple cider vinegar

Preheat the oven to 400°F and place a rack in the middle position.

Place the diced red pepper, poblano pepper, tomatillo, and onion in a 9 by 13-inch baking pan and spread them evenly. Drizzle the olive oil over the vegetables and toss to coat. Season with salt and pepper. Place the pan in the oven, uncovered, and bake for about 10 minutes. Stir the vegetables, and bake for another 10 minutes. Stir again, and bake for about 10 minutes more, or until the vegetables are fork-tender. Remove the vegetables from the oven and cool completely.

Once the vegetables are cool, combine with all the remaining ingredients in a nonreactive bowl and blend well. Chill for at least 2 hours or overnight in the refrigerator.

PEAR HONEY

Makes about 9 pints

12 large pears

2 cups sugar

1 (8-ounce) can crushed pineapple, with juice

Roughly chop the pears and run them through a Squeezo Strainer or a food mill to extract the juice. This separates the juice and pulp from the peelings, seeds, and skin. Add the sugar and crushed pineapple to the juice. Boil in a stainless-steel or other nonreactive pot until the mixture is reduced by about one-third. Pour it into hot, sterilized 1-pint canning jars, use a clean, damp cloth to wipe any drips from the rims of the jars, put the lids on, and let the pear honey cool.

MONTE JONES

Monte, aka Biscuits O'Bryan, gave us this recipe to go with plain homemade baking soda biscuits, served hot, or with made-from-scratch hot angel biscuits. Monte doesn't recommend the canned variety. He told us, "I made angel biscuits today for lunch, and my wife, my son, and I ate almost a pint of pear honey with them. It's really yummy." See Monte's recipe for Corny Cheese Chile Pepper Biscuits on page 105.

THE BONEYARD

277

KEN MISHOE

Ken made this recipe up. Sugar-free equals not sticky, not so filling, and lots fewer calories. Ice-cold margaritas are great when BBQ'n on a hot day—especially when grilling with Mexican rubs or grilling corn on the cob or peppers, stuffed or otherwise. They're also good served with Mexican pizza. Once you go this sugar-free margarita route, you'll never go back—whether you're dieting or not. They are just better. You won't use all of the Diet Mountain Dew.

SUGAR-FREE MARGARITAS

Makes 2 liters

1 (2-liter) bottle Diet Mountain Dew

1¾ cups tequila

2 scoops Country Time sugar-free lemonade

1 tablespoon orange extract

2 tablespoons fresh lime juice

2 tablespoons fresh lemon juice

Margarita salt (optional)

Pour the Diet Mountain Dew out of the bottle and into a separate container. In a small bowl, mix the tequila and lemonade powder well. Add the orange extract, lime juice, and lemon juice. Using a funnel, pour the tequila mixture into the Diet Mountain Dew bottle. Add enough Diet Mountain Dew to bring the liquid to the halfway mark. Cap the bottle tightly and shake well to mix it further and remove some carbonation. Fill the remainder of the bottle with more Diet Mountain Dew (or water if you like). Cap the bottle tightly and carefully shake it again. Chill before serving.

Wet the glass rims and dip them in margarita salt, if desired. Fill with the margarita mixture and serve.

Note: *This is slapstick funny if someone forgets to put the cap on the bottle well and shakes this recipe, forgetting about all the carbonation. When that happens, it's a good thing this is sugar-free and not sticky. Some folks like to cut back a couple of ounces on the tequila and replace those ounces with rum, which is also very nice. This recipe, like all margarita recipes, is not static. Play with it to taste.*

BARBEQUING AND GRILLING TERMS, A TO Z

180—A perfect score for appearance, tenderness, and taste in all meat categories; usually expressed with numbers.

Alder—A wood from the Pacific Northwest that is especially great for smoking salmon and other fish or meat.

Baby Backs—Pork ribs cut from the blade and center section of the loin.

Barbeque—As defined by the U.S. government, "Barbecued meats, such as product labeled 'Beef Barbecue' or 'Barbecue Pork,' shall be cooked by the direct action of dry heat resulting from the burning of hardwood or the hot coals therefrom for a sufficient period to assume the usual characteristics of a barbecued article, which include the formation of a brown crust on the surface and the rendering of surface fat. The product may be basted with a sauce during the cooking process. The weight of the barbecue meat shall not exceed 70 percent of the weight of the uncooked meat." 9 CFR, Part 319, Subpart C, Sec. 319.80 Revised as of January 1, 1985.

Barbeque Sauce—A flavored liquid blend of ingredients that enhances barbequed meats.

Baste—To moisten meat at intervals while cooking. The liquid used in this process is also called a *baste.*

Bear Claws—A pair of clawlike utensils used to "pull" meats, such as "pulled pork."

Big Rig—Large smoker, usually mounted on a trailer along with attendant bells and whistles per competition cooks' needs.

Bullet—A water smoker shaped like R2-D2.

CBJ—KCBS Certified Barbeque Judge.

Charcoal—Small pieces of wood or carbon that have been converted to char (burned in the absence of oxygen). The most common form is pulverized charcoal formed into briquettes. Also known as the second most famous invention of Henry Ford.

Charcoal Chimney—A round metal device with a handle used to light coals by igniting paper beneath the coals. Since no petroleum product is required, chimneys are an environmentally friendly way to light coals.

CMJ—KCBS Certified Master Judge.

Custom Smoker—A cooking unit custom-made to the specifications of the end user.

Direct Heat—Cooking directly over the heat source.

Dry—Barbequed meat that is covered with dry seasonings instead of liquid sauce. Most often used with reference to ribs, especially in Memphis.

Dry Rub—A blend of dry spices used to enhance the flavor of meats.

Entry Meats—Chicken, ribs (pork), pork (butt, shoulder, picnic), and beef brisket; required in all KCBS-sanctioned contests.

Fuel—Heat source—usually wood and/or charcoal.

Gas Grill—A grill whose primary fuel source is propane or natural gas. A no-no for KCBS competitions.

Glaze—A thin brushing of liquid to make the meat glisten (just before turning in a contest entry).

Grill—To cook food by direct or indirect heat on a barbeque grill. Cooking units are also called *grills.*

Hasty Bake—A smoker/oven developed by Grant Hasty of Tulsa, Oklahoma, in 1952.

Hibachi—An open brazier with a grate top. Commonly used for grilling steaks and other small portions of meat, vegetables, or fruit.

Hogmatism—A set of rigid doctrines based on the premise that the only true barbeque meat is pork.

Inject—A method of forcing flavored liquids into meats prior to the cooking process with a hollow needle attached to a syringelike plunger.

Instant-Read Thermometer—Inserted into barbequed meats to determine internal temperature at that moment.

Kamado—A ceramic egg-shaped cooking unit with a tight seal—a centuries-old Japanese design.

Kebab—Meat/fowl/fish and/or vegetables/fruit on a skewer for grilling.

Kiawe—Hawaiian version of mesquite.

Lighter Fluid—Petroleum-based chemicals in a can used to light charcoal. Leaves a terrible petroleum aftertaste if you do not let the coals "ash over" at least 80 percent.

Liquid Smoke—Wood smoke diffused in water. If you must use it, do so sparingly.

Log Book—A book in which you write notes on your barbeque cooking experience—meat, fuel, seasoning, technique, recipe, weather conditions, cooking time and temperature, and results.

Marinate—To soak meat in a mixture of liquid and spices prior to the cooking process.

Mop—A tool with cotton strands attached to a small broom-style handle that is used to baste meats. Silicone basting brushes are also used for this purpose. *Mop* may also refer to the act of basting with a mop and to the basting liquid.

Natural Lump Charcoal—Hardwood charcoal in its natural form. Burns cleaner and hotter than briquettes.

Open Brazier—An open grill with no lid, used for grilling.

Pellet—Compressed sawdust from hardwood or corncobs. Used in pellet smokers, which have an auger that automatically dispenses fuel into the cooker using a thermostatically controlled device.

Pelletheads—Barbeque jargon for cooks who prefer and use pellet cookers in barbeque cooking contests.

PETA—Acronym for People Eating Tasty Animals.

PhB—Doctor of Barbeque Philosophy, awarded by the Greasehouse University.

Pigot—One who fervently believes that the only true barbeque is pork barbeque.

Pig Tail—Metal rod with a curved hook at the end. Used for turning cuts of meat not easily handled with tongs.

Pit—Another name for the cooking unit.

Pretty Pig—A barbequed pig that is perfect in every detail. It is pretty in appearance—no flaws whatsoever such as torn or burnt skin or meat—with a golden, brown, or mahogany patina from the action of hardwood coals. All meat in a Pretty Pig is tender, with a perfect flavor balance of sweet meat and barbeque seasonings.

'Que—Shorter word for *barbeque*.

Rib Rack—Stainless-steel device for cooking ribs vertically to increase grill capacity.

Shiners—Ribs with exposed bones from improper cuts or overcooking.

Skinned Ribs—Ribs with the membrane next to the bony side removed.

Sop—Same as *mop*.

Spare—Ribs: The rib section from the belly with or without the brisket. A complete slab should contain eleven ribs.

Stick Burners—Barbeque jargon for cooks who use hardwood logs or chunks, sometimes with charcoal or briquettes, as their cooking fuel of choice.

St. Louis–Style Ribs—Spareribs that have the brisket bone and all skirt meat removed.

Three and Down—Slabs of ribs that weigh 3 pounds or less.

Tongs—Long-handled utensil with a spring-loaded hinge. Handy for moving meat, coals, etc. Should be heavy-duty.

Water Smoker—A cooking unit with a pan (for water or other liquids) between the meat and the fuel.

Wet—Barbequed meat that is covered with liquid barbeque sauce. Often used with reference to ribs, especially in Memphis.

"Where's Fred?"—A question that has become a generic call for help. The late Fred Gould was famous for being the go-to man at any contest. When something broke, Fred was there to fix it.

Wire Brush—A brush with stiff wire bristles used to clean the grill.

Wok Topper—A square ceramic-coated wok used to grill vegetables and small meats.

WSM—Acronym for Weber Smoky Mountain brand bullet cooker.

X Factor—Name of any closely guarded secret concoction that makes a barbeque chef believe he or she has an edge over another.

Yardbird—Competition jargon for chicken.

BARBEQUE TIPS FROM THE KCBS

SAFETY FIRST!
FOOD SAFETY TIPS

- When shopping for meat, fish, and poultry, put them in your grocery cart last.

- Load grocery bags with meat and other refrigerated foods in the air-conditioned section of the car, not the trunk.

- Take groceries home immediately or bring along a cooler with ice packs and place the meat in it. Refrigerate or freeze the meat as soon as possible. If you won't use meat, fish, and poultry within a few days, freeze it immediately.

- When carrying food to a picnic, a barbeque, the beach, or a tailgating party, keep it cold. That includes take-out foods—such as deli potato salad, coleslaw, and barbequed baked beans.

- Store refrigerated meat in the coldest part of the refrigerator in its original packaging.

- Thaw frozen food in the refrigerator, never on the counter; allow sufficient defrosting time.

- Hand washing is paramount.

- Keep raw meat, poultry, and fish and their juices away from other foods.

- Sanitize cutting boards and countertops with chlorine bleach (1 capful per gallon of water).

- Marinate foods in the refrigerator, not on the counter or outdoors.

- Boil any marinade for at least 3 minutes to destroy bacteria if you plan to baste with it or serve it with the cooked meat.

- Cook meat thoroughly! See the doneness chart on page 293 for suggested times and internal temperatures for several types of meat.

- Reheat foods or fully cooked meats like hot dogs by grilling to 165°F or until steaming hot.

- Trim excess fat from meat to avoid flare-ups; never char the meat.

- Refrigerate leftover food quickly (after no more than two hours) and use it within a couple days.

GRILL SAFETY TIPS

- Always read the owner's manual before using a new grill.

- Barbeque grills are designed for outdoor use only.

- Set up barbeque grills in an open area away from buildings.

- When using a barbeque grill, be sure all parts of the unit are firmly in place and the grill is stable.

- Use long-handled barbeque utensils to avoid burns and splatters.

- Use salt or baking soda to control a grease fire and always have an ABC-type fire extinguisher handy when cooking.

- Never leave a grill unattended once it's lit or on.

- Don't allow anyone to conduct any activities around the grill when the grill is in use or immediately following its use.

- Do not attempt to move a hot grill.

BARBEQUE MAINTENANCE

- You can clean your cooking grates or grids easily by covering them with a layer of aluminum foil weighed down with a rock or brick and heating them over a hot fire for 10 to 15 minutes.

- To minimize flare-ups on a gas grill, change your lava rocks once a season. You can also switch to using ceramic or porcelain briquettes, which minimize flare-ups.

- To grill chicken and pork or for other slow cooking, turn one side of the grill to low and cook the barbeque on the side opposite the warm rack for indirect cooking.

- When opening your propane tank valve, open only one turn so that you can turn it off in a hurry if you need to.

- You can help protect your grill body from the weather and minimize white spots and oxidation by coating the outside of the grill with a light coating of vegetable oil applied with a paper towel while cool.

- Spritzing ribs, chicken, or other slow-cooking barbeque with apple juice will keep the barbeque moist without changing the flavor.

GRATE/GRID/RACK MAINTENANCE

- To prevent food from sticking, lightly coat the grates with a high-smoking-temperature oil, such as peanut oil, before turning on the grill. Cooking spray also works.

- When the grill is completely cool, wipe up spills with damp paper towels. Grease and salt accelerate corrosion.

- Grates clean up best when slightly warm. After cooking, scrub the grates with a wire brush or a ball of heavy-duty aluminum foil held with long tongs. Use a brass wire brush on stainless-steel grates and stainless-steel brushes on cast-iron grates.

- For charcoal grills and smokers, discard ashes after they have completely cooled. For gas grills, regularly clean or change the catch-pan liner.

- Place a water-resistant cover over your grill after every use. Use a custom-made cover or a tarp.

INSIDE CLEANING

- Remove the grill racks, lava rocks, and burner assembly.

- Use a wire brush and warm soapy water to clean the inside of the grill and the grill racks.

- While the burner assembly is out, clean off all of the rust and corrosion with a wire brush and inspect carefully for any burner holes that may be clogged.

GRILL MAINTENANCE

- Use a garden hose to spray the exterior of the grill and then use hot soapy water to clean off any remaining grease or dirt.

- After the grill is completely dry, use fine sandpaper to remove any corrosion.

- Wipe off the grill and then use a high-temperature paint designed for the intense heat that grills emit.

- After the paint has dried, bake it on by turning the grill on to medium heat for a few minutes.

BASIC BARBEQUE CONTEST GEAR:
THE BARE ESSENTIALS TO TAKE TO THE CONTEST

Thinking about competing? Already sent your application and entry fee in and wondering "What's next?" Not to worry. The best way to relieve precontest anxiety is to—as our Eagle Scout friend Ron Buchholz advises—"Be Prepared."

Your essentials list may grow as you become a seasoned contest cook, but here's what the experts say is the bare minimum you should take to a contest:

- At least one grill/pit with enough capacity to cook all four meat categories. Some insist it's easier to dedicate one for brisket and another for pork butt, ribs, and chicken.

- Coolers for meat, food for the team and guests, and plenty of cold beverages.

- Meat. Don't forget the meat! And don't mess with it until it has passed inspection.

- Shelter from sun, rain, and whatever else Mother Nature will bring to you.

- Communication tools—cell phones with chargers, etc.

- Reliable clocks set to the official contest clock.

- Tool kit containing tongs, forks, thermometers, insulated gloves, aprons, napkins, oven mitts, disposable food-handling gloves, mops, sprayers, duct tape, and sharp knives.

- First-aid kit.

- Contest commissary of rubs, marinades, bastes, standard condiments, and finishing sauces, plus green leaf lettuce and/or curly parsley and cilantro if desired.

- Organization chart that spells out your team's division of labor: who is responsible for doing what, and when.

- Log book for keeping detailed notes so you'll know what worked and what didn't work.

- Contest checklist. Start with the list from world champion barbequers Phil and Linda Hopkins of Smokin' Guns BBQ (page 287) or develop your own based on your contest experience.

Finally, the most important essential is ATTITUDE. Be positive. Be there to have fun and make new friends. Sure, you want to win, but don't be obsessed with winning. Help other teams when they need help and gladly accept help when you need it.

CONTEST CHECKLIST

CONTEST CHECKLIST		CITY, STATE	
CONTEST		CONTACT PHONE	
CONTACT		DATE SENT IN	
ENTRY FEE		DATE	
CONFIRMATION RECEIVED		BEG. ODOMETER READING	
NUMBER OF TEAMS		END. ODOMETER READING	
		TOTAL MILES	

✓	NON–FOOD PRODUCTS	COST	✓	NON–FOOD PRODUCTS	COST	✓	FOOD PRODUCTS	COST
	Aluminum foil			Paper towels			Beer	
	Aluminum pans			Pillows			Briskets	
	Aprons			Plastic chairs			Chicken	
	Bleach			Plastic cups			Ice	
	Broom			Plastic wrap			Lettuce	
	Bug repellant			Pot holders			Parsley	
	Cooker			Silverware			Pop	
	Coolers			Sleeping bags			Pork butts	
	Cutting board			Spare cooker parts			Ribs	
	Dish pans			Spatulas			Rub	
	Dish rags			Spray bottle			Sauce	
	Dish soap			Table covers			Snacks	
	Duct tape			Tables				
	Electric knife			Tongs				
	Extension cords			Tool box				

BASIC BARBEQUE CONTEST GEAR: THE BARE ESSENTIALS TO TAKE TO THE CONTEST

✓	NON–FOOD PRODUCTS	COST	✓	NON–FOOD PRODUCTS	COST	GROCERY LIST	
						FOOD PRODUCTS	COST
	Fire extinguisher			Resealable plastic bags (gallon size)			
	Fire starter			Water containers			
	First-aid kit			Wet wipes			
	Flashlights (and batteries)			Trash bags			
	Fuel (charcoal, wood, pellets)						
	Gasoline						
	Generator						
	Gloves, latex or rubber						
	Hand soap						
	Knife sharpeners						
	Knives						
	Lawn chairs						
	Matches						
	Meat thermom-eters						
	Paper plates						
SUBTOTAL			**SUBTOTAL**			**SUBTOTAL**	
						TOTAL	

METRIC CONVERSIONS AND EQUIVALENTS

METRIC CONVERSION FORMULAS

TO CONVERT	MULTIPLY
Ounces to grams	Ounces by 28.35
Pounds to kilograms	Pounds by .454
Teaspoons to milliliters	Teaspoons by 4.93
Tablespoons to milliliters	Tablespoons by 14.79
Fluid ounces to milliliters	Fluid ounces by 29.57
Cups to milliliters	Cups by 236.59
Cups to liters	Cups by .236
Pints to liters	Pints by .473
Quarts to liters	Quarts by .946
Gallons to liters	Gallons by 3.785
Inches to centimeters	Inches by 2.54

APPROXIMATE METRIC EQUIVALENTS

VOLUME

¼ teaspoon	1 milliliter
½ teaspoon	2.5 milliliters
¾ teaspoon	4 milliliters
1 teaspoon	5 milliliters
1¼ teaspoons	6 milliliters
1½ teaspoons	7.5 milliliters
1¾ teaspoons	8.5 milliliters
2 teaspoons	10 milliliters
1 tablespoon (½ fluid ounce)	15 milliliters
2 tablespoons (1 fluid ounce)	30 milliliters
¼ cup	60 milliliters
⅓ cup	80 milliliters
½ cup (4 fluid ounces)	120 milliliters
⅔ cup	160 milliliters
¾ cup	180 milliliters
1 cup (8 fluid ounces)	240 milliliters
1¼ cups	300 milliliters
1½ cups (12 fluid ounces)	360 milliliters
1⅔ cups	400 milliliters
2 cups (1 pint)	460 milliliters
3 cups	700 milliliters
4 cups (1 quart)	.95 liter
1 quart plus ¼ cup	1 liter
4 quarts (1 gallon)	3.8 liters

WEIGHT

¼ ounce	7 grams
½ ounce	14 grams
¾ ounce	21 grams
1 ounce	28 grams
1¼ ounces	35 grams
1½ ounces	42.5 grams
1⅔ ounces	45 grams
2 ounces	57 grams
3 ounces	85 grams
4 ounces (¼ pound)	113 grams
5 ounces	142 grams
6 ounces	170 grams
7 ounces	198 grams
8 ounces (½ pound)	227 grams
16 ounces (1 pound)	454 grams
35.25 ounces (2.2 pounds)	1 kilogram

LENGTH

⅛ inch	3 millimeters
¼ inch	6 millimeters
½ inch	1¼ centimeters
1 inch	2½ centimeters
2 inches	5 centimeters
2½ inches	6 centimeters
4 inches	10 centimeters
5 inches	13 centimeters
6 inches	15¼ centimeters
12 inches (1 foot)	30 centimeters

COMMON INGREDIENTS AND THEIR APPROXIMATE EQUIVALENTS

1 cup uncooked rice = 225 grams

1 cup all-purpose flour = 140 grams

1 stick butter (4 ounces • ½ cup • 8 tablespoons) = 110 grams

1 cup butter (8 ounces • 2 sticks • 16 tablespoons) = 220 grams

1 cup brown sugar, firmly packed = 225 grams

1 cup granulated sugar = 200 grams

OVEN TEMPERATURES

To convert Fahrenheit to Celsius, subtract 32 from Fahrenheit, multiply the result by 5, and then divide by 9.

DESCRIPTION	FAHRENHEIT	CELSIUS	BRITISH GAS MARK
Very cool	200°	95°	0
Very cool	225°	110°	¼
Very cool	250°	120°	½
Cool	275°	135°	1
Cool	300°	150°	2
Warm	325°	165°	3
Moderate	350°	175°	4
Moderately hot	375°	190°	5
Fairly hot	400°	200°	6
Hot	425°	220°	7
Very hot	450°	230°	8
Very hot	475°	245°	9

Information compiled from a variety of sources, including *Recipes into Type* by Joan Whitman and Dolores Simon (Newton, MA: Biscuit Books, 2000); *The New Food Lover's Companion* by Sharon Tyler Herbst (Hauppauge, NY: Barron's, 1995); and *Rosemary Brown's Big Kitchen Instruction Book* (Kansas City, MO: Andrews McMeel, 1998).

HELPFUL CHARTS AND TABLES

BRINING

This timetable will give you a light brine without getting too salty. You can brine overnight in the refrigerator if you like. Be sure to rinse the brine off the meat with cold running water.

Shrimp and thin fish fillets	30 minutes
Whole chickens (4 pounds)	2 to 4 hours
Chicken parts	1½ to 2 hours
Cornish game hens	1 to 2 hours
Salmon fillets	1 to 2 hours
Whole turkeys	4 to 8 hours
Pork chops	2 to 3 hours
Whole pork loin	8 to 12 hours

MARINATING

Spare Ribs, Venison, Duck	6 to 8 hours
Beef Roast, Beef Brisket, Beef Short Ribs, Beef Ribs	5 to 7 hours
Beef Kabobs, Beef Steaks, Lamb Kebabs, Game Birds	4 to 6 hours
Turkey, Turkey Quarters, Flank Steak, Skirt Steak	4 hours to overnight
Pork Tenderloin, Pork Chops, Pork Loin	3 to 4 hours
Chicken Breast, Chicken, Chicken Parts, Chicken Wings	2 to 4 hours
Fish, Shellfish	30 minutes to 2 hours

COOKING WOODS

This chart gives the flavor properties and meat recommendations for a wide variety of woods used for smoking. You may want to use a water pan when smoking with woods; it helps to keep moisture in your cooker at all times. You can use an old bread pan or a heavy-duty aluminum pan. Keep in mind it should be large enough so you don't have to refill it while cooking.

ACACIA In the mesquite family. Strong. Good for most meats, beef, vegetables.

ALDER Delicate flavor, with a hint of sweetness. Good for fish, pork, poultry, light meat, and game birds. Great for salmon.

ALMOND Nutty and sweet smoke flavor, light ash. Good for all meats.

APPLE Slightly sweet, but denser, fruity smoke flavor. Good for beef, poultry, game birds, pork, and ham.

APRICOT Milder flavor and sweeter than hickory. Good for most meats.

ASH Fast burning, light but distinctive flavor. Good for fish and red meats.

BIRCH Medium-hard wood with a flavor like maple. Good for pork and poultry.

CHERRY Slightly sweet, fruity smoke flavor. Good for all meats.

COTTONWOOD Very subtle flavor. Good for most meats.

GRAPEFRUIT Medium smoke flavor with a hint of fruitiness. Excellent for beef, pork, and poultry.

GRAPEVINE Aromatic, similar to fruit woods. Good for all meats.

continued on page 292

HICKORY The most common wood used. Pungent, smoky, baconlike flavor. Good for all smoking, especially pork and ribs.

LEMON Medium smoke flavor with a hint of fruitiness. Excellent for beef, pork, and poultry.

LILAC Very light, subtle flavor with a hint of floral. Good for seafood and lamb.

MAPLE Mild, smoky, somewhat sweet flavor. Good for pork, poultry, cheese, vegetables, and small game birds.

MESQUITE Strong, earthy flavor. Good for most meats, especially beef. Also good for most vegetables.

MULBERRY Sweet smell reminiscent of apple. Good for beef, poultry, game birds, pork, and ham.

NECTARINE Milder and sweeter flavor than hickory. Good for most meats.

OAK The second most popular wood. Heavy smoke flavor. Many pitmasters consider red oak to be the best. Good for red meat, pork, fish, and heavy game.

ORANGE Medium smoke flavor with a hint of fruitiness. Excellent for beef, pork, and poultry.

PEACH Slightly sweet, woodsy flavor. Good for most meats.

PEAR Slightly sweet, woodsy flavor. Good for poultry, game birds, and pork.

PECAN More like oak than hickory, but not as strong. Good for most meats.

PLUM Milder and sweeter than hickory. Good for most meats.

WALNUT Very heavy smoke flavor, usually mixed with lighter wood, like pecan or apple. Can be bitter if used alone or not aged. Good for red meats and game.

OVEN TEMPERATURES

300°F (150°C) and below	Slow oven
301°F to 349°F (151°C to 179°C)	Moderately slow oven
350°F to 399°F (180°C to 199°C)	Moderate oven
400°F to 449°F (200°C to 229°C)	Hot oven
450°F to 499°F (230°C to 249°C)	Very hot oven
500°F (250°C) and above	Broil

THE BARON'S COOKING TIMETABLES

BEEF BRISKET	9 to 12 pounds	16 to 18 hours
PORK SHOULDER	12 to 14 pounds	13 to 16 hours
PORK BUTT	5 to 7 pounds	10 to 14 hours
PORK LOIN	8 to 10 pounds	5 to 8 hours
PORK SPARE RIBS	3.3 pounds and down	6 to 8 hours
PORK LOIN BACK RIBS (BABY BACK RIBS)	2.0 to 2.25 pounds	4 to 6 hours
WHOLE HOG	75 to 85 pounds	20 to 24 hours
WHOLE SALMON	4 to 5 pounds	4 to 5 hours
WHOLE CHICKEN	3.25 to 4.5 pounds	4 to 5 hours

FOOD DONENESS AND TEMPERATURE

FOOD	DONENESS	INTERNAL TEMPERATURE ° F
BARBECUED PORK	Sliceable and Chopped	180°F (82.2°C)
SHOULDERS, PICNICS	Sliceable, Pullable, and Chopped	185°F (85° C)
BOSTON BUTTS	Pullable	195° to 205°F (91° to 96°C)
BARBECUED BEEF BRISKET	Sliceable	185°F (85°C)
BEEF STEAKS	Rare	135°F (57°C)
	Medium-Rare	140°F (60°C)
	Medium	145°F (63°C)
	Medium-Well	160°F (71°C)
	Well Done	170°F (77°C)
BEEF ROAST	Rare	130°F (54°C)
	Medium-Rare	140°F (60°C)
	Medium	145°F (63°C)
	Medium-Well	160°F (71°C)
	Well Done	170°F (77°C)
CHICKEN		
Whole or Pieces	Done	170°F (77°C)
Breast	Done	165°F (74°C)
CORNISH HEN	Done	170°F (77°C)
DUCK	Done	170°F (77°C)
GROUND MEAT	Medium	165°F (74°C)
BEEF, PORK, LAMB	Well Done	170°F (77°C)
HAM		
Fully Cooked	Well Done	140°F (60°C)
Not Fully Cooked	Well Done	160°F (71°C)
LAMB CHOPS AND RACK	Rare	120°F (49°C)
	Medium-Rare	125°F (52°C)
	Medium	130°F (54°C)
	Medium-Well	140°F (60°C)

HELPFUL CHARTS AND TABLES

293

FOOD	DONENESS	INTERNAL TEMPERATURE ° F
LAMB ROAST	Rare	115°F (46°C)
	Medium-Rare	125°F (52°C)
	Medium	130°F (54°C)
	Medium-Well	140°F (60°C)
PHEASANT	Well Done	165°F (74°C)
PORK CHOPS	Medium-Rare	130°F (54°C)
	Medium	140°F (60°C)
	Medium-Well	150°F (66°C)
PORK TENDERLOIN	Medium-Rare	135°F (57°C)
	Medium	140°F (60°C)
	Medium-Well	150°F (66°C)
SAUSAGE	Well Done	170°F (77°C)
TURKEY		
Whole	Done (Check Thigh)	175°F (79°C)
Breast	Done	165°F (74°C)
Dark Meat	Done	175°F (79°C)
VEAL CHOPS AND ROAST	Medium-Rare	125°F (52°C)
	Medium	140°F (60°C)
	Medium-Well	150°F (66°C)
VENISON	Medium	160°F (71°C)

IMAGE CREDITS

Most of the images are the property of the authors. The following people have also contributed photos:

Jeremy Ravenshaw Fowler: 214-215

Matthew Shropshall: 252-253

Mike Tucker: 143

Rich and Bunny Tuttle: 1, 22, 114, 196

Dave Conti: 204

Jennifer B. Stanley: 101

Harry Soo: 115

Duane Daugherty: 72

Eric Abraham: 64

Karen Walker: vi (Jack Daniel's); xviii (chicken); 1 (tent); 14 (three women); 46 (Murphysboro poster and pig bus); 86; 97; 106 (tour bus); 175 (Chris Roylance); 236 (cheesecake, tent, demo, Carolyn Wells and Monty Spradling); 247; 248; 272 (awards)

Ruben Gomez: 42

Ron Harwell: 52

Jubon's: 99

DennyMike Sherman: 117, 130 (logo by T.Doc Creative)

Lew Miller: 156

Don Przybyla: 160

Chris Roylance: 175 (lamb)

INDEX OF CONTRIBUTORS

Kell Phelps—Douglas, Georgia

Michael and Diane Phillips—Montreal, Canada

Don Przybyla—Calumet City, Illinois

John Raven—Johnson City, Texas

Anne Rehnstrohm—Des Moines, Iowa

Billy Rodgers—Overland Park, Kansas

John Ross—Prairie Village, Kansas

Steve Rowan—Murfreesboro, Tennessee

Chris Roylance—Forbes, New South Wales, Australia

Fred Sauceman—Johnson City, Tennessee

Mike and Carol Sawyers—Caddo Lake, Louisiana

Paul Seabrook—Woodstock, Ontario

DennyMike Sherman—York, Maine

Ron Shewchuk—North Vancouver, British Columbia

Mathew Shropshall—Staffordshire, England

Tana Frensley-Shupe—Tullahoma, Tennessee

Guy Simpson—Shawnee, Kansas

Perry Skrukrud—Nisswa, Minnesota

Harry Soo—Diamond Bar, California

Brad and Susan Sparr—McKinney, Texas

Monty Spradling—Leawood, Kansas

Jennifer B. Stanley—Richmond, Virginia

Mason Steinberg—Elkhorn, Nevada

Mike Stines—Cape Cod, Massachusetts

Tony Stone—Cookeville, Tennessee

Jim and Kathleen Tabb—Tryon, North Carolina

Howard L. Taylor—Richardson, Texas

Mike Tucker—Ankeny, Iowa

Rich and Bunny Tuttle—Pleasant Hill, Missouri

Walt VanStone—Arlington, Texas

Jay "The Snail" Vantuyl—Claycomo, Missouri

Drew Volpe—Boston, Massachusetts

William E. Wall—Red Keg, Michigan

Carolyn Wells—Grandview, Missouri

William Wright—Topeka, Kansas

Joe Yonan—Washington, D.C.

TEAM CONTRIBUTORS

AM and PM Smokers—Kansas City, Missouri

Beaver Castors—Bellevue, Washington

Big Bob Gibson Bar-B-Q—Decatur, Alabama

Butt Shredders—North Vancouver, British Columbia

Feeding Friendz—Deerfield, New Hampshire

Jaw Breaker BBQ—Yarmouth, Maine

K Cass BBQ—Pleasant Hill, Missouri

Pa and Ma's Kettle—Wauconda, Illinois

Lotta Bull BBQ—Marietta, Oklahoma

Team Smoke E ZZ—Itasca, Ilinois

Holy Smokers Too—Knoxville, Tennessee

Chubbs Bar-B-Que—Rogers, Arkansas

Sin City Chefs—Las Vegas, Nevada

Doc K's BBQ—Rose Hill, Kansas

Diva Q—Ontario, Canada

Steve's Smoke Shack—Murfreesboro, Tennessee

The Will Deal Catering and BBQ Co—Topeka, Kansas

Pok N' Da Ribs—Wichita, Kansas

Demon Pig BBQ—Stewartville, Minnesota

INDEX

J

Jack Daniel's World Championship Invitational Barbecue
        Contest, 179, 184
    journalist-pig fries story at, 27
Japanese Marinade, 214–15
Jasper the Pig, 178–79
Jaw Breaker BBQ, 53
Johnston, Jay
    background, 157
    Skillet-Grilled Potatoes and Italian Sausage, 157
Johnston, Nancy, 157
Jones, Monte
    background, 105, 277
    Corny Cheese Chile Pepper Biscuits, 105
    Pear Honey, 277
journalist-pig fries story, 27
judges, 6, 102, 107, 120, 153, 252, 255
    oath, 18
Juiced-Up Chicken, 162

K

K Cass BBQ, 22, 196
Kansas City Barbeque Society (KCBS). *See also individual cooks*
    CBJ, 279
    CMJ, 280
    current membership, xiii
    customs, 179, 184, 227
    definition, xiii
    entry meats, 280
    history, ix–xiv
    humor, 27, 88, 123, 206, 209, 227, 259
    incorporation, x
    KCBS-sanctioned barbeque contests, x, 6, 8–9
    mission, xiii, xvi, 51
The Kansas City Barbeque Society Cookbook: Barbeque . . .
    It's Not Just for Breakfast Anymore, xi–xx
Kansas City Bullsheet, xi, 179
Kansas City Star, 56
Kathy's Pig Powder Sauce, 233
K.C. Rib Doctor's Baked Beans, 54
KC Masterpiece Sausage Balls, 25
KCBS. *See* Kansas City Barbeque Society
KCBS Certified Barbeque Judge. *See* CBJ
KCBS teams
    AM and PM Smokers, 40
    Beau Hog BBQ, 37

    Beaver Castors, 199
    Best British BBQ Cookery Team, Company and Trade,
        252–53
    Butt Shredders, 39
    Feeding Friendz BBQ Team, 116
    the Licks, 37
    Lotta Bull BBQ, 43
    Sin City Chefs, 138
    Slap Yo' Daddy, 115
    Sue-B-Q BBQ Team, 208
    Swine Flu, 3
    Team Kansas City, 122–23
    Ziggy's Piggys, 22
KCBS-sanctioned barbeque contests
    attending, 6
    cooks, 6
    fuel for, 3
    green lettuce in, 4
    judges, 6, 18, 102, 107, 120, 153, 252, 255
    judges' oath, 18
    locations, 8–9
    organizers, 6–8
    purpose, 9
    rules, 1–4

N

O

INDEX

333